The Visual Arts and Early Childhood Learning

Edited by
Christine Marmé Thompson
University of Illinois at Urbana-Champaign

1995

About NAEA

Founded in 1947, the National Art Education Association is the largest professional art education association in the world. Membership includes elementary and secondary teachers, art administrators, museum educators, arts council staff, and university professors from throughout the United STates and 66 foreign countries. NAEA's mission is to advance art education through professional development, service, advancement of knowledge and leadership.

Cover: *Untitled* by Brian Adams. Kindergarten, 1993. Marker drawing, 8–1/2" x 11".

ISBN 0–937652–80–6

This anthology is dedicated to Marilyn Zurmuehlen.

Acknowledgments

This anthology was conceived and initiated during David W. Baker's term as President of the National Art Education Association (NAEA), and completed with the support of the NAEA Board of Directors and Executive Director, Thomas A. Hatfield. On behalf of all who believe in the fundamental importance of children's first encounters with art in educational settings, I thank them for their vision and their unwavering commitment to this project. To all those who contributed to this volume, I add my appreciation for your willingness to share inspiring work and my admiration for the intelligence and sensitivity you exemplify in word and action. Special thanks to my students, my colleagues, and my family, for all they have done to shape this book as they shared its journey.

Table of Contents

Chapter 1
The Visual Arts and Early Childhood Learning: Changing Contexts and Concepts

Christine Marmé Thompson
University of Illinois at Urbana-Champaign

Slightly more than a century ago, a number of astute adults noticed that young children clustered around walls and fences were up to something that seemed suspiciously artistic. Since that time, artists, educators, psychologists and parents have admired and encouraged, collected and catalogued, studied and supported young children's work with art materials, for reasons as varied as the forms of relationships existing between adults and children. Many adults continue to encounter children's art without preconceptions or theoretical preparation, when a child they know and love entangles them in an activity which seems to matter to that child in some potent, if mysterious, way. For some, including many art educators, that initial, visceral fascination evokes curiosity, presents questions, and inspires more systematic study. Much of the work that art educators do, with great commitment and zest, involves the examination and the explication of children's drawings and the sharing of enthusiasm and understanding with others. We art educators continuously find ourselves echoing sentiments expressed by Walt Whitman as we assure the parents, teachers, and researchers who are our audiences, students, and colleagues, "What I have loved, you will love, and I will show you how."

Early Stages of Artistic Development

Art making is a natural occurrence of childhood, an activity young children discover and pursue even in the absence of adult prompting. In fact, it was children's untutored, completely voluntary engagement in the creation of visual images that first attracted attention and inspired documentation. Thus, child art exists independently of any efforts to probe its character and meaning. Yet it becomes more clear every day that the nature of children's experience with art depends crucially on the adults who are responsible, by design or default, for guiding the course of artistic development and learning. This is particularly true for young children, who depend upon adults for basic access to workable materials, as well as for the encouragement to use them.

As Jo Alice Leeds (1989) demonstrated, children and their teachers operate within a history of attitudes toward child art, conditioned by prevailing conceptions of the nature of art and of childhood. The theory and practice of art education in elementary and secondary schools have varied through the years, in response to these (and other) aspects of the cultural milieu. Yet art educators have remained remarkably consistent in their interpretations of young children's art and their recommendations on the children's behalf.

Through the years art educators have succeeded in describing the evolution of young children's art and in explaining the significance of the subtle transitions of form and meaning that mark the earliest stages of artistic development. This is an important and enduring function of the profession: Images that mystify as thoroughly as young children's often do can be dismissed as meaningless without proper introduction to the complexities of thought and action involved in their making. Even those adults predisposed to appreciate the workings of young hearts and minds often find child art difficult to comprehend or to value.

Difficulties seem to emerge, however, when these descriptions of children's art fail to yield the prescriptions for classroom practice that the teachers of young children expect and need. Art educators have long assumed that "developmentally appropriate" instruction in early childhood originates in a firm understanding of children's spontaneous approaches to art making. Methods courses and textbooks typically provide meticulous, sequential descriptions of the stages and substages of children's art, accompanied by suggestions concerning materials compatible with the intentions children may hold at various ages, advice about classroom contexts, supplementary experiences, and resources for teaching. The teacher's role is characterized as active, but reserved and responsive. As Howard Gardner (1980) suggests, adults provide the equipment and the encouragement that will allow children's natural artistry to unfold.

While few art educators have counselled a completely noninterventionist approach to early art education, many placed emphatic limits on the teacher's involvement in the process of "spontaneous self-instruction" (Froebel, in Kellogg, 1970, p. 62) through which children teach themselves to draw. Many of these cautionary statements seem to persist powerfully in memory. Many teachers of young children accept them as guides to practice which conform to the traditions of nursery school education and seem to satisfy young children's hunger for unencumbered play with responsive materials.

This guidance is fundamentally sound and perfectly appropriate for very young children. Experience has shown that it can be the basis for effective teaching. It is clear, however, that many early childhood educators find it vague and insubstantial. The daily realities of teaching young children, amid the perceived expectations of parents and administrators, often entice teachers to abandon the experiential approach to art activities. Intuitively seeking more structure and more uniform results, many teachers gravitate toward lessons that are directive and mechanical. The use of art materials to complete designs prepared and distributed by teachers is all but universal in preschools and the primary grades. Like the consumption of junk food, this activity thrives without endorsement and in spite of expert advice, and reduces the capacity, if not the appetite, for more substantial fare.

Art educators are notoriously, and often justifiably, critical of much that is done in the name of art in preschool and the primary grades. We may, at the same time, recognize that the tenacity of the practices and projects we deplore testifies to the complexity of life in schools and to the extraordinary difficulty of transposing theory to practice. Part of what seems to be lost or garbled in the translation is a fundamental sense of the contribution which artistic experience makes to the lives and the learning of young children. Lacking a more profound conception of what art might be or do, many teachers operate on the assumption that art activities are merely a form of play, a break in the day's routine, an opportunity for children to flex small muscles and exude raw emotions. When art experiences are offered among several, equally enticing alternatives, when art teaching is reduced to "the provision of materials" (New, 1991, p. 28), when teachers accept neutrality and disengagement as professional duties, precious opportunities for immersion, reflection, and dialogue are lost, to children and their teachers. When art activities are overly directive and designed to produce reasonable facsimiles of an adult model or close approximations of an adult vision of the world, children are deprived of much, if not all, that art has to offer.

New Developments

As the form and content of this volume attests, a subtle but significant shift in thinking about the nature and the possibilities of art in early childhood has occurred. The chapters to follow may seem to be a dramatic departure from the emphasis on "self-taught child art" (Kellogg, 1970, p. 145) that long characterized the advice that art educators offered in regard to young children. A largely undocumented ferment of experience and reflection has brought art educators to a point where adults figure more prominently in early art education and children are seen as capable of creating complex artistic forms and of responding to forms and meanings created by others.

Much of the wisdom contained in this volume emerged through practice, through contact with young children in classroom settings, through conversation with others similarly involved and interested in the artistic learning of young children. It is a celebration and a testimony to changes long underway, to the emergence of a consensus that promises to alter young children's earliest encounters with art.

In the past several decades, as women's participation in the work force increased dramatically and the demand for child care outside the home became insistent, services for young children exp half of 3- and 4-year-old children in the U.S. now spend their days in education or care settings outside the home. Day care centers—only one among countless provisions available—serve approximately 4 million preschool children and provide after-hours havens for an additional 1 million school-aged children (Willer, 1992). The children of working parents may spend 35 hours or more each week in the company of children and adults beyond their immediate families, absorbing routines and rhythms far different from those which once seemed typical of a young child's day. Formal preschool experience, once an exception, has become the rule for the great majority of today's youngest children. Society is just beginning to contemplate and understand the impact of early education on children's socialization and learning. (See, for example, Elkind, 1987; Kagan & Zigler, 1987; Suransky, 1982.)

The term "early childhood education" designates a tremendous variety of arrangements for the care and education of children from birth through age 8, from center-based day care to more traditional part-time preschools to enrichment programs in museums, community centers, universities, compensatory programs and special services, and classroom instruction in public and private schools. Early childhood educators and developmental psychologists agree that children in the first 9 years of life—children in the process of "becoming at home in the world" (Vandenberg, 1971, p. 63)—require forms of education significantly different from those serving older children in traditional elementary classrooms. Many early childhood specialists see exploratory play and self-initiated and self-directed activity as young children's primary means of coming to know their world, and they recommend that the structure of academic learning be introduced gradually, as children approach middle childhood. The inclusion of children in the primary grades within the rubric of early childhood reminds us that children require "special treatment" long after they enter formal schooling, and that education in the primary grades must retain the concrete engagements with materials, teachers, and peers that characterize preschool education.

Responding to the Changes

In response to the tremendous and apparently irreversible demand for early childhood services, programs to certify teachers of young children have multiplied. Art educators are involved in the preparation of early childhood teachers more directly and intensely than ever before, providing preservice methods and practicum courses, workshops, publications, instructional materials and informal advice and counsel to a constantly burgeoning audience. This is an exceptionally important and challenging task, an opportunity which we must recognize, a responsibility we should welcome. Although art educators and early childhood educators have much in common, the relationship between the two fields is somewhat asymmetrical. Art educators seem destined to serve young children indirectly, through the mediation of classroom teachers who are more directly and continuously involved with young children and their art. Few preschools, and even fewer day care centers, include art specialists among their professional staffs. Even those teachers who hold baccalaureate degrees—slightly more than half of those responding to a recent national survey (Willer, 1992)—may have little or no formal background in the theory or practice of art education. The situation is much the same in 42% of U.S. elementary schools (Center for Education Statistics, 1988), where classroom teachers are solely responsible for any art teaching that occurs. Art educators' role in early art education is, largely, advisory: Our greatest and most immediate sphere of influence includes teachers more often than it does children.

Teachers of young children are a most receptive and concerned audience. Preschool teachers, responding to a survey recently conducted by David Baker (1992), estimated that the children in their care spend between 30% and 50% of their active school day engaged in art, or "art-like," activities. Although the exact nature of these activities remained unspecified, the fact that so many teachers accepted art as a featured activity in children's school day is heartening. Other trends in early childhood education suggest that a pervasive reevaluation of art's contribution to children's learning is occurring within the early childhood community. A new appreciation of the role of visual expression in children's efforts to make sense of their experiences is gaining currency and credibility.

Artistic activity became a decidedly peripheral and neglected concern in classrooms focused on academic, or "preacademic" (Katz, 1977, p. 19), routines. Few educational scholars favored the introduction of highly structured lessons, rote memorization, worksheets and drill in preschool or kindergarten. Yet the movement seemed to emerge and thrive, briefly, at the grassroots level. Pressure to emphasize early academic learning appeared to be a logical corollary of research indicating that young children were far more capable of solving classic Piagetian tasks when those problems were presented in contexts that made "human sense" (Donaldson, 1978), that is, in situations that were meaningful to young children. The intrinsic limits that, Piaget maintained, constrained the thinking of preoperational children proved to be less rigid and impermeable than once believed.

As researchers began to explore the competencies of young children, many teachers and parents succumbed to the inevitable temptation to believe that anything was possible, that children could be taught to perform the most complex mental operations if only they were sufficiently challenged. The nature of this challenge was, most often, equated with the very structures of academic learning that failed to provide the "human sense" required by young children. As Lilian Katz (1977) observed, the tendency is to overestimate young children's capacity for academic work while underestimating their appetite for intellectual challenge.

Advocates of several highly influential and compatible strains of curriculum reform—writing process, whole language, the project method, thematic units or cycles—evince renewed faith in children's inclinations to explore and to make sense of the world, to discover and sustain involvement in meaningful tasks, and to direct their own learning with the assistance and support of teachers and peers. Artistic activity is virtually taken for granted as one of the most comfortable and fluent means of investigating and interpreting experience that young children have at their disposal. Art is back to the center of many classrooms because of academic goals that support activities like

- The voluntary drawings encouraged by writing process teachers as forms of "rehearsal" (Graves, 1984) for the dictation or writing of stories.

- The clay models and murals and sketches children create as they conduct multimedia studies of grocery stores, the inner workings of a school bus, or the nature of seasonal change (Katz & Chard, 1989).

One program has inspired unprecedented interest in the role, and the possibilities, of art in early childhood learning. In the 22 municipally supported preschools of Reggio Emilia, a town in northern Italy, children spend their days in the company of a small group of adults, including, in every case, one teacher whose specialty is art. Every preschool has a large studio, equipped with an incredible array of materials, including many normally reserved for much older children. Every classroom has a miniature studio as well because drawing, painting, modelling, and constructing are integral to every activity the children pursue (New, 1991). The children participate in extended inquiries, often originating in interests they discover and always in some phenomenon that touches their experience. The children's teachers claim that intervention is seldom necessary as the children create images consolidating and expressing what they have learned: So much has gone before, in the form of dialogues, field trips, preliminary sketches, planning, documentation, and discussion, that the children proceed independently.

Additional support for more meaningful forms of early art education comes from the National Association for the Education of Young Children (NAEYC; Bredekamp, 1987; NAEYC, 1991) in recent statements which define and clarify the concept of "developmentally appropriate practice." The NAEYC supports regular and frequent experiences which promote young children's artistic expression and aesthetic responses. Bredekamp (1987) is openly critical of projects which reflect the teacher's thinking more clearly than the child's. She singles out the coloring of predrawn images, the cutting and assembly of prepared patterns, and the enforced emulation of adult models as particularly, and equally, inappropriate.

In a subsequent paper, the NAEYC (1991) offers a description of the cycle of learning which is retraced throughout life whenever we confront a new topic or process of thought or action. The authors suggest that all learning begins in awareness of a phenomenon and proceeds through a process of personal exploration to more structured forms of inquiry, moving finally toward utilization of the knowledge and skills thus acquired. This version of the progress of learning begins and ends in a social context: Teachers must provide occasions for children to encounter new ideas and activities, and must finally help them master conventional approaches to their application and use. Between these two poles, however, stretches a leisurely expanse in which children must be free to manipulate new materials, to test and measure, combine and compare, experiment and explore in personally meaningful and playful ways. This theory provides support and structure to experiential modes of artistic learning which may otherwise strike teachers as amorphous and slow to yield results.

A New Synthesis

Underlying most, if not all, of these recent trends in educational thought and practice is a conception of children and of the pedagogic relationship they share with adults that departs from the Piagetian vision of the solitary child exploring the world. A new synthesis has emerged in which the unfolding of children's innate capacities is seen as dependent upon teaching, in which development is seen not as preliminary to learning nor distinct from it, but as a process facilitated by the challenges which teachers, peers, and materials offer. The writings of L.S. Vygotsky (1962, 1978) have been particularly influential: His emphasis on the social, cultural, and historical influences which surround and enable early learning mediates many of the enduring disputes between developmentalists and advocates of more direct instructional intervention. Vygotsky proposed that children's "actual developmental levels," demonstrated by their capacities to act independently, should serve as the foundation for teaching rather than its boundaries. He recognized peers, teachers, and parents as partners in children's learning, collaborators whose participation and assistance allows children to accomplish more than they might left to their own devices.

The social nature of early learning, the "sociocentric" (Bates, 1975) nature of young children, is documented in the writings of William Corsaro (1985, 1988), Anne Haas Dyson (1986, 1989), Vivian Gussin Paley (1984, 1988, 1990) and others who have recognized and come to appreciate the profound influence that young children exert upon one another when they gather in classrooms, to work and play in close proximity, to exchange opinions and ideas, to help one another make sense of a puzzling world. Similarly, the role that adults play in "giving meaning to the child's experience" (Tizard & Hughes, 1984, p. 22) has been recognized and articulated more clearly, perhaps, than ever before. Barbara Rogoff and J.V. Wertsch (1984) summarized this role by remarking that adults serve young children much as tour guides assist travellers in a foreign land. We plan itineraries, call attention to certain landmarks, and steer our charges clear of others. We translate unfamiliar phrases, explain local customs, and convert the currency children bring with them to other, more common and negotiable coins. We stand between children and their destinations, doing what we can to ensure that their journeys are enjoyable and enlightening, comfortable and yet challenging.

In the prevailing climate of thought about young children's capacities and the conditions which support their learning, the problems and the possibilities of early art education, the place of the visual arts in early childhood learning, have evoked renewed debate. In the midst of such discussions I remember the 8-year-old boy, frustrated by his preschool-aged brother's resistance to drawing instruction, who voiced what may well be the central dilemma of early art education: "I wonder," Erik said, "how you teach those little guys anything." I answered Erik as art educators are wont to do, assuring

4

him that in due course the single line that so offended his conception of a properly depicted snake would acquire volume and curvature. I did not, however, answer the question he posed, a question which had to do with learning and teaching and the expansion of possibilities that one, more experienced person might offer to another, younger and less experienced.

Ensuing Chapters

In this volume, there are answers to this and other fundamental first questions. There are significant contributions to our understanding of "how you teach those little guys anything," and vivid accounts of the wonders than can happen when we accept the responsibility of doing so. The authors of the chapters which follow found or invented opportunities to work with young children and their teachers, in classrooms, on playgrounds, in museums and workshops, in preschools, elementary schools, colleges and universities. Each chapter presents a single perspective on early art education as it is, a unique vision of what it might be. Taken together, these chapters provide a comprehensive index of the topics that have emerged and persisted in this portion of our field.

The many circumstances in which young children make and encounter art, the subtle influences exerted by classroom rituals and routines, the important roles adults play as they enable and enrich children's experiences are pervasive concerns. The nature of artistic activity in early childhood, its contribution to children's attempts to explore and to create meanings, the intimacy of its relation to the undifferentiated surge of learning which young children accomplish are recurring issues throughout this text. The extent and the limits of children's understanding of adult works of art, their sense of history and of culture, of differences and similarities, connections and chasms, are explored within. Models, examples, concrete possibilities, theoretical insights, and practical wisdom are interwoven through the pages that follow. These authors convey a shared commitment to young children as capable creators of artistic forms and meanings and to the adults who create conditions in which children's natural affinity for artistic experience may find sustenance, support, and stimulation.

References

Baker, D. W. (1992, September). *Toward a sensible education: Inquiring into the role of the visual arts in early childhood education.* Keynote address presented at Making Meaning through Art: Art in Early Childhood Education Symposium, University of Illinois at Urbana-Champaign.

Bates, E. (1975). Peer relations and the acquisition of language. In M. Lewis & L. A. Rosenblum (Eds.), *Friendship and peer relations* (pp. 259-292). New York: John Wiley & Sons.

Bredekamp, S. (1987). *Developmentally appropriate practice in early childhood programs serving children from birth through age 8.* Washington, DC: National Association for the Education of Young Children.

Center for Education Statistics. (1988, May). *Bulletin CS 88-417.* Washington, DC: U.S. Office of Education.

Corsaro, W. (1985). *Friendship and peer culture in the early years.* Norwood, NJ: Ablex.

Corsaro, W. A. (1988, January). Routines in the peer culture of American and Italian nursery school children. *Sociology of Education, 61,* 1-14.

Donaldson, M. (1978). *Children's minds.* New York: Norton.

Dyson, A. H. (1986). Transitions and tensions: Interrelationships between the drawing, talking, and dictating of young children. *Research in the Teaching of English, 20,* 379-409.

Dyson, A. H. (1989). *Multiple worlds of child writers: Friends learning to write.* New York: Teachers College Press.

Elkind, D. (1987). *Miseducation: Preschoolers at risk.* New York: Alfred A. Knopf.

Gardner, H. (1980). *Artful scribbles.* New York: Basic Books.

Graves, D. (1984). *A researcher learns to write (Selected articles and monographs).* Exeter, NH: Heineman.

Kagan, S. L., & Zigler, E. F. (Eds.). (1987). *Early schooling: The national debate.* New Haven: Yale University Press.

Katz, L. G. (1977). *Talks with teachers (Reflections on early childhood education).* Washington, DC: National Association for the Education of Young Children.

Katz, L., & Chard, S. (1989). *Engaging children's minds: The project approach.* Norwood, NJ: Ablex.

Kellogg, R. (1970). *Analyzing children's art.* Palo Alto, CA: Mayfield.

Leeds, J. A. (1989). The history of attitudes toward child art. *Studies in Art Education, 30*(2), 93-103.

National Association for the Education of Young Children. (1991). Guidelines for appropriate curriculum content and assessment in programs serving children ages 3 through 8. *Young Children, 46*(3), 21-38.

New, R. (1991). Projects and provocations: Preschool curriculum ideas from Reggio Emilia. *Montessori Life, 3*(1). 26-28.

Paley, V. G. (1984). *Boys and girls: Superheroes in the doll corner.* Chicago: University of Chicago Press.

Paley, V. G. (1988). *Bad guys don't have birthdays: Fantasy play at 4.* Chicago: University of Chicago Press.

Paley, V. G. (1990). *The boy who would be a helicopter: The uses of storytelling in the classroom.* Cambridge, MA: Harvard University Press.

Rogoff, B., & Wertsch, J. V. (Eds.). (1984). *Children's learning in the "zone of proximal development."* San Francisco: Jossey-Bass, Inc.

Suransky, V. P. (1982). *The erosion of childhood.* Chicago: University of Chicago Press.

Tizard, B., & Hughes, M. (1984). *Young children learning.* Cambridge, MA: Harvard University Press.

Vandenberg, D. (1971). *Being and education.* Englewood Cliffs, NJ: Prentice-Hall.

Vygotsky, L. S. (1962). *Thought and language* (E. Hanfmann & G. Vakars, Eds. & Trans.). Cambridge, MA: MIT Press.

Vygotsky, L. S. (1978). *Mind in society* (M. Cole, V. John-Steiner, S. Scribner & E. Souberman, Eds.). Cambridge, MA: Harvard University Press.

Willer, B. (1992, January). An overview of *The Demand and Supply of Child Care in 1990. Young Children,* 19-22.

Chapter 2
The Narrative Quality of Young Children's Art

Marilyn Zurmuehlen
The University of Iowa
Larry Kantner
University of Missouri

Crawling about the base of a clothing display while his parents shopped, three-year-old Ben softly narrated, "He said...," "Then she said...," "She got in the car, then he got in the car." This barely audible, rudimentary story clearly was not intended for any audience beyond himself, although the form of his narrative quite evidently derived from a social context: children's storybooks read aloud to him by his parents, their friends, other relatives, and teachers at the preschool he had attended since infancy. Unlike these sources, however, Ben accompanied his elementary story with physical enactments so that his speech was more akin to a voice-over narration than

Figure 1. *Boundedness and repetition in drawing.*

to direct storytelling. Later, while riding together in a car, I noticed him absorbed in a similar *sotto voice* monologue that complemented his seatbelt-constrained movements of toys across the car interior's vinyl surface.

Barbara Hardy (1975) contended that "narrative imagination is a common human possession" (p. vii). Ruth Weir (1962) established how early and spontaneously such self-narration begins when she recorded the presleep monologues in which her two-and-a-half-year-old son talked to himself while lying alone in his crib. She described these dialogues as "vocalized inner speech which is essentially social" (p. 100). Even when their

teller is the only hearer, these vocalized narratives conform to the children who construct them their individual relationships with objects and spaces, their commonality with other storytellers who frequent their lives, and their experience of the kind of praxis Maxine Greene (1978) defined as a dialectic between critical reflection and action. Although critical reflection in these self-narratives is incipient, any expression of contingency, such as one character's response to another's statement, or even of succession, such as the choice of "then," can occur sensibly only with recourse, however brief and intuitive, to some sort of reflection.

In instances like those recounted about Ben, where self-narration complements a young child's actions, a particular statement may be the immediate progenitor of a barely succeeding action with which it merges, while other pieces of this dialogue may initiate accompanying movements so that the whole verbal and physical enactments are constructed from a counterpoint of kinesthetic and speech sequences whose sustaining structure is a rudimentary critical reflection.

Narration and Art

Adults who witness preschool children making art are aware that these early artists often accompany their mark making and constructing activities with narratives, at times musing to themselves as audience, then addressing and not infrequently engaging in dialogue with responsive teachers, observers, or caretakers. Such commentaries may be primarily denotative, naming and so affirming a sometimes only momentarily specific representational symbol, or self-directing a succeeding action by voicing a particular verbal intention. Four-year-old Leigh's narrative while working with clay is typical.

I'm going to make something. (She squished up the large flat piece and a larger ball.) Now I'm going to make a nose person. (She rolled more clay into the ball. She continued rolling, and added this piece to the larger one. She repeated the procedure, making a large ball and adding it to the smaller one.) I'm making a little person. A big, fat nose. Me put a mouth on.

I'm going to put a mouth on it. See? Put a mouth on. See? (She next rolled a short coil.)

That's a dumb mouth. (She took off the one already there and added the coil.) It's hair. I'll show you how I am making his mouth. Know what? Here's his mouth. I'm walking along. I'm walking along. Come on. Let's get going. (She walked around the room with the little figure.)

I want to make another little ballie. I'm making a baby person. (She added smaller balls for the eyes, nose and mouth, and a coil became the hair. The figure was identical to the first one, only a little smaller.)

Now I have a little person and a daddy. I want to take them home (Hindes, 1981, pp. 74-75).

Clearly, Leigh's vocalized repetition, "I'm walking along," inspired her to actually walk around the room while holding the little clay figure she had constructed, and this imperative relationship between vocalized narrative and action is even more apparent in Leigh's additional urging, "Come on. Let's get going." Critical

Figure 2. Boundedness and repetition in drawing.

reflection, too, is directly manifested when she commented, "That's a dumb mouth," and removed that portion of clay she had so negatively described.

On other occasions the narratives which young children relate while they make art may evolve from connected connotations as poetic transformations emerge in a chain of unpremeditated images and words. Four-year-old Mila engaged in such mental play, displaying the fluidity that often characterizes early symbolic representations.

This is a small tree. (She drew a black zigzag circle.)
I'll put one color at a time. It's so small. (She filled in the red trunk.)
The tree is going to be all colored up.
This is you. (She drew a small green figure.)
I'm making you green. Then everyone will miss you. Then I'll clean you off.

Now I'm making coconuts. Yup. Nope. These are going to be flowers. (She made a black line extending from three of the black spots.) This is how the flowers grow. I'm making them for me. They went through the tree and one coconut on the tree. I'm not done yet. (She used the green marker and made spots.)

I'm making them in a line. (She continued down the page with the green.) Then I'm coming down here. It's going through the tree trunk. It gets black in the tree trunk. It's getting a line together. If the tree falls, this one will pull it up. It's a rope. (She made horizontal green spots.) The boy is afraid. Here's another rope. So he won't be afraid. There's three ropes. (She indicated the green figure which she designated previously as the teacher.)

He's eating a lollipop and eats it up. He throws it down in the garbage. (She indicated the middle black lines.) Now there's four ropes. Now I'll color on the side of the garbage.

I'm done. (She stopped drawing abruptly, picked up the picture and left the observation room.) (Hindes, 1981, pp. 63-64)

Of course, Mila's narrative also contains voiced imperatives that propel the progress of this visual narrative in stated intentionalities: "I'll put one color at a time," "The tree is going to be all colored up," "Now I'll color on the side of the garbage." However, in many of her statements, Mila concurrently described drawing actions in which she was engaged, providing access to the artist's stream of consciousness that

Figure 3.
Boundedness and repetition in movement.

now understand that the figure Mila previously represented as her teacher had been reconstituted as the frightened boy. When Mila next portrayed this boy as eating a lollipop, she may have constructed the eucastastrophe, or happy ending, that Spencer (1976) regarded as typically essential in children's stories; however its introduction is a disjunction in her narrative. Mila seemed to intuitively recognize and remedy this break in coherence by incorporating a structural connection with earlier parts of her story. "Now there's four ropes" repeats and extends a theme from other portions of her narrative.

Beittel (1973) hoped might be revealed even with young children. Obvious instances of such commentary are "This is you," and "Now I'm making coconuts." These statements are simply denotative, but others reveal Mila's consciousness of visual and compositional qualities: "I'm making them in a line," and "It's going through the tree trunk."

While occasionally Mila's comments convey her surprise at the outcome of some drawing action—"It's going through the tree trunk. It's black in the tree trunk"—most of her transformations manifest a poetic playfulness. In these circumstances she saw new possibilities, connected connotations between a previously designated image and another interpretation suggested by her continually evolving visual and spoken narrative. Her statement, "It's getting a line together," followed by, "If the tree falls, this one will pull it up," is such an instance, and this transformation is confirmed in her next designation, "It's a rope." Her succeeding utterance, "The boy is afraid," appears to lack any transition until her following sentences provide a new context: "Here's another rope. So he won't be afraid. There's three ropes." Readers can

"Boundedness" and Repetition

Repetition is fundamental to rudimentary stories by preschoolers (Zurmuehlen, 1983). It can serve to elaborate an object or event, or it can be used to structure events, objects, or feelings primarily by means of opposition or contrast. A story told by a two-year-old boy incorporates such opposition in the repetition that gives form to his elementary narrative:

Monkey jumped into the water. He jumped out.
He jumped back in the water. He jumped out.
He jumped in and out (Pitcher & Prelinger, 1963, p. 32).

Children also structure their early drawings by repeating a line or shape, perhaps elaborating on either by increasing or diminishing its size or by changing colors, at other times contrasting the original lines or shapes with new repetitions in such familiar oppositions as zigzag lines alternating with multiple dots.

"Boundedness" and repetition are paramount aspects that young children apprehend in the forms of pictures and stories, and they spontaneously structure their own visual and verbal explorations on their understandings (Zurmuehlen, 1983). These qualities are readily apparent in two successive drawings by four-year-old Megan (Figures 1 & 2).

A variety of repeated shapes, as well as representations of Megan and her mother, are bounded by the outline of her house which itself is contained at its base by another rectangle in the first drawing and by repetitions of flowers in the second.

Crites argued "that the formal quality of experience through time is inherently narrative" (1971, p. 291). Thus, even in such apparently simple situations as a two-year-old's painting orange on a paper, actions are intentions realized, repeated, and as the visible orange strokes—records of those intentions and actions—change the image that painting child sees, new intentions arise in this experience through time: The story of art for that child changes from doing to making (Zurmuehlen, 1990).

Observing the Children at Play

On a mild May afternoon a group of children were happily playing in a large enclosed area behind the preschool they attended. Their individual intentionalities were at first glance disguised by the rapidly coalescing and dissolving groups of boys and girls as they clustered around one activity area, then surged or drifted to another. One little girl paused to pick a dandelion in full seed, then with delicate concentration she gently blew so that its seeds dispersed into a nearly ephemeral diffusion, simultaneously enacting her individual intention and realizing the effect of her action on this heretofore taken-for-granted object from her environment. Another child bent to carefully pluck clovers that bloomed in the grass underfoot. Standing, she earnestly and with remarkable facility began tying stem to stem, forming a chain that while nearly universal in conception was enacted from her individual intentionality. The first child was engaged in doing; the second child's praxis shifted into making.

Other children focused their attention on more structured items presented in their physical environment: plastic and metal containers at the water table, a wand with its accompanying liquid for blowing bubbles, the slide permanently situated in the playground, and a patchwork quilt brought that day to the preschool. One child realized her individual intention in doing by pouring water from a metal pitcher, while a considerable volume splashed alongside the receiving bucket and was contained by the surrounding sides of the water play table. Doing continued to be the paramount intention of the child who earlier had blown dandelion seeds into the surrounding atmosphere; next she blew through a bubble wand, her breath propelling the thin film of liquid from its wand frame into an amorphous form, itself rapidly transformed by the reciprocal pressures from her breath and the enveloping air. A small girl, wearing over-sized goggles on her forehead, climbed to the familiar slide's top step. From this vantage she struggled to drape the patchwork quilt over the slide's highest point, adding a bedsheet to make a rudimentary enclosure structure in which she and other children sat and played intermittently throughout the afternoon. Although this accommodation originated as a private environment it quickly evolved into the kind of shared shelter that appeals to many young children (Kantner, 1989).

Doing shifted into making when a young boy with a ball of twine in his hands began walking around a large tree, binding its girth with twine while his movements also enscribed a circular path around its trunk (Figure 3). After several repetitions, he veered across the playground toward another tree, the taut twine recording his new direction and repeated his previous binding actions. Returning to the first tree, still pulling the twine, he marked his path with its parallel lines, slightly raised above the ground. In response he stepped in and out of this newly defined enclosure as he alternated his binding intentions between the two trees. Here a child structured his experience of movement and materials through time by means of the boundedness and repetition with which young children form their pictures and stories.

When young children make and talk about their art they manifest the narrative quality of once...now...then that permeates and grounds all human consciousness.

References

Beittel, K. R. (1973). *Alternatives for art education research*. Dubuque, IA: Wm. C. Brown.

Crites, S. (1971). The narrative quality of experience. *American Academy of Religion, 39*, 291-311.

Greene, M. (1978). *Landscapes of learning*. New York: Teachers College Press.

Hardy, B. (1975). *Tellers and listeners: The narrative imagination*. London: The Athlone Press.

Hindes, N. F. (1981). *Drawing and modeling: Dialogue with the young child*. Unpublished master's thesis. The University of Iowa, Iowa City.

Kantner, L. (1989). Beginnings: Children and their art. In S. Hoffman & L.L. Lamme (Eds.), *Learning from the inside out: The expressive arts* (pp. 44-47, 50-51). Wheaton, MD: Association for Childhood Education International.

Pitcher, E. G., & Prelinger, E. (1963). *Children tell stories*. New York: International Universities Press.

Spencer, M. (1976). Stories are for telling. *English in Education, 10* (1), 16-23.

Weir, R. H. (1962). *Language in the crib*. The Hague: Mouton.

Zurmuehlen, M. J. (1983). Form as metaphor: A comparison of aesthetic structure in young children's pictures and stories. *Studies in Art Education, 24* (2), 111-117.

Zurmuehlen, M. J. (1990). *Studio art: Praxis, symbol, presence*. Reston, VA: National Art Education Association.

Chapter 3
Significance of Adult Input in Early Childhood Artistic Development

Anna M. Kindler
University of British Columbia

Artistic development in the early childhood years has received a significant amount of attention from psychologists, educators, and others concerned with the arts. The breadth and intensity of this interest are not surprising, for the tendency to create visual images in the relatively early stages of life seems to transcend cultural, social, and economic boundaries (cf., Gardner, 1976; Kellogg, 1970).

Viewing Artistic Growth

The phenomenon of artistic growth has been addressed from at least three perspectives. The first is centered around the natural, genetically preprogrammed unfolding of dispositions controlled by maturation. The second is based on considerations of the learning processes which interact with natural maturation and precipitate or alter artistic growth. The third is concerned with the nature of art, aesthetic value, and the unique properties of images produced by children. This chapter takes these perspectives into account while discussing a contemporary disparity between what is known about the nature of childhood and artistic development and the approaches that parents and preschool teachers take in addressing the issue of artistic growth.

For decades, Piaget's conception of developmental stages in human development influenced researchers in the area of developmental psychology. Piaget (1926, 1928, 1952, 1969) identified a sequence of developmental changes in children's mental structures associated with four fundamental, and qualitatively different, stages in human development. Piaget suggested that transitions between stages could be explained in terms of four factors which contribute to development: biological maturation, equilibration, experience, and social transmission.

Although Piaget was specifically concerned with the intellectual development of children, his theory indicated that cognitive structures formed logical groupings which together composed an integrated whole. It seemed logical to assume that the stages Piaget identified applied to other domains of human development as well. This position, however, has been questioned by several researchers (e.g., Gardner, 1976; Hardiman & Zernich, 1988) concerned with children's artistic development. Gardner (1976) argues that during the sensorimotor stage, infants and toddlers involved in sensory explorations and the mastery of motor skills are not in any way involved in the arts. Gardner's conception of the arts as integrally concerned with symbol systems precludes authentic artistic involvement before children come to understand the meanings of concepts and acquire the ability to manipulate them. Gardner also suggests that 7-year-old children, at the very onset of the concrete operational stage, possess structures necessary to become artists and that no qualitatively different stages are required to fully participate in the artistic process.

Other theorists, including Lowenfeld (1952), maintain that qualitative changes in artistic development occur well into the formal operational stage. Some researchers emphasize the role of quantitative changes as well. Hardiman and Zernich (1988) note the role of quantitative differences within qualitatively different stages and propose that the stages should be regarded "as being in the process of becoming and not ending" (p. 363). These researchers agree with Gardner (1976) that the formal operational stage in intellectual development has no equivalent in artistic development.

The crucial period in children's artistic growth, then, corresponds to Piaget's preoperational and early concrete operational stages. If, in fact, it is at some point between the second and ninth or tenth birthday that children acquire the structures that henceforward guide artistic endeavors, it is surprising how little attention is given to the active enhancement of artistic growth in the first half of this time span.

Explanations for this lack of active investment in preschool children's artistic development can be found in the recent history of art education. Efland's (1976) review of changing positions on the issue of children's artistic development and their impact on art instruction describes some of the historical conditions that still bear on today's practice.

According to Efland, childhood was not recognized as a unique stage in artistic development until the end of the nineteenth century. In Walter Smith's Massachusetts Normal Art School, or in institutions influenced by the philosophy of Arthur Wesley Dow, children were seen as untrained and unskilled miniature adults, who needed to develop good habits and learn proper drawing skills. Teaching approaches were based on considerations of the nature of art (e.g., Smith, 1875) rather than the special needs of children.

The Child-Centered Approach

Only with the increase of interest in child studies at the turn of the last century did emphasis in art education begin to shift. As often is the case, what was previously unappreciated and neglected became the centerpiece of a new philosophy. The "child centered-approach" quickly became the doctrine to follow in art education. The philosophy of Franz Cizek (cited in MacDougall, 1926 & Rugg & Schumacher, 1928) was especially attractive to educators representing the progressive front. Cizek believed that "method poisons art" (Efland, 1976, p. 71) and that teachers should only "take off the lid" (Efland, 1976, p. 71) and allow the child to develop from within. Victor Lowenfeld (1952), whose views significantly influenced practice in art education after World War II, agreed with Cizek on many points, including the belief that any input from the outside world is potentially negative. Lowenfeld held that every child had an inborn creative impulse, which was inhibited by the outside world.

Much has been written and researched in the areas of education and art education since the first edition of Lowenfeld's *Creative and Mental Growth* appeared (e.g., Burton, 1980; Eisner, 1976; Wilson & Wilson, 1977). However, in many schools across North America, teachers continue to leave young children undisturbed, hoping that their art will unfold naturally with as few external influences as possible. This noninterventionist philosophy is even more universally held by preschool teachers. Tarr (1989) argued that Cizek's approach to early childhood art education coexists in today's North American schools with models influenced by Pestalozzi (1915) and Froebel (1887). Tarr observed that, in setting up art centers, preschool teachers often resort to art activities reminiscent of Pestalozzi's "gifts and occupations." They do so, however, while professing a noninterventionist philosophy.

The child-centered approach to education brought attention to the unique abilities and needs of young learners. However, it also carried several undesirable side effects. The philosophy of "unfolding" was instrumental in reinforcing the common (and convenient) belief that artistic development takes care of itself. Little or no art training was necessary for teachers who would subsequently expend little effort on behalf of artistic learning. The undeniable expedience of this approach may account for the fact that contrary recommendations by many contemporary leaders in the field (e.g., Eisner, 1976; Wilson & Wilson, 1982) seem to pass unnoticed.

The Role of Adults

Life provides strong evidence that artistic learning is not the automatic result of maturation and self-guided experience. Many young adults, graduates of child-centered programs and "products" of noninterventionist approaches to art education, complain of their lack of insight, understanding, and ability in the realm of artistic expression. They feel illiterate and inadequate in one of the fundamental domains of human experience.

Adult intervention may not only be useful, but essential, to children's artistic development. L.S. Vygotsky (1978) argued that many curriculum ventures are founded on major theoretical positions which do not adequately describe the role of learning in the developmental process. Vygotsky disagreed with Piaget's claim that the process of development was essentially independent of learning, dismissing the notion that learning was not actively involved in, nor influenced by, the pattern of development.

Vygotsky argued that the process of development lagged behind learning, resulting in what he called a "zone of proximal development." Vygotsky (1978) proposed that "learning awakens a variety of internal developmental processes that are able to operate only when a child is interacting with people in his environment and in cooperation with peers. Once these processes are internalized, they become part of child's independent developmental achievement" (p. 90).

According to Vygotsky, then, experiences which are tailored to children's actual developmental level do not sufficiently promote growth. A laissez-faire approach to learning encourages the child to stay in place rather than to move ahead toward areas well within the child's reach if he or she receives appropriate assistance. Vygotsky's theory supports educators' concern with the learner and his or her present developmental abilities, while it looks ahead toward the child's potential at any given point in time within a particular domain. In that sense, Vygotsky's theory is both child-centered and discipline-based.

The zone of proximal development can be seen most clearly, perhaps, in young children's language acquisition. Adults, including parents and care givers, are undeniably instrumental in early speech development. Although children may seem to invent their first sounds, linguists believe that most children are truly responding to external input. Undoubtedly, these sounds are mastered and acquire meaning through social interaction, as others interpret the child's intentions and respond according to these interpretations. Parents do not passively listen, but constantly present new and challenging tasks. Children are exposed daily to language rules and structures by listening to adult conversations. They are stimulated to venture into the zone of proximal development, rather than to remain at an already attained level. This form of instruction is remarkably efficient and effective. Rapid language acquisition in the early childhood years has been documented by Chomsky (1965), Nelson (1980), Bruner, Roy, and Ratner (1982), and many others.

Although most adults, especially parents, find great delight in listening to children's babbling sounds, they do not attempt to preserve such a state forever. Common sense dictates that the beauty and innocence of the young child's earliest speech should not be preserved at the expense of communication. No one suggests that early attainment of a verbal vocabulary is detrimental to a child's ability to use language in a creative fashion later in life. In fact, depriving a child of those essential early learning experiences would be considered an abusive practice.

Yet, artistic development seems to be regarded in dramatically different terms. The "discovery" of children's art in the beginning of the century, and particularly the fascination with the spirit and process through which children create, made admiration of young children's art a social phenomenon. Today few argue that children's art is devoid of natural beauty, that it does not have an enviable sense of directness, purity, sincerity, and intensity. On the other hand, it may be useful to consider to what extent admiration for, and fascination with, young children's art can blind parents and educators to children's actual needs: their needs to be stimulated and challenged; to acquire skills and abilities that permit fluent use of visual symbols; and to operate at the level of a zone of proximal development.

Some researchers draw clear lines dividing childhood into periods that should be approached differently, in terms of the necessity of adult intervention. Gardner suggests that "during the natural artistry of the preschool years, active intervention is unnecessary"

(1982, p. 89) and that "during this period the approach of unfolding, or giving full rein to natural development, seems indicated" (1976, p. 108). Gardner implies that only children of school age benefit from or require active external investment in their artistic development. Gardner is certainly correct that when children between the age of two and five years are provided with materials, time, and opportunity to engage in artistic tasks, they do so readily. However, there is no evidence that appropriate external input would not enhance such "natural" unfolding.

The very idea of "natural" unfolding seems flawed, in that no matter how completely children are sheltered and protected from external influences, they do not grow up in a visual and aesthetic void. From the very beginning of their lives, children are exposed to and influenced by visual images, many of them produced by adults. Therefore, Lowenfeld's (1952) idea that "if children developed without any interference from the outside world, no special stimulation for their creative work would be necessary" (p. 1) cannot be tested. Nor can his call ever be answered: "Don't impose your own images on a child!" (p. 3). Aesthetic growth is subject to external influence, if only because children's experiences with art occur in a social context. What matters, then, is not the presence, but rather the quality, of external input.

The possibility that adult assistance might foster aesthetic growth has been discussed and demonstrated. As early as 1931, Alma Jordan Knauber studied art ability of nursery-school to third-grade children. She concluded that "proper stimulation toward creative activity would produce more and better trained artists and also a people versed in the appreciation of beauty" (p. 71). Subsequent research supports this proposition.

Pemberton and Nelson (1987), for example, demonstrated that graphic dialogue facilitates children's acquisition of drawing skills. These researchers used two strategies based on paradigms designed for verbal dialogues with young children: "growth recast" and "challenge continuation." Growth recasts immediately followed a child's production and involved an adult making a drawing that maintained the same basic reference and some structural detail, but at the same time structurally varied or "recast" the forms, "so that the child was exposed to structures more complex than those in the child's current system" (p. 31). Challenge continuations, which also presented structures challenging the child's current level, did not closely follow the child's production, but instead evolved around the general topic of the dialogue. The idea of presenting children with graphic forms "slightly above the child's current level of performance" (p. 39) was influenced by language input studies (Nelson, 1980), as well as by the ideas of Wilson and Wilson (1982). In

Vygotsky's terms, Pemberton and Nelson's study represented an attempt to provide children with an opportunity to perform within the boundaries of the zone of proximal development.

Burton (1980) discussed the instrumental role adults play in the "beginnings of artistic language" (p. 6), describing verbal interchange between a child and a teacher as a means of enriching and expanding artistic learning. Burton demonstrated how a teacher, recognizing that the child is learning to control and vary actions and reinforcing the child's terminology through dialogue, can offer the child an opportunity to pause and reflect, which in turn intensifies the learning experience. The interventions that Burton recommended were intended not to tell the child what to do, or to provide specific directions, but rather to encourage conscious choice making.

Wilson and Wilson (1977, 1982) have been among the most vocal advocates of active involvement in young children's artistic development. They argue that children draw primarily from images derived from popular culture even before they reach school age. Wilson and Wilson conclude that learning from adult-made images is an integral part of the process of artistic growth. They suggest that:

> Without models to follow there would be little or no visual sign making behavior by children.... The child learns to form configurational signs of his own mainly through observation of the configurational-sign-making-behavior of others, by noting initially that other people make drawings, then observing the way in which they are made, the variety of configurational signs that are made, and the diverse forms that these signs take in our culture (1977, p. 6).

Evaluating Children's Progress

One of the major difficulties in promoting adult's active involvement in young children's artistic development is understanding what constitutes progress in terms of artistic growth in early childhood years. The value attributed to children's spontaneous art has created a situation in which any departure from this artistic convention is regarded as a loss. Extensive analysis and study of children's art (e.g., Arnheim, 1954; Golomb, 1974; Kellogg, 1970; Lowenfeld, 1952) created a number of taxonomies that define the genre of "child art". As Wilson and Wilson (1977) observed, the concept of child's art is often associated with "those things which fit our image of a 'natural' or a 'creative' or a 'spontaneous'" expression but "we are turning a blind eye to the

very drawings—the copied ones—that could reveal the true nature of artistic learning" (p. 5).

Adults look at children's art much as twentieth-century audiences approach works of art from the past. Savile (1982) argued that works of art must be understood in the light of values and concepts relative to the period when they were created, and that any importation of ideas not present at that time for the purpose of interpretation is historically inappropriate. Richmond (1992) indicated, however, that this type of historical viewpoint was in reality impossible, as some essential factors shaping such an outlook are no longer accessible to a contemporary audience. Similarly, one may argue that adults' life experiences and expectations provide a perspective for interpreting children's art that differs greatly from a child's perspective. Is it possible to prevent adult ideas and conceptions from being imported into the process of interpreting children's art? Richmond's (1992) implication that "the modern viewer cannot, as a matter of logic, acquire the interpretive sensibilities and feelings for the qualities of life necessary for authentic understanding of artistic legacy" (p. 12) suggests that adult accounts of children's artistic efforts may never be fully accurate. Wilson and Wilson's (1977) observations are certainly congruent with this position.

The persistent influence of adult conceptions of children's artistic development is manifested in current educational practices derived, surprisingly, from child-centered philosophy. The model that emerged from this tradition, and which continues to influence many preschool teachers, recommends organization of art centers in children's play environments. The role of teacher is reduced to one of "dispenser of art materials and fountain of emotional support for the child" (Eisner, 1976, p. 7). It is assumed that the child will spontaneously approach the centers and explore the available media with little or no guidance or supervision. This is certainly what adults would do in a similar situation. Provided with several activity centers, most of us would circulate among them, often in a systematic manner, and take advantage of learning opportunities. Do young children, however, behave in the same manner?

Significance of Adult Input

For 9 months, I spent an hour-and-a-half each Wednesday morning at my youngest son's daycare. The program in which 12 children, 18 months to 3 years of age, were enrolled, was guided by child-centered philosophy. The facility's physical design allowed for organization of several "centers," including areas devoted to exploration of art materials. The teachers took great care to ensure that a variety of materials was offered on different occasions: tempera paints, differing collage materials and glue, playdough with rolling pins, cookie cutters, and so forth.

Although opportunities for art materials exploration were plentiful, the children took little advantage of them. On many occasions the "art centers" remained untouched, and the amount of their use seemed to be closely associated with the teacher's physical presence at the table. Unlike the housekeeping corner or the car racing area, the art centers were rarely approached by children on their own, and even fewer children spent any significant amount of time at them. Most of the "explorations" that I witnessed involved dipping a brush in paint and making one or two marks, before embarking on a more exciting adventure in other areas of the daycare. Only when a parent or a teacher stayed with a child and became involved in a dialogue related to actions that the child was performing, did a child seem inclined to truly explore the available materials and tools, or to experiment with their use. Although more systematic observations and research are certainly needed to substantiate this claim, I would submit that the mere availability of materials in early childhood classrooms is not a sufficient condition for the enhancement of artistic growth. My observations clearly suggest that adult input is essential to young children's artistic explorations.

Once the necessity of such input is recognized, the nature of adult intervention needs to be carefully defined. I agree with Elkind (1991) who opposes the idea of formal instruction in the early childhood years and insists that "the education of young children has to be in keeping with their unique modes of learning" (p. 183). There is, however, a great difference between total nonintervention and teaching 3-year-old children the rules of linear perspective. In the same way that parents and daycare teachers assist a young child in language acquisition, they can become instrumental in enhancing artistic growth.

Although several types of possible intervention have been described by researchers (e.g., Golomb, 1974; Pemberton & Nelson, 1987; Wilson & Wilson, 1982), there is an urgent need for more efforts to propose, implement, and test models which promote the artistic development of young children. Art educators must convince parents and preschool teachers of the significance of aesthetic growth in human development. We must also clarify and stress the fact that active adult participation in this process of growth need not be detrimental and may well be, in fact, absolutely necessary.

References

Arnheim, R. (1954). *Art and visual perception.* Berkeley: University of California Press.

Bruner, J., Roy, C., & Ratner, H. (1982). The beginnings of request. In K. E. Nelson (Ed.), *Children's language* (Vol. 3, pp. 91-138). Hillsdale, NJ: Lawrence Erlbaum Associates.

Burton, J. M. (1980) Developing minds: Beginnings of artistic language. *School Arts,* 6-12.

Chomsky, N. (1965). *Aspects of the theory of syntax.* Cambridge: MIT Press.

Efland, A. (1976). Changing views on children's artistic development: Their impact on curriculum and instruction. In E. Eisner (Ed.) *The arts, human development, and education* (pp. 65-86). Berkeley: McCutchan.

Eisner, E. (1976). What we know about children's art—and what we need to know. In E. Eisner (Ed.) *The arts, human development, and education* (pp. 5-18). Berkeley: McCutchan.

Elkind, D. (1991). An essential difference. In J. W. Noll (Ed.), *Taking sides: Clashing views on controversial educational issues* (6th ed., pp. 183-192). Guilford, CT: Dushkin Publishing Group.

Froebel, F. (1887). *The education of man.* New York: D. Appelton.

Gardner, H. (1976). Unfolding or teaching: On the optimal training of artistic skills. In E. Eisner (Ed.), *The arts, human development and education* (pp. 99-110). Berkeley: McCutchan.

Gardner, H. (1982). *Art, mind, and brain: A cognitive approach to creativity.* New York: Basic Books.

Golomb, C. (1974). *Young children's sculpture and drawing: A study in representational development.* Cambridge: Harvard University Press.

Hardiman, G.W. & Zernich, T.Z. (1988). Some considerations of Piaget's cognitive-structuralist theory and children's artistic development. In G.W. Hardiman & T. Zernich (Eds.), *Discerning art: Concepts and issues* (pp. 335-365). Champaign, IL: Stipes Publishing Company.

Kellogg, R. (1970). *Analyzing children's art.* Palo Alto: Mayfield Publishing Company.

Knauber, A.J. (1931). A study of the art ability found in very young children. *Child Development, 2*(1), 66-71.

Lowenfeld, V. (1952). *Creative and mental growth.* (2nd ed.). New York: Macmillan.

MacDougall, A.R. (1926) Developing of artists through imagination. *Arts and Decoration, 24.*

Nelson, K.E. (1980). Theories of the child's acquisition of syntax: A look at rare events and at necessary, catalytic, and irrelevant components of mother-child conversation. In V. Teller & S. White (Eds.), *Studies in child language and multilingualism* (pp. 45-67). New York: Annals of the New York Academy of Sciences.

Pemberton, E.F. & Nelson, K.E. (1987). Using interactive graphic challenges to foster young children's drawing ability. *Visual Arts Research, 13*(2), 29-41.

Pestalozzi, J. (1915). *How Gertrude teaches her children.* Syracuse, NY: C.W. Bardeen.

Piaget, J. (1926). *The language and thought of the child.* New York: Harcourt, Brace.

Piaget, J. (1928). *Judgement and reasoning in the child.* New York: Harcourt, Brace.

Piaget, J. (1952). *The origins of intelligence in children.* New York: International Universities Press.

Piaget, J. (1969). *The mechanisms of perception.* New York: Basic Books.

Richmond, S. (1992). Historicism, teaching, and understanding of works of art. *Visual Arts Research, 18*(1), 32-41.

Rugg, H., & Schumacher, A. (1928) *The child centered school.* Yonkers on Hudson, NY: World Book Company.

Savile, A. (1982). *The test of time.* Oxford: Clarendon Press.

Smith, W. (1875). *Freehand drawing.* Boston: James R. Osgood and Company.

Tarr, P. (1989). Pestalozzian and Froebelian influences on contemporary elementary school art. *Studies in Art Education. 30*(2), 115-121.

Vygotsky, L.S. (1978). *Mind in society.* Cambridge: Harvard University Press.

Wilson, M. & Wilson, B. (1977). An iconoclastic view of the imagery sources in the drawings of young people. *Art Education, 30*(1), 4-11.

Wilson, M. & Wilson, B. (1982). *Teaching children to draw.* Englewood Cliffs, NJ: Prentice Hall.

Chapter 4
Art at Home: Learning From a "Suzuki" Education

George Szekely
University of Kentucky

At age 4, my daughter Ilona announced that she wanted to be an artist and teacher just like her dad. Delighted at the prospect, I began to involve her in many of my daily activities, discussed my art ideas and lesson plans with her, and took her shopping for

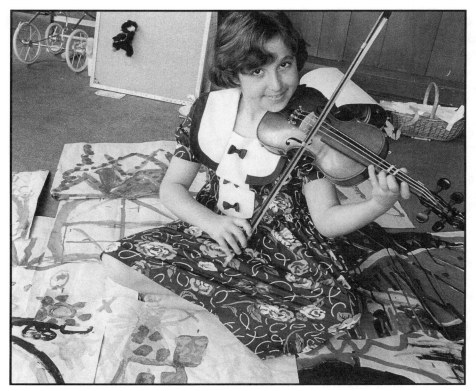

Figure 1

art supplies. At that time, Ilona was interested in every aspect of art and worked tirelessly on her creations. However, when she started school, her art making at home declined steadily.

When Ilona was 5, she attended a school concert of young musicians and pointed to the

violin, proclaiming, "I want to play this, too." The violin became an important part of her life as she was introduced to the Suzuki method of music education. As I sat back, waiting for Ilona's art to reblossom, I began to consider the possibilities of the Suzuki methodology for learning art at home.

Mr. Suzuki, a respected Japanese educator, believes in training young children in the skills, coordination, patience, respect and knowledge of musicians. Suzuki education is based on the concept that "the parent and teacher need to develop a musical environment that supports and inspires a child's natural musical talents" (Mills, 1984, p. 6). Each child is treated, and expected to act, as a serious adult musician. Talent is not an issue since, according to Suzuki, music is the "mother tongue": All children can enjoy and express themselves through their natural gift. Music education in the Suzuki style involves a close partnership between the music teacher, parent, and student. Parents not only attend all classes with the children, but also serve as music teachers during home lessons. Music develops in the close company of at least one caring parent who fully participates in every lesson, rehearsal, and performance. A Suzuki parent is a special breed of dedicated and determined individual who deeply cares about every detail of the child's musical studies. Parents learn not only about the violin but, more importantly, about their children as learners and people. They become totally familiar with the problems of artistic development such as difficulties in learning, recall, manipulation, and posture, and learn to diagnose and deal with such difficulties. Parents are constantly searching for new and innovative teaching ideas to make each practice session more exciting and productive.

As full participants in the process, Suzuki parents not only appreciate the joys of performance, but are aware of what it takes to get there. Suzuki trained children deeply feel their parent's concern and values in dedicating themselves to music. The child lives the life of a musician: practicing daily, attending "repertory" or small group sessions, and giving periodic recitals.

Parental cooperation is an equally necessary ingredient for young visual artists. How rewarding it would be for an art teacher to work with a comparably dedicated group of parents who were familiar with every aspect of art instruction. Total commitment of parents to visual art studies would convey a sense of the subject's importance to the child. Children's school art programs would be greatly improved if they came to class with confidence and ideas from regular home practice. If parents took an interest in providing an exciting visual diet at home, school art instruction would begin with a greater appreciation for beautiful things. The professional attitude toward work, practice, patience, and the idea of slowing working toward accomplishment (which musicians learn quickly) would also be of great assistance in learning to view and make art.

Many parents feel that art learning is mysterious, sacred, unteachable, and unique in its development. Some teachers even advise parents against "tampering with art." I believe all parents can be effective art "teachers" in many subtle, yet explicit ways. Visual artists who show their pride in being self-taught often leave the mistaken impression that they learned their art in spite of school and art teachers, as if they needed no assistance from anyone. Yet, when artists reminisce, they are the first to recall the important individuals at home and in the schools who helped them formulate crucial attitudes and respect for their work. Parents can, and should, play an important role in the artistic development of their children.

Anyone visiting our home is invited to a concert. Special persons like grandparents are asked to participate in more intimate practice sessions. During special occasions, the family is serenaded by young violinists. At the comple-

tion of a music book, the entire family celebrates. During quiet evenings, music is heard throughout the house. In the car traveling anywhere, the violin tapes go into the stereo before the car begins to roll.

Ilona's music flourishes in a caring, supportive environment. All art made by young people is created for someone special; usually the child is working hard to please a receptive parent. The number of supportive responses and kind words our children receive during each violin session far exceeds the supportive responses they would receive in a large school class. Performing artists needs this much attention: They need a willing listener who is visibly excited and sometimes moved by their music.

Yet, what effort is made in the home to appreciate the visual art works of children? The brief praise a work receives as it is hung on the refrigerator door is simply not equal to the reception music receives. The strong relationship between parents and children in the course of Suzuki studies affords a greater opportunity for the child to realize that art is worth giving. But with visual art, what extended occasions do we have to receive a child's dreams, listen to artistic plans, or participate in discoveries? Parents who want to enhance the visual art development of their children will need to create sustained opportunities for praise and support by making a long-term commitment to the child's visual art endeavors.

Of course, there are interesting problems to art reception at home. So much of the child's art is tied to play that parents often do not see art as a creative performance needing support. Parents assume that art, like play, is self-inspired and self-nourished, so that neither receives great attention. While children in and out of school meet many art critics, they seldom have good audiences. Support for art in the home requires that parents clearly express how they feel about art. Parental support of the child's creative words, gestures and play with art builds enthusiasm and an appetite for greater artistic challenges.

What art opportunities exist in the home and how can young visual artists be challenged? Home art teaching requires finding opportunities in everyday tasks to plan, select and develop a sense for the visual in everyday events. It involves seeking moments of visual pleasure, such as looking up to see a special cloud or examining an old doorway during a walk. There needs to be a sense of importance to living with and being surrounded by beautiful things and discovering or collecting interesting objects. An awareness of beauty can be made evident in clothing choices, in selecting fabrics for a new chair, or in shopping for any new object we live with. Parents can lead the way in being visually alert and excited by a new color or a striking new form or object. Children often find objects of visual interest such as a pine cone on a daily walk or a shiny rock to fill their pockets; parents need to support such searchings and provide a spirit which inspires such artistic values.

Home is the place where basic artistic skills are learned and have the most opportunities to flourish. Basic construction, display, or packaging skills, for example, are learned through home tasks. Skills that become important in art are learned by the child who is allowed to be a parent's apprentice in using a paint roller, hammer, or car-repair kit or in baking or cake decorating. Children who have access to the family camera, typewriter, sewing machine, or computer frequently use them in creative ways. Each home activity has artistic extensions and can be discussed via the child's creative adaptations. Each home tool, from a spatula to a hair dryer, is an art tool in disguise. Each home space is a studio and each home occasion has possibilities of becoming an artistic celebration. Home tasks become art tasks when children view themselves as artists and are encouraged to exercise creative thoughts and judgments. Home chores that allow children to play, select, arrange and display forms through active investigations have great artistic merit. Each home purchase or repair, from replacing a watering can to fixing the roof, involves visual choices and design decisions which can involve a young artist. The many visual comparisons required at home can become "on the job" training for a young designer.

Space

Since our Suzuki musical beginning, the living room has shifted from a company space to the room devoted to music. It made me realize how seldom children's visual art works merit the living room as their place of display. Too often, their art is considered unprofessional and not important enough to be featured in the family's primary living space.

Suzuki practice sessions, in fact, frequently move to all parts of the house as violinists stroll on the porch, enter the dining room, or serenade a bather in the tub. In search of air, light, or an unusual echo, children practice violin where inspiration may lead them. Wouldn't the artist in the family also benefit from such flexible space allowances?

Art, created at home, has the advantages of interesting spaces—closets, stairways, the bathtub, or the laundry room—all seem to inspire crawling through, hiding inside, or climbing over. Space is an invention in children's play and in their art and they experience spaces through direct sensory means. Their art is the creation of a controlled and make-believe world within a real one. My own children's favorite space is under the table where they build elaborate arrangements with pillows and blankets. Children also structure with chairs covered with blankets or umbrellas creating unique architectural spaces within a room. Clubhouses, play spaces and forts turn a home's furnishings upside down, but such inventive architectural structures should not only be tolerated, they should be encouraged. These primitive-looking structures allow children to grapple with space ideas, to discover architectural relationships, and to create spaces with imagination when they begin to make two-dimensional art. Using chairs as spaceships, tents, or forts under the table, kids create unusual views and unique forms and spaces that will later be described in their art works. These experiences, rather than adult formulas in perspective drawing, present to children a significant space experience.

The first step in gaining control over one's art is the ability to understand and manipulate the environment around the work. Children should understand the qualities of a work space—its shape and size, lighting, openings and surfaces—because these contribute to and suggest what is to be made within it. A space that is understood contributes to the art and ideas conceived within it. Spaces with low ceilings may suggest working on the floor while a long space may recommend working on a long roll of paper. Instead of seeking a formula for a perfect space, each space needs to be lived in and adjusted for art work. Parents can play an important role in the child's artistic development by helping children locate work spaces and supporting their unorthodox "studios."

Time

Even though time may be available for little else, there is always time for music practice in a Suzuki home. My wife, our resident Suzuki teacher, in pre-arranged negotiations with the children ensures that practice takes place each day at the agreed time. Recognizing that children are just as busy as adults with demands imposed by school, home responsibilities, and self-committed time for recreation, Suzuki families know that finding practice time is difficult. To practice violin, however, this family cooperates by withholding interruptions and focusing attention to the needs of our musicians. Daily rehearsal is a requirement and regular work is the key to improvement, a doctrine accepted by all Suzuki students.

Visual artists would certainly agree with Suzuki in emphasizing the values of daily practice in the development of skills and ideas. They know that art involves routines, schedules and commitment to rehearsal time. Unfortunately, while this is readily accepted in music and dance, it is an idea not readily associated with the visual arts.

In the visual arts, regular work habits are important, but parents should understand that time spent "practicing" the visual arts, unlike music practice, should not be relegated to a specific time frame at a designated hour each day. Art rehearsal involves more than skill building: It includes gathering ideas and materials, a combination of physical and idea creation. Time for art-making needs to be flexible. Parents and students can discuss personal preferences in time use, recognizing, for example that some people work best in the morning, others at night; some work best at a fast pace while others prefer to work more slowly. An understanding of an individual's "inner time" preferences in relationship to art-making helps in determining the most effective use of time.

Parents need not nag their children to work, nor must they remain completely uninvolved in their children's art. Parents need to be committed and involved in every aspect of home art, including the scheduling of art time. Simply put, the more time spent on art, the better. If parents indicate their personal involvement and interest in children's art, then helping the child allocate time to work will not be seen as interference.

It is important, however, for parents and children to recognize and discuss the developmental nature of art. Unlike time spent on school activities in pursuit of finished products, usually one project per period, artists do not work in a prescribed time frame because art making is a lifelong activity. Time breaks from art are simply momentary pauses as ideas continue. Young artists need to become more aware of their inner timing as creative people, by making their own decisions as to when to start, how long to continue, and when to stop the art clock. Being in charge of one's art requires the ability to be aware of time and able to control it, and the recognition that art has to be dealt with on a regular basis.

Materials and Tools

After much searching through catalogues, perusing advertisements, and following up recommendations, our family purchased our first violin. It was a fine sounding instrument, a reproduction of a more famous ancestor. Then there was the search for a piano, looking through antique stores and showrooms, invit-

ing both music teacher and piano tuner to inspect and give their opinions. Other musical purchases also were made to broaden the children's musical interests—a synthesizer and a guitar. Each of our instruments is specially cared for, frequently dusted and polished, and kept in a protective environment away from humidity or extreme temperature. Materials required for music studies also receive prompt sincere attention. The purchase of recording tapes and violin strings becomes a priority. We have acquired numerous tape machines for the home and car to reproduce quality sounds.

In direct contrast, most families purchase art supplies at discount stores with little attention to quality or longevity. Few homes contain more than a box of crayons, and children are expected to make art from whatever home scrap is available. Parents and children seldom experience the excitement of searching for fine chalks or handmade paper which could be sources of inspiration to the young artist.

When a child wants to make art, yet lacks the tool or material, parents seldom rush to the store or feel that they have to research the best materials available. Why is there not the same enthusiastic willingness to provide the funds for art that seems to always exist with music education?

Nevertheless, children can learn to practice art by exploring the wide range of art supplies available in the home. Consider the various papers ready at hand: Toilet paper, paper towels, sandpaper, lens cleaning tissues, memo pads, wallpaper, stationery, bags, wax papers, and so forth. These varied surfaces form a richer variety than may be found in schools or art supply stores. In other areas of art such as painting, parents can suggest using food colors, nail polishes, cake decorating tubes, graphite powder, and many other unusual and inexpensive household substances. For sculpting, children can use bricks, toothpicks, hair curlers, clothes clips, shingles, or floor tiles. These ideas are just the beginnings of the home supplies that work well as art media. As children sculpt with a garden hose or draw with a sprinkler, they are at the forefront of contemporary art inventions. Substances found at home, such as ice, earth, stones, or shaving cream, can be explored as art works without the restrictions of traditional media or art forms. In playing with home art supplies, children recognize the values of environmental substances in defining a new art.

Reading and Listening

In our home the bookshelves contain many illustrated biographies of great composers to serve as inspiration for our young musicians. The daily music study is expanded through the works and ideas of other musicians, critics, and commentators. Suzuki parents provide musical accompaniment to daily activities, with music turned on as a background to play, or as a lullaby in going to sleep. According to Suzuki philosophy, the child's inner strengths are developed by providing daily opportunities for listening.

Parents could enhance children's visual art education by helping them to encounter beautiful things each day, through making exciting visual works available through books and reproductions. Good quality art books can be purchased or explored at the public library. Collecting books can become a family matter when beautiful books with exceptional reproductions are given as holiday gifts. Looking at pictures and reading about artists and their works can occasionally replace bedtime stories. Artists' biographies offer an important source of camaraderie and sharing of experiences which are often recognized by even the youngest person involved in art. Museum gift shops, antique and used book stores as well as flea markets are lively places to discover books with interesting illustrations.

Leafing through a picture book with a child may require little commentary by parents, since the power of shared seeing cannot be overestimated. Frequently searching through an old book store and sharing one's visual findings can be simply phrased "Isn't this beautiful?" or "Look at this." Sharing beautiful images is an important act to which explanations sometimes get in the way. Children learn to accept our simple visual cues and respond to them.

Art learning at home is exciting in that art and play-related subjects can be introduced as they arise. An old plumbing supply catalog may inspire new art interests and collections while introducing kids to a new world of windmills, old barns, castles or light houses. What constitutes an "art book" lies in the imagination of the artists—exciting collections can be built from medical illustrations, scientific journals, or a catalog of old playground equipment.

Since books are such an important part of every artist's life, I have encouraged each member of our family to work on his or her own book. My son, Jacob, has just completed one of his many series of transformer adventure books. My daughter, Ilona, is working on an illustrated book of poems, and our four-year-old, Ana, is already showing an author's interest by eagerly stapling all of her pictures and cutouts into a book. Whenever our children complete a book, they select their own cover and we xerox the book so copies can go on bookshelves or be shared with friends.

Collecting

My Suzuki musicians, Ilona, Jacob and Ana, have collected violin pencils, sweaters, figurines, stickers, memo pads, and a special chocolate violin! In addition, we have dozens of music tapes and instruments, including an antique metronome with a bakelite plastic case reminiscent of old radios of the 1940s. When music becomes an important life activity, children begin collecting their share of music-related souvenirs.

In art, collecting is usually related to an individual's art work, since each piece requires specific visual choices and research. An artist's collection is a valuable clue to his or her art ideas. Children's drawings are often visualized from their toy and other collections and exist in the play setups before they begin to appear on paper. Through collections, displays, and arrangements, children's art ideas are observed, compared, and decided on. There are great similarities in the collecting habits of adult artists and children. Neither views collections as an investment and both may be highly eclectic in their choices. Looking for collections goes hand in hand with looking for art ideas. For the child, collecting is a first step toward appreciating more sophisticated museum collections.

Children need the freedom to collect without being judged by the tastes and standards of others, especially those of adults. When collections are in conflict with adult tastes, it is easy to label them junk or to place prohibitions on them. The beauty of a rusty spring or a weathered work glove may be obvious to its discoverer, but unclear to the parent who is asked to live with it. Yet, as parents, our approval of collections is a significant means of supporting young artists' imaginative development. In fact, art discussions should stress the connections between Garbage Pail Kids cards, plastic charms, and rock collections with art interests and ideas. And a parent who picks up a crushed can in a parking lot because it looks interesting demonstrates the sensibilities of a collector and, importantly, appears supportive of a child's collection.

Freedoms of Investigation

Oh the busy life of concert musicians! We rush to recitals, attend workshops to improve musical skills, and play in front of new audiences. The calendar is dotted with lessons and musical events. There is great jazz, Broadway shows, ballet and even a performance of barber shop harmonizing. At each concert, we meet other Suzuki-taught pupils. They play their instruments in the mall, a park, a senior center and a farmers' market. Suzuki students are treated as professional musicians so their confidence develops before real audiences. Wherever we travel, we move with violins in hand; even a brief vacation includes three violins! A holiday is simply a new place to play, with new spaces for our musicians to hear their sounds and get new perspectives on their work. Thus far, our children's most unusual concert was a performance for the pilot and crew of our delayed airplane held for repair at Kennedy Airport.

Do the parents of young visual artists fill their calendars regularly with art activities and encourage them to visit exhibitions and galleries to meet with artists? Do young artists have the occasion to work and/or display art in front of a variety of audiences? Are they free to visit different places in order to collect ideas and respond to new and exciting environments? Do young artists carry their cameras or sketchbooks every place they go? Is each vacation an opportunity to reflect about art? Art making should be an ongoing investigation of life's arenas, with the freedom to go anywhere and search faithfully through every aspect of the environment for inspiration, new audiences, and ideas. Art requires being in front of newly created art work, in new places and new settings, as well as being far removed to see it through one's memory. Art requires constant shopping for possibilities and visions. Recognizing this, parents should encourage young art students to roam and wander through favorite places, search for colors, experience smells and feel new sensations.

Working Alone

As Suzuki musicians mature, violin practice sessions extend in time and the students learn to practice alone. Old pieces are reviewed while new pieces are explored. The move toward working by oneself occurs gradually over many years. As Suzuki-trained children seek greater independence, they begin to welcome the challenge of independent working and its responsibilities.

Would it not be wonderful if art students experienced a similar process and discovered the joys of independent art making? In music, the goals and techniques to be practiced alone are decided by the teacher. In art,

one not only has to face the difficulties of working alone, but also has to decide what to do when alone. Working by oneself in art requires the ability to take charge of the entire art process—to discover ideas and manage the process of acting on these new ideas.

It is sometimes difficult to convey the pleasure of working alone to children. Children who have good work spaces and interesting rooms will declare, "I am afraid to be in my room alone." Rooms filled with exciting toys are not enough to keep children from whining, "I have nothing to do." For people whose lives have been scheduled and organized from infancy on, deviating from set routines, whether for a day off, a vacation, or retirement, and being alone can be difficult, even frightening.

To accustom our children to working alone, we allow them to deviate from their routines and follow their own ideas for the day. I try to share with them the joys of personal walks and the pleasures of experiencing a creative idea and having an opportunity to work it out by oneself. Artists need to learn at an early age the value of doing things by themselves. Being able to work alone is vital to the ability to make art.

It is often difficult for children to face unassigned challenges, or even to take their own thoughts and ideas seriously enough to confidently act on them without adult guidance or advice. To become an artist, one must learn to appreciate the pleasure of working for oneself, of not being dependent on others. A primary goal of all art teaching is to prepare children for the notion that art can exist without an art teacher. Parents can offer important assistance in planning for student's independent works by helping them to schedule time, locate places, and explore material opportunities. Parents can listen to and discuss a child's goals and preparatory thoughts. The many decisions and choices made in the process of art making at home can become overwhelming when compared to the relatively few independent decisions a school art project requires. Parents need to understand this and work to build the confidence and the sense of importance attached to independent working.

An Introduction to the World of Performing Artists

Whenever a line of autograph seekers forms backstage after a concert or performance, young Suzuki musicians are well represented. These children have many opportunities to speak to world famous musicians from Lionel Hampton to Itzhak Perlman. As my children discussed their practicing concerns with the great Lionel Hampton, I could not help but think of the many creative concerns that a child could discuss with visual artists. When children make art in school, they seldom consider that their activity has a great deal in common with a group of people called "artists." Can similar "stage door" meetings be arranged for the young visual artist?

A young artist would profit by visits to an artist's studio to witness his/her rehearsal and performances in preparation for an art work or an entire exhibit. Parents can work with local galleries and museums, especially university galleries, to arrange for children to witness preparations for a show. Children can talk to the artists and learn how artists work with a gallery, select works for an exhibit, and choose display materials. Parents can help to link the child to an art world through an awareness of other artists.

Because young artists learn to work alone, there is a greater need to know that their initiatives are shared by a larger art community. They need an enlarged art group to serve as models, mentors, and guides. Artists at any age need to know there are others who think art making is important. Even the most solitary artists needs to be able to compare and contrast his or her work, as well as to visualize beyond the works of others. Interests and ambitions are stirred by other artists, so that even when one works alone, there is an invisible audience responding to each work. All unique views and ideas develop against this background as we differentiate ourselves from others. A child who is lucky enough to be befriended by an artist gains one of the most important connections to art that one can have.

The Private Lesson

Suzuki-taught children have great advantages. They have a private music teacher to work each week with them. Each child is the exclusive center of attention for a period of time, as teacher and child discuss the young musician's needs and progress. The teacher assigns daily practice lessons, overseen by a concerned parent who continues at home where the private teacher left off. My children, for example, spend a half-hour each week in private sessions and an hour in group lessons, in addition to their daily practice at home. An incredible amount of time and attention is paid to the child's music education.

How many parents go through the same trouble of seeking a private artist to work with their children's visual art studies? Would parents be willing to pay and spend time on such special instruction? It is rare that an art stu-

dent receives the full, individual attention of a professional artist on a regular basis. Although Saturday morning art classes do exist, these are instructions for large groups, similar to school art, and often taught by novice art teachers. While parents of young musicians do a great deal of research in checking the credentials and reputation of their music teacher, few parents know more than the name of their Saturday morning art teacher.

Engaging a private artist to work with a child can have benefits much like those in Suzuki training. Goals, interests, values, and work habits can be talked about while the essential caring of an experienced artist-teacher is generally inspiring. As relationships develop between the child and the artist, unique learning occurs. Many artists would like to work with a child and would generously give of themselves if asked, yet parents must initiate such relationships.

In artist-to-artist sessions, mutual respect and trust are built through the interest demonstrated for each other's works. A private teacher can expand the child's art interests as he or she shares unique experiences and perspectives. As an artist working with my children, I am never certain who is learning from whom; I simply try to treat the children's art and ideas with respect without trying to steer or change them.

Keeping Records

Our family has kept photographs of each child's first music practice session and films and videos of each concert. Color movies of both performances and rehearsals provide valuable comparisons of the childrens' development to demonstrate to all the results of hard work. We have numerous scrapbooks filled with pictures and concert programs, autographs and mementos that recall the thrill of meeting famous musicians. We have noted the words spoken at these events, such as my son, at age 4, shaking hands with Itzhak Perlman and saying, "You know I play the violin, too." The first violins, of course, were never sold and are taken out occasionally to be viewed, touched, played by the children who are amazed that they once held such tiny instruments.

How many parents keep their child's first scribblings? Of course, far fewer keep their first drawing tools. Do parents have records of the child's first paintings? Or do we even recall these with the same fondness as the early musical beginnings? Is there anything in family scrapbooks reflecting the growth of the young artist? With all the visual media that each family has available today, do they keep visual records of the children's art?

The young visual artist may have had an art work displayed on a school bulletin board, but bouts with fame, exposure to audiences, and opportunities to experience the excitement of a show are rare indeed. Art exhibits are excellent teaching tools and even the youngest child would learn a great deal by preparing and developing an exhibit. But children's art work is often displayed where few can share it—on classroom walls and refrigerators.

Parents play an important role when they document and preserve children's art. I am proud to have a complete set of my daughter's paintings from her first year of exploring the media. Some of her works fell apart quickly, but they have survived through photographs. We store art projects in drawers, folders, and envelopes for easy access and encourage her to return to them again and again. Caring for art work in this fashion demonstrates that we value her art.

Parents may want to keep written journals of the child's progress. These records may encourage children to talk about their art and share perceptions of it. Videotaped records of children's art, places of work, and the acts of making a work can become a journal type activity as the young artist describes and reflects on his or her creation of a particular piece.

Children's works can be shown in the home, in the parent's place of work, or even in community exhibits. Work can be framed professionally or, through the use of plastic box frames, by the artist.

When a child's art is considered among the family's valued possessions, it will be well preserved, thoughtfully exhibited, and supplemented by exciting records of art-related experiences.

A Final Thought

The experience of writing this chapter helped my family to recognize that in our children's musical education, which we originally intended as a supplement to their art, greater accomplishments are being made. As a family, we give more energy and time to the children's music than to their art. This assessment and comparison to Suzuki music experiences has helped make some long overdue adjustments in the many things we encourage and do in art at home. It is my hope that a similar process could be encouraged in classrooms and homes to properly support home players-artists, their collections, space needs, object and material interests, and their parents, the first art teachers of all of us.

Reference

Mills, E. (1984). *In the Suzuki style*. Berkley, CA: Diablo Press.

Reading Suggestions

Adcock, D., & Segal, M. (1983). *Play together—grow together*. New York: Mailman Company.

Clark, G., & Zimmerman, E. (1984). *Educating artistically talented students*. New York: Syracuse University Press.

Gardner, H. (1973). *The arts and human development*. New York: John Wiley.

Hartley, J. & Goldenson, M. (1978). *The complete book of children's play*. New York: Thomas Y. Crowell.

Paley, V. G. (1981). *Wally's stories*. Boston, MA: Harvard University Press.

Szekely, G. (1981). *Recollections of home by contemporary artists*. Unpublished paper presented at the Doctoral Association of New York Educators Convention, New York University.

Szekely, G. (1988). *Encouraging creativity in art lessons*. New York: Teachers College Press-Columbia University.

Szekely, G. (1991). *From play to art*. Portsmouth, NH: Heinemann-Boynton & Cook.

Timmerman, C. (1987). *Journey down the Kreisler highway*. Memphis, TN: Ivory Palace Music.

Chapter 5
Preschool Children's Socialization Through Art Experiences

Patricia Tarr
University of Calgary

ncreasingly, researchers acknowledge the role that external influences—images absorbed from television and comic books, as well as ideas borrowed from peers and adults—play in children's artistic expression. The impact of external influences is usually discussed as it relates to the graphic forms, modes, or strategies which children adopt for their purposes of expression (Duncum, 1984; Gardner & Wolf, 1987; Wilson & Wilson, 1987). These influences may become apparent as soon as children pass the scribbling stage of development (Alland, 1983). Influences related to the meaning, purposes, values, and assumptions about the art making process occur simultaneously with visual influences, and are transmitted through human interactions.

This chapter will explore some ways 3- and 4-year-old children acquire cultural understandings about the nature and representational potential of art materials. According to G. H. Mead (1934) and Herbert Blumer (1969), meaning about objects and ideas is created through human interactions. Children come to understand art making in the preschool classroom as a direct result of their interactions with teachers and peers around the experience of using art materials, as well as the experiences they derive from interactions between family members and the general community. This understanding, or acquisition of meaning, plays a direct role in what children do with the art materials, how they respond to them during the process of making art, what kind of product results.

The Art Program

School art forms its own unique art world (Efland, 1976). This chapter explores some of the assumptions and values guiding the human interactions that comprise this specific art world for young children. According to Efland (1976), "school art" is "art that is produced in the school by children under the guidance

and influence of a teacher" (p. 37). It tends to stress manual rather than mental activity, is quickly produced, and allows for diverse products to be accomplished by simple skills. Early childhood curriculum texts such as *Helping Young Children Learn* (Pitcher, Lasher, Feinburg, & Braun, 1979) and art texts focusing on early childhood (Haskell, 1979; Herberholz & Hanson, 1990; Lasky & Mukerji, 1980; Schirrmacher, 1988) present activities and methods for providing art experiences for young children which conform closely to Efland's description of school art. Embedded in the manner and methods teachers use to provide art experiences in the preschool classroom are taken-for-granted assumptions (Garfinkel, 1967) about the ways in which children acquire meaning about art.

The examples of teacher-child and child-child interactions in this paper come from observations made over 2 months of the art program in a preschool class. Fourteen children between the ages of 3 and 4 years attended the class which met four afternoons per week for 2 1/4 hours and was taught by two teachers. Sharon, the Head Teacher, had a Master's degree in Child Development and over 20 years experience teaching children's programs in the United States, Canada, and England. Her Assistant Teacher, Mary, was a graduate student in education. After each classroom observation, Sharon and I discussed her goals and reactions to the day, and I shared my observations with her.

The Creation of Meaning about Art

Classroom Routines and Rituals

Programs for young children are structured around a daily routine or schedule which happens in a predictable way on a day to day basis. The daily routine for the 3- and 4-year-old class described began with outside play followed by circle/group time, free play (including art), clean up, snack, and departure. Early childhood educators assume that such routines give teachers and children security and freedom to function effectively throughout the day. These routines can also be seen as a means of transmitting cultural values and providing structures for the creation of meaning. Blumer (1969) supports this possibility, stating that meanings are "creations that are formed in and through the defining activities of people engaged in social interaction" (p. 5).

Sociologists define ritual as "any regular pattern of interaction" (Abercrombie, Hill, & Turner, 1988, p. 209). Both routines and rituals are vehicles for the construction of meaning within the preschool classroom. Meaning can be constructed both in circle or other group activities, and in interactions between two individuals. Group activities are apt to be structured in a ceremonial or ritualistic manner, containing consistent elements, such as songs or stories, but varying in content from day to day. Other interactions may appear more spontaneous and yet retain a common structure across occurrences. There are two kinds of rituals operating within this preschool class: those set out as routines by the teachers and those occurring within these routines which could be mutually constructed between children and teachers.

The most clearly ritualized interaction between teacher and child around art making occurred as a child completed an art work. Each child took the completed piece to one of the teachers. Usually the teacher would respond with a comment like, "Beautiful," "Lovely," or "I like...(all the colors you used, the fish, etc.)." Sometimes teachers would engage in a conversation about the subject matter of the work, such as "That looks just like a squirrel," or "Tell me about your picture," but the majority of the comments were general adjectives like "beautiful."

Several strands of meaning construction operate within this ritual. First, children seek out the teachers for validation or acceptance of their work. It was not apparent from my observations how the process originated in this classroom, but it was clear that these interactions serve to foster children's understanding about the kind of work which is acceptable. What teachers respond to as art reinforces particular aesthetic values (Efland, 1976; Rosario & Collazo, 1981). Teachers express cultural reinforcement for "school art," with its particular child art quality, through responses such as "beautiful" or "lovely." Representational subject matter is encouraged through the teacher's comments about the representational characteristics of the work (Rosario & Collazo, 1981).

This form of indirect teaching contrasts to cultures, such as China, where classroom teachers guide children through step-by-step lessons to depict objects in traditional painting styles (Gardner, 1991; Winner, 1989). Efland (1976) equates the teacher-child interaction to a "client-patron" (p. 41) relationship in which the teacher (patron) accepts the commissions or art projects produced. To extend Efland's model even further, the teacher frequently acts as a curator who selects certain works for display, acts on behalf of other clients (parents) to encourage acceptable art work, or interprets the art produced to these clients. This is the second strand of meaning construction. The teacher-parent interaction sequence then impacts on parent-child interactions around the art experiences and products. During each junction/interaction sequence, meaning is redefined between the participants.

The third strand relates to the child's sense of self, which is constructed from the interaction between teacher and child (and also between parent and child). Mead (1934) wrote that an individual's notion of self as an object distinct from the physical body is constructed through interactions with others. As children take their products to the teacher, they are also acquiring a concept of self with regard to their ability to use art materials and to participate in this process of making school art in an acceptable way. It is for just this reason that teachers respond with such remarks as "lovely," "beautiful," and "Tell me about your picture." To encourage children's positive view of themselves, teachers respond positively to their art. What teachers are not doing when they respond with these generalized comments is teaching children anything about art or art skills. Learning about art or acquiring art skills would contribute to children's ability to create art and to their self concepts as artists.

As Mead and Blumer emphasize, this transmission of meaning is not simply a stimulus-response interaction in which the teacher reinforces a particular form of behavior. Rather the interaction requires interpretation by the individuals participating in the interaction—in this case a teacher and child—to form a common definition of the situation in order for both parties to engage in the creation of meaning (Blumer, 1969; Mead, 1934). The following examples demonstrate how this occurs.

In some situations the teacher's comment may serve to reinforce and motivate continuation of a specific behavior. For example, when the assistant teacher commented to a child gluing tissue on the work, "I like the way you have done it with so many pieces of tissue," the child seemed stimulated to continue to add tissue to the work.

However, in another situation, the child rejected the teacher's suggestion. Following a trip to the aquarium this child began to draw a shark. The teacher inquired,"How will you do it? Eyes and teeth? Remember the shark we saw yesterday?" The child responded, "I'm not making the teeth."

In each of these situations, the child (and teacher) "selects, suspends, regroups, and transforms the meanings in the light of the situation in which he is placed and the direction of his action" (Blumer, 1969 p. 5).

Instructional Strategies

One form of interaction through which children construct meaning about art is from the instructional strategies of the teacher. Sharon, the teacher, stated that she did not believe in direct teaching in art. However, teachers employed other instructional strategies such as modelling an action by the teacher. When sponge printing was set up, I observed Sharon playfully printing her fish-shaped sponge across the paper. In this manner she was demonstrating a printing technique to children who sometimes scrub back and forth, rather than stamp with materials ostensibly set out for the purpose of printing. As in the example of the child drawing the shark, the children must construct meaning from the situation, in this case Sharon's action, and then decide whether they will transform their own actions to match her technique.

On another day, during circle time, a teacher explained the process of constructing stuffed paper fish. However, this situation precluded children's immediate personal responses to her instructions. This was one of the few examples from my observations when she told children how to do something. Her instructions to the entire group carried the implicit meaning that this was an important project in which everyone would participate (although participation would not be forced), and to do so successfully would mean following the appropriate steps.

A third instructional strategy the teachers employed was that of making positive comments about a work in the presence of other children. The following example illustrates this technique,

> Sam has made an outline of a house using wooden stir sticks. He has left this on the table. Stephanie is in the process of making a similar house when Sharon comments, "Well, Stephanie, what are you up to?" Stephanie, "I'm making a house." Sharon, "That's a good idea. Where did you get that idea?" Stephanie, "From that," pointing to Sam's house. Sharon comments to Sam, "Stephanie thought that was a good idea and she's making one too."

We have seen how meaning about art is created overtly through interactions between teachers and children. However, additional meanings and cultural values are also transmitted through art activities besides those which structure the kind of art created in school. Not only were the teachers dealing with unspoken values, but they also continually faced contradictions in the

dialectical relationships of process-product (ownership), and messy vs. non messy activities.

Meaning about Ownership

One of the values the teacher stressed in her art program, and one generally accepted by practitioners in the field, is the importance of process over product. This belief is closely related to the Piagetian notion that the child constructs knowledge about the world through interactions with it. In this case, the child will learn to do art by doing it and it is this process of working with materials which is important. The child's representations will change and become more realistic as he or she gains experience with the materials.

However, observations of this classroom, and knowledge of my own teaching practices, suggest that this emphasis on process is routinely contradicted in practice. The child's ritual of taking an art work to the teacher for acknowledgment is the beginning of the contradiction. The teacher acknowledges not the process, but the product. The teacher compounds this acknowledgment by either putting the child's name on the work or suggesting that the child do so. In addition, the teacher frequently suggests that the child put the work in some safe place. This is indicative of a valuation of product and property. The name identifies the object with the self. The child and the work become part of each other. If teachers really believed in the primary importance of the process, the completion of a work would become a time of separating of the child from the work rather than a time of reinforcing a sense of ownership with the work. This notion of product and production is further reinforced by parents who ask children, "Did you make something to bring home today?"

Messy Art

One assumption held by North American preschool teachers is that children need to be messy and that good programs provide opportunities for this. Art activities are one means of meeting this need. Sharon stated in an interview that she firmly believed it was important to provide messy art activities such as painting because children might not have these activities at home. One of the prime concerns expressed by teachers is keeping art activities within acceptable limits of messiness or maintaining a balance between order and disorder acceptable to themselves and to parents. Douglas (1969) equates dirt with disorder and suggests that the elimination of dirt is a "positive effort to organize the environment" (p. 2). She concludes, "Dirt is the by product of a systematic order and classification of matter, in so far as ordering involves rejecting inappropriate elements" (p. 35).

In this situation Sharon defined "messy art" through categories of inclusion and exclusion: Things that are wet, gooey, or sticky, such as those using paint or glue, comprise messy activities; activities with dry components, such as crayons, comprise nonmessy activities. The classification of the activity as messy meant that certain conditions would apply: It would take place on the large rectangular table (although glue was used at the round table in conjunction with children's free choice activities), aprons would be provided, and provision for clean up would be easily accessible. The table designated for messy activities was situated so that there was clear space around it to keep paint away from other furniture and equipment. Chairs were often removed.

Many of the teachers' comments to children were concerned with maintaining a balance between neatness and mess. Comments like, "No painting with glue, remember. You have far too much glue," seemed to be related as much to concern for order as for economics. "If you are going to do painting (black paint on paper maché whale) you desperately need an apron, sleeves pushed way up," was another typical comment by which the teacher was attempting to set limits as to how materials should be used and to contain messiness to easily washed surfaces.

Children are also involved exploring this dangerous ground between messy and clean. Although there were several situations of children painting their hands when at the easel, one situation between two boys clearly demonstrates their pushing the boundaries of acceptable messiness, and how it became dangerous territory for them:

Stuart draws on his hands with felt pens while Nathan watches. Stuart asks him, "Want to color yourself?" Nathan tries drawing on his hand with a green felt pen, then changes to a red one, draws, and selects a brown pen. Stuart continues to draw with a single color over his hand and fingers. They continue to draw on their hands for a few minutes before one of them says, "When we get through we'll have to wash it up, right?" The other remarks, "Yeah, but we like it." Nathan suggests, "It'll never come off, right?" When Mary, the assistant teacher, sees the boys drawing on their hands, she intervenes, "What are you doing? Remember, these are not for coloring hands. Time to wash up." As the boys stand at the washbasin, one comments, "It won't come off." Mary concludes the episode, "It'll come off when you have a bath tonight. You must remember not to paint your hands with the felts. It doesn't come off."

If we consider this in light of Douglas's definition of dirt as an offense to order, it becomes apparent that painting on hands is a deliberate challenge to the accepted norm of order and safety. It is acceptable to get felt pen or paint on one's hands during an activity because order can be restored by washing one's hands after the activity. However, drawing on hands deliberately or painting them deliberately is frequently, although not consistently, seen as an unacceptable activity. Sharon acknowledged the inconsistency, saying that whether it was acceptable depended on her mood and the tone of the day. However, the activity was not encouraged and often redirected. (Perhaps it would be a more acceptable activity if North American culture valued body decoration in the forms of tattoos or other painted decorations.)

Children are also becoming aware of cultural notions of color symbolism, in this case the view that black has negative connotations relating to dirt or death.

Diana, remarking to Stuart, "I knew you were going to make a rainbow." Tim, "He always puts black in it, right?" Another child comments about black in rainbows (inaudible). Tim concludes, "It's a nice color, but it isn't so nice."

There are less obvious reasons for providing messy art activities to children. Preschool teachers do this as part of the socializing process of teaching children to become orderly, and therefore neat and clean. Each of these messy activities becomes a ritualized means of providing an opportunity for children to be messy within acceptable limits, because teachers do believe that being messy is important.

Periodically teachers offer one activity which seems to serve as a ritualized cleansing ceremony. This ceremony involves the messiest art activity teachers provide preschool children: fingerpaint. Teachers and textbooks have constructed elaborate accounts about the value of fingerpainting for children's gross and fine motor development, and the opportunities it provides to explore color mixing, printmaking, and line formations without the necessity of an intervening tool. I suspect, however, that deep inside, teachers believe that if children have this opportunity to muck in paint, they will become cleansed or purged of this desire and other painting opportunities will remain neat and orderly. Teachers often provide fingerpaint when they notice children beginning to paint their hands or paint with their hands. After a fingerpainting experience teachers often say to a child something like, "Paint the paper, not your hands; we had finger painting yesterday." This reflects the underlying notion that the ceremonial opportunity for this experience has been provided, and now the children should be able to use brushes and other tools for painting, rather than their hands.

Conclusion

Efland (1976) suggests that the school art style has changed little in the past 50 years because this tradition reflects the culture and purpose of schools. Although teachers provide colors, textures, and shapes for children to use, these are used in the manner prescribed by the school art tradition. Art as it exists in this preschool classroom says more about cultural values of order, ownership, and assumptions about preschool as a place of cultural transmission than it says about artistic creation as skill acquisition, self expression, the acquisition of critical skills to look at art, or knowledge about the rich artistic heritage of our culture.

Through person-to-person interactions around art media, preschool children are learning far more than how to create their own symbols and schemas for recognizable objects within their environment. They are negotiating issues about the acceptance of specific kinds of art forms, self-concept, the work-related value of production, and order. These components comprise an important, often overlooked aspect of children's artistic development.

Acknowledgments

I gratefully acknowledge Dr. Glen Dixon, Director of the Child Study Centre, University of British Columbia, for granting permission to undertake this study. I want to thank the children, parents and teachers who allowed me to observe, with special thanks to Sharon for the hours she spent talking with me and reviewing my transcripts. The names of the teachers and children have been changed to protect their anonymity.

References

Abercrombie, N., Hill, S., & Turner, B. (1988). *The Penguin dictionary of sociology* (2nd ed.). Markham, ON: Penguin Books Canada Ltd.

Alland, A. (1983). *Playing with form: Children draw in six cultures.* New York: Columbia University Press.

Blumer, H. (1969). *Symbolic interactionism: Perspective and method.* Englewood Cliffs, NJ: Prentice Hall.

Douglas, M. (1969). *Purity and danger.* London: Routledge & Kegan Paul.

Duncum, P. (1984). How 35 children born between 1724 and 1900 learned to draw. *Studies in Art Education, 26*(2), 93-102.

Efland, A. (1976). The school art style: A functional analysis. *Studies in Art Education, 17* (2), 37-44.

Gardner, H. (1991). *To open minds.* New York: Basic Books

Gardner, H., & Wolf, D. (1987). Symbolic products of early childhood. In D. Gorlitz, & J. Wohlwill (Eds.), *Curiosity, imagination and play,* (pp. 306-325) Hillsdale, NJ: Lawrence Erlbaum.

Garfinkel, H. (1967). *Studies in ethnomethodology.* Englewood Cliffs, NJ: Prentice Hall.

Haskell, L. (1979). *Art in the early childhood years.* Toronto: Charles E. Merrill.

Herberholz, B. & Hanson, L. (1990). *Early childhood art* (4th ed.). Dubuque, IA: Wm. C. Brown.

Lasky, L., & Mukerji, R. (1980). *Art: Basic for young children.* Washington, DC: The Association for the Education of Young Children.

Mead, G. (1934). *Mind, self and society.* Chicago: University of Chicago Press.

Pitcher, E., Lasher, M., Feinburg, S. & Braun L. (1979). *Helping young children learn* (2nd ed.). Columbus, OH: Charles E. Merrill.

Rosario, J., & Collazo, E. (1981). Aesthetic codes in context: An exploration in two preschool classrooms. *Journal of Aesthetic Education, 15*(1), 71 82.

Schirrmacher, R. (1988). *Art and creative development for young children.* Albany, NY: Delmar.

Wilson, B., & Wilson, M. (1987). Pictorial composition and narrative structure: Themes and the creation of meaning in the drawings of Egyptian and Japanese Children. *Visual Arts Research, 13*(2), 10-21.

Winner, E. (1989). How can Chinese children draw so well? *Journal of Aesthetic Education, 23*(1), 41-62.

Chapter 6
The Case of the Easter Bunny: Art Instruction by Primary Grade Teachers

Liora Bresler
University of Illinois, Urbana-Champaign

Bunny is for Easter

9:26. Today's project is bunny hats in preparation for tomorrow's "Spring Frolic," an annual play for parents and guest classes. The second grade teacher takes out crayons as students move chairs to form horizontal lines facing her. She holds high her model bunny hat. "Let me show you what we're going to do." She motions to Johnny to stand up and places the hat on him. "What do you think you look like?" Johnny, switching from leg to leg: "I look silly." Teacher protests: "You're not looking at yourself. Trust us. You look cute. [To class]: Do you want to do one of these? [Approving voices.] I already traced the pattern. First you need to put some eyes on it. I'm going to give you a choice. You can have pink eyes or blue eyes."

With heavy demand for pink, the teacher gets more pink paper from her desk and hands it to Matt to distribute. Ears, eyes, nose and whiskers are manufactured in that order. The teacher instructs: "Okay, I want you to hold it so that the ears are going down on your paper. No, turn it around, put it flat down, so that the ears are down. Now, where do you think the eyes should go?" Lucy suggests right in the middle. A teacherly caution: "Don't put them too high. Put them about half way, about like that. You can make them as big or as small as you want. Now we need a nice, big pink nose. Then you're going to cut the black paper in some skinny strips and make some whiskers. If you have your scissors—Remember? Yesterday I reminded you, I said, you need scissors and glue—if you've got your scissors, you may start cutting your pink, your blue and your black. How many whiskers do you think you should cut?" Matt says three, other voices echo. Michael says six. "Why six, Michael? Everybody else is saying three, how

come you said six?" Michael: "Three on one side, three on the other." Teacher: That's right. Maybe you could do eight. But don't do any more than eight because then it will be all whiskers."

Bunnies multiply and proliferate as children cut, glue, and paste. Jeff comes to show a paper-cut finger, with a pain- and pride-mingled expression and is told he can go wash it in just a few minutes. At 9:45, the teacher reminds the children to put their names on the back of the hats. Passing from one student to another, she checks that things have been done correctly, compliments ("I see some real nice bunny ears here.") and, the final sanctification, staples the hat. Now she holds high the finished products: "O.k. Our first bunny. Yeah!!!" Josh, the creator, smiles. "And here is another bunny." More high voices enter in, "I'm done." "I'm done," answered by a lower, articulated "I'm coming." Children put their bunny hats on, show their bunnies to friends. Small groups of children are talking softly. For those who are finished, the math lesson starts like a stretta (an overlapping of themes in contrapuntal compositions). There is some tidying up. Most students are doing math at this point, with bunny hats on.

This vignette is taken from a 3-year study (Stake, Bresler, & Mabry, 1991) carried out under the auspices of the National Arts Education Research Center and funded by the National Endowment of the Arts. This study aimed to explore and analyze the learning opportunities provided in arts instruction in U.S. elementary schools. This chapter examines classroom practice in the primary grades, K-3, focusing on contents, structures, pedagogies and evaluation practices (Eisner, 1991). A special place is given to the contexts in which arts programs operate—in particular to the values and goals of the schools and to teachers' beliefs about the arts. These contexts are crucial to understanding what is happening in the classroom. The questions asked in the study and described here are: What is the role of the arts in these primary grade levels? What different functions are served by the arts within the school system and the society? What are the similarities and the differences between arts curricula in the primary, versus the middle and upper, grades? How compatible is art (as perceived by teachers) with school values and goals?

This chapter focuses on the visual arts in three ordinary elementary schools, selected to touch a variety of demographics. Armstrong school, located in the north part of Chicago, housed 780 students in grades K-8 and 37 certified faculty. Minority students comprised 74% of the school population: 40% blacks, 20% Hispanics, and 13% East Indians. In Danville, Illinois, a small blue-collar town, Washington school housed 820 students in grades 2-5 as well as most of the special programs in the Danville district and 60 certified faculty. Prairie, K-1 school, housed 440 students and 20 certified faculty. Minority students in both schools comprised 42% of the school population: 28% blacks, 10% Hispanics, and 3% Asians.

The emphasis here is on classroom teachers rather than specialists, because nonspecialist classroom teachers are largely responsible for teaching visual arts in elementary schools. U.S. elementary school students usually lack access to a visual art specialist: 42% of the student population are not served at all, 32% are served part-time, and 26% are served full-time (National Endowment for the Arts, 1988). With recent budget cuts, the number of specialists is decreasing (Leonhard, 1991). While there is some excellent research on arts specialists' practices (e.g. May, 1989, 1990), there is little literature on classroom teachers teaching the arts.

Altogether, I spent 120 hours in each setting from October through June. I observed 15 primary grade classrooms between 1 and 4 times where art was taught by classroom teachers and conducted interviews with 39 classroom teachers including the 15 classroom teachers observed. The observations encompassed different ability levels, from the gifted through the "average" to the lowest tracks, including special education classes.

The opening vignette was, in many ways, representative of most classrooms observed. For the most part, the ambience of art classes was cheerful, the teacher caring and attentive to students' needs. Tasks and activities were well articulated, expectations were clearly presented. There was much good will and often extra effort on the teacher's part. The arts scene observed, as in many other schools throughout North America, reflected the progression of seasons and holidays: Halloween witches, pumpkins, and turkeys earlier in

the year; Valentine hearts, Easter bunnies, and painted roses for Mother's Day later on.

Lessons were typically 45 minutes long, varying from once per week to once every four weeks. The projects, primarily the making of craft objects, were one-time activities, with no continuity or development. Evaluation consisted mostly of checking that directions had been followed and expressing personal likes or dislikes, with no reasoning or attempts for justification. The great majority of the products seemed to be oriented towards popular cultural symbols, with little attempt to convey expressivity, to broaden associations. For the most part, products appeared standardized, reflecting diverse ability levels rather then diverse visions and ideas. A third-grade teacher summed it up in a sentence: "It is seasonal, cut-paste, color, draw, and I usually do it on Friday afternoon."

Occasionally, the theme of an arts lesson was unrelated to a holiday. One teacher's paint project consisted of coloring half a page with water colors, then folding the page to make a mirror image. The lesson required pre-planning and special effort on her part, to cope with messiness like handling aprons and stained shirts in an otherwise clean class. It was obviously enjoyed by most of her kindergartners. From a disciplinary point of view, however, this was a missed opportunity: Not once did the teacher draw attention to the concepts of symmetry or mirror-image, nor to any other aesthetic quality. When I asked this teacher, as well as others, about the goals or motives behind arts activities, they typically spoke of change of pace, promotion of creativity and of the uniqueness of the child, and the expression of self and imagination. Technical goals included eye-hand coordination and the beneficial impact of art on writing skills. If teachers aimed at an aesthetic dimension it was intuitive, unverbalized, and difficult to detect from their interaction with the children, whether in instruction or in evaluation of children's art work. They rarely drew students' attention to artistic ideas and concepts like form, repetition, and variation. There was little guidance or encouragement to explore and experiment with materials, even less with ideas and aesthetic qualities.

Let us now examine a classroom representative of different pedagogies, embodying beliefs about free expression and open-ended activities.

Art as an Open-Ended Activity

1:40. A second grade teacher pours glitter, yarn, cotton balls and other materials into little plastic bowls, and arranges them neatly on a back table between scissors and pine cones. Laura makes green stems from yarns and cones.

Christopher glues cones on a newspaper. Allison glues glitter on a cardboard. Mark folds paper for a magnificent lamp, each fold separately; Sarah helps. Children visit with each other and are interested in what the others are doing. The teacher summons Allison to help assemble more bowls on the table. Jacob accidentally hits a box and the water colors spill out. Teacher in a soft voice: "Just clean up, please." Children are scattered all over, in natural patches, which bring to mind the arbitrariness and artificiality of straight lines. The teacher, young and graceful, moves from one group to another: "Now what I can do, is I can cut that out, and I can put glue there, and I can glue the paper, then it will be a little Christmas tree. And if I wanted now I could glue it and it would be ornaments. Would that be an idea?" "What are you doing? Ooh, that's nice. Do you have lots of paper to put them on or do you like them like that? Are you going to glue them to this paper? Why don't you do glitter or glue on one side?" "Do you need some help? Are you going to put some glitter before you finish that? Why don't you paint this and wait on this for a little?" Occasionally, a dialogue takes place:

Teacher: "It's not a telescope any more. What is it now?"

Natalie: "A pole, maybe?"

Teacher: Hm, maybe it is a pole."

Natalie: "I don't know. Maybe it's a statue. Maybe it's a piece of art."

Children crowd around ("I want to see it, I want to see it.") Jeff complains about Santa's eyes sliding down.

Teacher: "Yeah, its kind of tough to make eyes on cotton balls. Look at all the Santa Clauses here. Cotton ball beards. Pretty neat."

The total freedom seemed to confuse some students, who just stand and look at the teacher. One little boy asking for help with the glitter commented that he does not like glitter. When asked why he chose it, he explained that, unsure what to do, he chose the material encouraged by his teacher and the other students. The teacher encouraged the self-conscious guy: "Your things look a lot better than you think they do. I am sure it looks fine. O.k. now you are ready? Is that what you wanted? Is that how you wanted it?"

During the activity, the teacher explained:

These are their own art projects. They can make anything they want. Somebody made a computer out of cardboard boxes; we have many Christmas trees from magazines. What I told them in the beginning of the week is to bring any supplies they want to, anything that they would like for art. They can pick up three items over there [motions to the table with supplies] to start, and they can go there later after everybody has their chance.

Her own art supplies, she indicated, occupy two big drawers on the side of the room. "When they closed two schools in Danville, nobody wanted these supplies" and she just "came and took them." I sense her pride in her special supplies and her enthusiasm as she points out the little shelves housing a variety of materials.

2:20. Teacher: "It's time to start picking up." [Disappointed little sounds]. Lou comes and wants to give her his art work. Teacher: "I think you should go home and put it up on your Christmas tree. Put it by the light and all the sparkle will shine. Won't that be pretty?" He insists and she accepts. I hear from a number of teachers that some parents throw away the children's art work immediately. By giving it to the teacher, these children get, at least, the acknowledgement of the gift.

This lesson was one of those which clearly invited individual ideas and projects. The tone was gentle and teamwork was not discouraged. There was greater variety in art work: Some of the items were remarkably different from the rest in their ideas and execution. Still, the majority of products were strikingly similar to each other and to the products of more highly directive lessons. The explanation lies perhaps in the fact that here too there was little teaching of skills, of new, deeper ways of looking and seeing. Children need explicit teaching and guidance of alternatives, especially if in fact giftedness needs nurturing and teaching to overcome the otherwise routine school environment. My observations showed that in the open-ended lessons, students were not presented with opportunities to learn a set of skills and knowledges specific to the arts.

Art routines in the two classes described in this chapter's vignettes have similar structures, contents and evaluation practices. Holidays and seasons prevail and the projects are single, isolated experiences with little attempt at sequentiality or the development of skills. The activities employ lower level skills, use similar directions, and result in routinized products. Evaluation typically consists of positive feedback ("I like that," "How pretty") with little attempt to substantiate the evaluation on aesthetic qualities. In both, lessons are production-oriented: It is the rare lesson that ventures into art appreciation, even rarer one that gets into history or criticism.

The routinization of activities and products is especially surprising in light of the teachers' stated beliefs about art. Most of them highlighted its uniqueness and self-expressive qualities, emphasized meaningful, personal experiences for the children (Bresler, 1988). Yet most of their art lessons do not fit these aspirations.

Barriers to Improved Arts Instruction: School Priorities

What are the hindrances to better, more frequent, more substantive arts programs? The following section points to different factors operating within classroom teaching.

Pressure for Academics

Role of classroom teachers.

Most teachers interviewed for this study did not see their role as including the arts, saying explicitly that they did not feel responsible for teaching art. Twenty years ago there were art specialists in many Illinois schools. In teachers' minds, the arts still belong to specialists. Even though many classroom teachers were involved in arts activities in their private life, most lacked specialized artistic skills, background in arts history, and critical expertise in the arts. The acquisition of these skills required more than a reasonable effort for teachers who struggled to survive the difficult conditions in a typical school system. The result was a void in the function of a teacher responsible for the visual arts.

In contrast to the arts, all teachers felt heavily responsible for academics. The demand for academics was brought up by teachers across different grade levels. They mentioned feeling guilty about taking time away from academic subjects, when there was so much emphasis on and so little time in the school day for "the basics." Thus, teachers created their own balance between the pressures (where art can be seen as taking away from the basics) and their own ability and motivation to teach art. That balance varied from classroom to classroom, but the reduction of arts instruction was a general trend.

Visual art was not the only victim of that pressure. Whatever activity did not contribute directly to measured achievement was diminished, sometimes eliminated. Such was the fate of building blocks in first grade: "The less distractions we have, the more work we get done," said a first-grade teacher. Music also suffered, although not having a specific place in the curriculum, visual art suffered the most.

Integration of art into academics.

Many teachers saw integrating art into academics as a possible solution, so it would not "take" academic time. Ms. M., a second-grade teacher stated:

> I integrate art with the subjects as much as I can, but with the elementary age level, here in school, the time you spend with reading and math seems to take up most of your day. And so you really have to make a special effort to get the art subjects in. It's very difficult at times. You almost feel pressured to keep the children advanced enough in their reading and math. At the same time, [you strive to] meet their other needs, needs that they have to express themselves in other ways. And so you really have to integrate it, or else you just have to take special time aside and just work on art.

The pressure for academics leads to the use of art as a vehicle rather than a subject in its own right. How are arts activities integrated into the academics? Geometric designs and collages for math were popular activities. Again Ms. M., expressing a "menu" representative of many, explained:

> In math, when we talk about geometric designs, I usually try to have them make a geometric design, using squares and circles and rectangles and that type of thing. It's cute, you know, and they like that. [She pauses for a minute to reflect.] We often talk about the difference between animal and mineral and vegetable. Then I take magazines and I have them do collages. And I have them separate those that are animal and those that are vegetable. That turns out to be a pretty nice artistic type of thing, depending on the child.

The low priority of art within the school (and the lack of intellectual challenge associated with it) are clearly reflected in her words: "I know a lot of teachers like to work on Fridays especially, because by this time, their brains seem to be draining, and it's a good way for them to kind of relax and end the week."

Echoes of the pressure for academics were reiterated by every teacher. A veteran kindergarten teacher who has seen the curriculum change in the last 20 years could elaborate on these changes and the emotional cost for children. Others were more laconic but not less intense. A second- and third-grade Reading Improvement teacher said with great emphasis: "We slack off on the arts and sciences, especially in the primary grades. We have to read, read, read!!!" Typically, primary grade teachers lamented the decrease in the arts, while upper grade teachers often felt that teaching art in the school was not a priority, considering all that students need to know in life.

At what grade level does the pressure for academics start? I began examining the lowest grade level, kindergarten, expecting only minimal pressure. To my surprise, a kindergarten teacher pointed to two kinds of pressure: the first coming from the top, that is from administrators, superintendents, parents, and curriculum guides—a pressure which I called "vertical"— and the second, more subtle but not less powerful, coming from peers, which I called "horizontal" pressure:

> Sometimes it's comforting to hear about other people in the same spot, but at the same time, there are always a few who like to stick it at you: 'My children are on page such and such and my children do this and my children do that.' Kindergarten teachers get some pressure from first-grade teachers. When they get your kids they put you down. They say, 'I want to ask you about Joe Smith, didn't you have him last year? Well, he just does not know his letter sounds.' Because some of the teachers have so much pressure and some of them are so academic, they start the year with full force [and no review].

Thus, the pressure for academics seems to permeate the whole school setting. Initiated from the top, it now envelops the teachers and community to reinforce and shape a particular climate. And, in such a climate, subtler, horizontal pressures become hard to resist. This is a prime example of a mutual shaping of factors, a self-reinforcing cycle, rather than cause and effect.

The pressure for academics is part of a larger value system—extending down to kindergarten—advocating "back to the basics," directly measurable achievements, and accountability as a primary value. Spodek (1991) places these changes in a broad educational context:

> As kindergarten education has expanded during the past several years, there have been pressures to change the kindergarten curriculum. Since most children now enter kindergarten with prior early childhood educational experience the traditional play-oriented kindergarten curriculum was seen as denying them a valid educational experience. It was also felt that beginning academic instruction one year earlier would increase the probability that the children would learn to read (p. 10).

Limited Resources

Art's low priority within the school is manifested in the low budgets allocated to it. In these days of tight budgets, administrators and teachers mention the lack of financial resources. Because there is no money for arts specialists, visual arts are taught by classroom teachers who may lack any formal background in the arts, or, at best, have taken one or two art courses, which often were not considered relevant at the time and the content of which they have long forgotten. That lack of background affects teachers' ability to draw on curricular organizers such as textbooks, curricular guides, and other resources the district and school provide.

My own observations did not detect any existing textbooks for art (e.g., Chapman, 1985) in the teachers' rooms or school libraries. Conversations revealed that teachers were not aware of such books nor of art curriculum guides (typically located at district offices). When teachers used resource books for their arts activities, they usually relied on a potpourri of popular magazines, in-service materials, and craft books purchased with their own money or borrowed from others. While textbooks usually offer a structure and a systematic approach, the available resources left the burden of creating a pedagogically sound curriculum out of an arbitrary collection of sources to teachers who lacked the requisite background. Apparently, the lack of sequence and development of knowledge and skills was not perceived as a problem. Here, the teachers' lack of art background combined with the lack of resources shapes arts practice: Teachers chose projects that were mainly easy to teach, easy to manage, and attractive to youngsters. In accordance with their sources, the result was a series of short projects and no development of or building on previously learned skills.

The frequency of arts instruction in K-3 grades ranged widely, varying from school to school, influenced by building leadership as well as individual teacher commitment. One of the principals in Danville required arts products to be publicly presented in the school corridors and changed every month. This decision, although unpopular, required teachers to include arts lessons every two weeks. The other Danville principal stated that she did not regard the arts as a priority. That statement added to the general message that art could be dispensed with in the general curriculum. The Chicago principal, although generally supportive of the arts, had no specific demands and little close monitoring of the amount of arts instruction in that school. A number of teachers chose not to include art in their classrooms. In all three schools, the primary grades, and in particular kindergarten classes, had more arts instruction compared with the middle and upper grades, although contents, activities, and evaluation were strikingly similar across grade levels (K-8). Because kindergarten children lack academic skills and are seen to have shorter concentration spans, kindergarten traditionally is more play-oriented and, therefore, by school definition of art, more oriented to the arts.

School Goals and Underlying Values

The pressure for academics is directly related to what is widely considered as the primary role of school: the development of students' cognitive faculties. Academic subjects are at basis of what is valued by school life. School art, however, does not include academic substance. Accordingly, arts curricula are often lacking in intellectual substance. Rather than deal with a body of knowledge and skills, arts curricula are decorative, trivial, and typically associated with the less important aspects of school life. Art does not share in the school's primary values.

A second clash between art and school values occurs at a rather subtle level. Schools, by their definition and functions, are heavily structured environments, centering around discipline, evaluation, and the following of rules (cf. Dreeben, 1968; Henry, 1966; Jackson, 1968). Schools aim to produce similitude of results, to inculcate rules rather than break them. They are places of clear and well-defined standards. But these are the very opposites of the values that teachers associate with art. The open-endedness, self-expression, and creativity which teachers highlighted in their views of art are incompatible with schools' omnipresent practice of evaluation and the production of results for which teachers and students are held accountable. Equally unacceptable in school is the expression of unique feelings and emotions (and their manifestations: noise and chaos). The school aims to shape and mold these feelings (at least, their outward manifestations) rather than nurture and promote them.

As a result of these conflicting goals, teachers find themselves in a double bind when called upon to integrate the arts into the curriculum. Two sets of values are at dissonance: the open-ended, criteria-free, individualistic, experiential and exploratory arts on the one hand; the predetermined, rule-governed, authoritative, disciplinary and structured school on the other. How do these discrepancies resolve themselves in classroom practice? Time and again, the unique, open-ended aspects of art are given up in favor of the disciplining aspects of school. Assignments are chosen based on product imitation, where criteria are clear and easy to judge even if formal evaluation never takes place. The reconciliation of the need to evaluate with teachers' disdain of negative feedback in the arts is achieved by giving unchallenging assignments in which everybody who tries, can succeed. Open-ended lessons are few and far between and certainly not enough to neutralize other messages.

And so arts programs include two opposing sets of values: (a) the Lowenfeldian (1939) values promoting self-expression, creativity, and uniqueness, manifested in teachers' goals and in some of the more open-ended lessons (see the second vignette in this chapter), and (b) the structured activities manifested in the Halloween dittos, outlined turkeys, precut penguins, Valentine hearts, and bunny hats. While arts educators value art because it provides an outlet for expressing the inner being (and the ideals of Lowenfeld are especially attractive these days, because of the lack of such opportunities in the school), it is extremely difficult to integrate in the existing school culture.

In adjusting their art concepts to classroom practice many teachers sacrifice an important and, perhaps, their most cherished perception of art—its expressivity and creativity. In the ever-lasting pendulum swing between Basics versus Holistic education, the current emphasis is on isolated skills, clearly measurable achievements and standardized test-scores. Meaningful experience is often neglected within the school. Teachers and principals alike sense the loss and lament the imbalance. The arts, symbolizing the essence of experience and intuition, are regarded by teachers as capturing these lost qualities. Introducing more of the arts into the school promises for many to restore some balance.

But the discrepancy seems too large, and the pressure towards school values much too strong, for art to be legitimized. Only those few teachers who have a professional artistic background, those who have practiced art seriously, have an alternative, discipline-rooted set of schemas and paradigms for teaching the arts. Only they have specific knowledge of subject-matter content and the skills to communicate that knowledge. These teachers can provide a middle ground between the extremes of rigidity and open-endedness, creating a domain where feelings can be conceptualized in materials and different modes of presentation. They can address the core of arts disciplines, drawing on conceptual organizers inherent to the arts. For the rest, an easy way to resolve the conflict is to adhere to recipe-like activities that imitate what is done in other subjects, where contents specific to the arts are eliminated.

Coda

Deep-rooted ideas shape our aspirations and behaviors. As long as the primacy of the arts in human knowledge remains unrecognized, art lessons are likely to remain as they are. To change practices of art instruction requires "consciousness raising":

- Acknowledging that much of what is expressed in art is rooted in our culture and learned symbol systems.

- Dispelling the belief that the arts are merely entertaining and decorative.

- Countering the notion that no learnable body of knowledge and skills exists.

But a raised consciousness is only a starting point. The next stages concern the development of arts curricula for the classroom. It requires the translation of visions into realistic goals and classroom practices. This process calls for teachers' critical examination of ideas about art, an examination of aims from which contents and activities can be derived. The translation of visions to practices requires specific knowledge of subject matter and appropriate pedagogies.

Interestingly, the more recent view of art and arts education as a cognitive activity, advocated by philosophers and prominent arts educators (e.g. Broudy, 1972; Cassirer, 1944; Eisner, 1982; Gardner, 1983; Gombrich, 1960; Goodman, 1968; Langer, 1957; Perkins, 1977), lends itself more easily to school values. A cognitive approach, emphasizing higher order skills and problem solving in a variety of media and modes of representation, is more congruent with the academic goals of the school. At the same time it offers concrete knowledges and skills drawn from art as a discipline.

An important part of our mission in preservice teacher education is to discuss and negotiate realistic goals, to teach the skills of deliberating and developing a curriculum adjustable to changing classroom realities, and to acquaint teachers with available materials and textbooks upon which they can draw. The ultimate goal, in my opinion, is not the creation of a standardized curriculum, but one that critically enhances personal beliefs and cherishings (Bresler, 1991; Stake, Bresler & Mabry, 1991) and places them within a planned, sequential arts curriculum.

ACKNOWLEDGEMENTS: I am deeply indebted to Robert Stake who provided the inspiration for this study. Many thanks to Bernard Spodek, Christine Thompson and Daniel Walsh for providing insightful comments on the manuscript.

Note: An extensive account of this work with a theoretical emphasis appeared in the Fall 1992 issue of Early Childhood Research Quarterly, 7 (3).

References

Bresler, L. (1988). *Arts education in Danville, Illinois* (Report for the National Endowment of the Arts). Urbana-Champaign: University of Illinois, National Arts Education Research Center.

Bresler, L. (1991, April). *Using autobiography in aesthetic education teacher training.* Paper presented at the annual meeting of the American Educational Research Association, Chicago, IL.

Broudy, H. (1972). *Enlightened cherishing.* Urbana, IL: University of Illinois Press.

Cassirer, E. (1944). *An essay on man.* New Haven, CT: Yale University Press.

Chapman, L. (1985). *Discover art.* Worcester, MA: Davis.

Dreeben, R. (1968). *On what is learned in school.* Reading, MA: Addison-Wesley.

Ecker, D. (1963). The artistic process as qualitative problem solving. *Journal of Aesthetics and Art Criticism, 21*(3), 283-290.

Eisner, E. (1982). *Cognition and curriculum.* New York: Longman.

Eisner, E. (1991). *The enlightened eye: Qualitative inquiry and the enhancement of educational practice.* New York: MacMillan.

Fullan, M. (1982). *The meaning of educational change.* New York: Columbia University Press.

Gardner, H. (1983). *Frames of mind: The theory of multiple intelligence.* New York: Basic Books.

Gombrich, E. (1960). *Art and illusion.* Princeton, NJ: Princeton University Press.

Goodman, N. (1968). *Languages of art.* Indianapolis: Bobbs-Merrill.

Henry, J. (1966). *On education.* New York: Random House.

Jackson, P. (1968). *Life in classrooms.* New York: Holt, Rinehart and Winston.

Langer, S. (1957). *Problems of art.* New York: Charles Scribner's Son.

Leonhard, C. (1991). *Status of arts education.* Urbana, IL: Center for Research in Music Education.

Lowenfeld, V. (1939). *The nature of creative activity.* London: Degan Paul, Trench, Trubner.

May, W. (1989). *Understanding and critical thinking in elementary art and music* (Elementary Subjects Center Series No. 8). East Lansing: Michigan State University, Center for the Learning and Teaching of Elementary Subjects.

May, W. (1990). *Whose content, context and culture are in elementary music textbooks?* (Elementary Subjects Center Series No. 23). East Lansing: Michigan State University, Center for the Learning and Teaching of Elementary Subjects.

National Endowment for the Arts. (1988, May). *Toward civilization: Overview from a report on arts education.* Washington, DC: Author

Perkins, D. (1977). *The arts and cognition.* Baltimore, MD: Johns Hopkins.

Spodek, B. (1991). What should we teach kindergarten children? In B. Spodek (Ed.), *Educationally appropriate kindergarten practices* (pp. 10-22). Washington, DC: National Education Association.

Stake, R., Bresler, L., & Mabry, L. (1991). *Customs and cherishing: Arts education in the United States.* Urbana, IL: Center for Research in Music Education.

Chapter 7
Developmentally Appropriate Practice in Early Art Education

Cynthia B. Colbert
University of South Carolina

More children each year enter kindergarten with several years of early childhood education already behind them. Visual arts educators must become familiar with the goals of early educational programs and the experiences that children are likely to have prior to kindergarten and first grade. Art educators also must assume a more active role in developing the visual arts education curriculum for early childhood education programs and in providing for the special developmental needs of children in the lower primary grades.

In recent years, there has been a national trend toward formal instruction of academic skills in early childhood programs, a trend based on what many experts feel are misconceptions about young children and how they learn (Elkind, 1987; Kamii, 1985). Well meaning parents, often ambitious for their children's academic success, demanded programs with stringent academic standards and content. These parents complain vociferously if worksheets involving mathematical skills, letter recognition, and letter formation are not sent home with their children regularly. Unfortunately, many schools complied with these parental demands, rather than trying to educate parents about developmentally appropriate practices that enhance their children's growth and development.

A growing body of research in early childhood education suggests that children learn most effectively when they engage in activities that are both concrete and playful. Learning activities for young children, offered in the context of play, should be concrete, real, and meaningful to the lives and the needs of children (Almy, 1975; Biber, 1984; Evans, 1984; Forman & Kuschner, 1983; Kamii, 1985; Kline, 1985; Piaget, 1972; Schickendanz, 1986; Seefeldt, 1986; Smith, 1985; Weber, 1984). Research studies such as these, supported by publications and texts addressed to parents (Elkind, 1987) and by the efforts of the National Association for the Education of Young Children (NAEYC), have initiated a national reappraisal of the needs of young children in educational programs.

Pressures to discontinue inappropriate early academic instruction of young children are being felt in schools and in district and state offices of education.

A developmentally appropriate curriculum is one that meets the needs of children within the class grouping and is implemented in a relaxed, comfortable, and playful fashion with attention to children's general and individual needs, interests, and development. The developmentally appropriate curriculum offers an integrated approach to education, addressing children's physical, emotional, social, and cognitive development. The NAEYC promotes developmentally appropriate practice encompassing instruction that is

1. Age appropriate, based on the universal sequences of growth and development that occur during the first 9 years of the child's life.

2. Individually appropriate, acknowledging that each child is unique and that the child's growth, learning style, and family background should be considered (Bredekamp, 1987).

A developmentally appropriate art curriculum for young children reflects many of the same concerns.

This chapter focuses on visual arts education for early childhood settings and on fitting this education into the philosophies and suggested practices for educating young children. Quality early childhood programs center on the child, rather than the content of the instruction to be introduced to the child. The child-centered approach in visual arts education stays with the historical wisdom of the field, following the ideas of Lowenfeld (1947), Kellogg (1969), and others who emphasized the child's abilities, interests, and needs in relation to the visual arts. Subscribing to child-centered approaches to visual arts education does not mean abandoning the study of art as a discipline nor eliminating the experiences that encourage children to talk intelligently about art. It is possible to reconcile the field's current shift toward subject-centered approaches with the specific needs of children; to accommodate children's interests, skills, and abilities, and to follow the practices that best meet their needs while offering substantial information about the visual arts.

Recommendations for Appropriate Practices

The following recommendations for appropriate practices in curriculum development and instruction have been selected from the NAEYC guidelines, *Developmentally Appropriate Practices in Early Childhood Programs* (Bredekamp, 1987), and feature research findings that address issues of significance to the teaching of art to young children.

Guidelines for the development of appropriate curriculum for young children

A. *Developmentally appropriate curriculum addresses all areas of children's development through integrated approaches to learning.*

While important for study in its own right, art lends itself well to integrated approaches to learning. The use of language skills in describing spatial relationships in works of art and the introduction of art concepts such as symmetry and asymmetry help children develop a general understanding of spatial concepts and a vocabulary to describe spatial relationships. Because spatial concepts are a focus of early childhood programs for preliterate children, many early childhood teachers enjoy using art experiences to encourage students to demonstrate their understanding of spatial concepts and art reproductions in guided discussions of spatial concepts such as near, far; inside, outside; above, below; in front, behind (Frostig, 1961; Salome, 1968).

Young children benefit from opportunities to use art materials in the early educational setting. The introduction of art concepts and the use of art reproductions with young children is appropriate and has been shown to enhance children's acquisition of an art vocabulary, increase perceptual awareness, and strengthen descriptive powers of language. Researchers have also established relationships between drawing and language development in young children (Colbert, 1984; Golomb, 1974; Goodnow, 1977; Litt, 1977; Lowenfeld, 1947; Willats, 1977).

Self-awareness and self-esteem can be enhanced by focusing on the self in many art experiences. The relationship of artistic and aesthetic development to language, reading, perceptual, and math skills is well documented in research conducted by both art educators and early childhood educators (Colbert & Taunton, 1990, xix).

B. *Appropriate curriculum planning is based on teachers' observations and recordings of each child's special interests and developmental progress.*

Teachers can set realistic curriculum goals and plans based on their own continuous assessment of individual and class strengths, needs, and interests. Through teachers' own assessments of children, they can plan activities that enrich and broaden the curriculum for all children. If, for example, children become excited about mixing colors using tempera paints, the teacher might plan to extend that unit of study for several additional class periods so that students could have time to further their explorations. If students have had relatively few experiences in modeling three-dimensional forms and the teacher noted students experiencing some difficulty in modeling, he or she might include additional playful experiences with clay or dough that involve students in rolling balls and coils and patting flat forms. This would be added to the curriculum based on the teacher's observations that students needed more experiences with clay prior to modeling three-dimensional forms. Teachers monitor students' progress and adjust their plans according to the students' needs. For this approach to work in the classroom, teachers need to be confident of their opinions of student needs based on their observations and they must remain flexible in their approach to planning lessons and units. Flexibility might include allowing a group of children to continue with one activity while encouraging another group to work on a different one.

C. *Curriculum planning emphasizes learning as an interactive process and is based on children's development and interests.*

Research has shown that young children are capable of creating, perceiving, and discussing the visual arts (Taunton & Colbert, 1984). Young children need guidance in using materials to create art and in looking at art works—whether their own, their peers', or the work of a professional artist. Children benefit from searching for visual elements in their environment and discussing what they see and what they value. A strong, systematic approach to planning instruction that focuses on young children's natural abilities to perceive, create, and appreciate the visual arts will engage, excite, and perhaps introduce children to a lifelong interest in art (Colbert & Taunton, 1990).

The sequence of lessons within and between units of study should accommodate children's interest spans, skills, and capabilities. Art experiences should be varied enough to sustain children's interest, yet organized so that concepts and skills introduced in one unit are reinforced and built upon in later units of study. Selected concepts and skills from the early part of the curriculum should be reintroduced in a new context later in the year.

The art curriculum should provide young children many opportunities for learning to create art, to experiment with a variety of media, and to create both two- and three-dimensional work. Children can begin to understand the importance of selecting, controlling, and using a variety of tools and processes. Children need to experiment with a variety of sources of inspiration for creating works of art, such as observing nature and the constructed environment, using imagination and memory, and trying experimental approaches to materials.

Children also need to learn how and why other people create works of art, what place art holds in everyday life, and why people value art. Learning to perceive and respond to works of art helps children to better express themselves verbally and to develop language and vocabulary skills. Viewing and discussing works of art encourages children to share their ideas about what they see, to listen to other children, to learn from what others see, and to become aware that other people may have views that differ from their own (Colbert & Taunton, 1990).

D. *Learning activities and materials should be concrete, real and relevant to the lives of young children.*

Learning takes place when children interact with materials and people. It occurs as they touch, manipulate and experiment with materials. Learning is especially meaningful when children have a part in deciding what they will do and how they will go about doing it. Children's active participation in self-directed play using concrete and real-life experiences has been found to be central to motivated and meaningful learning in the preschool and early elementary school years (Bredekamp, 1987).

Because art activity at the early childhood level often involves manipulating art materials to create two- and three-dimensional forms, concreteness offered in visual arts instruction is easily demonstrated. Much of young children's art activity is hands-on, using a variety of materials intended to stimulate the senses and the creation of images and forms. Children's ideas and memories take concrete form when they are transformed into symbols that are drawn, painted, or modeled. When art instruction involves children in talking about works of art, those works or reproductions of them should be present to be touched and closely viewed by the children.

Teachers are cautioned against using worksheets, coloring sheets, workbooks, and adult-made models for children to copy. Although this is especially true for children younger than six years, older children have also demonstrated benefits from being actively engaged in concrete, real-life experiences (Bredekamp, 1987; Kamii, 1985).

E. *Programs provide for a wider range of developmental interests and abilities than the chronological age range of the group would suggest. Adults are prepared to meet the needs of children who exhibit unusual interests and skills outside of the normal developmental range.*

In any classroom, the age will vary from 9 to 12 months. And the normal developmental-age range for any group may be as much as 2 years. In some classrooms the range will be even greater. This means that teachers must be prepared to offer materials that vary in complexity and that reflect the age span of the group (Bredekamp, 1987). Units of study must be planned in a open-ended fashion that allows children with varying skills and abilities to interpret the goals of the lessons for themselves. Teachers need to offer a range of materials and to plan variety in room arrangements and in grouping students to work together. Again, teachers must be confident in using their observations of student progress to plan educational experiences that meet the needs of all students.

F. *Teachers provide a variety of activities and materials; teachers increase the difficulty, complexity, and challenge of an activity as children are involved with it and as children develop understanding and skills.*

Teachers can observe, listen, make notes, and interpret the work of children as they are engaged in manipulation of materials or other activities. Teachers become facilitators of children's involvement in an activity by asking the children questions or by making suggestions or adding more complex ideas or additional materials to the learning environment (Bredekamp, 1987).

Art teachers usually work in just this manner. They introduce the major concepts and demonstrate an activity or discuss a visual attribute before encouraging children to work on their own. As children begin their work, the art teacher circulates, asking probing questions and offering encouragement. Art teachers push students who they know can add more to a piece and they probe for students' ideas about their work (Taunton, 1983). Teachers may offer further examples of different ways of working as they go around the room and see how various students have interpreted the activity for themselves.

G. *Teachers provide opportunities for children to choose among a variety of activities, materials, and equipment, and time to explore through active involvement. Teachers facilitate children's engagement with materials and activities and extend learning by asking questions or making suggestions that stimulate children's thinking.*

The teacher's role in settings where children can choose their own activity is to create an environment that is inviting, stimulating, and challenging for the children and to facilitate their engagement in the activities offered. Teachers also set the limits for the amount of time children can become involved (Taunton, 1983). Children need periods of uninterrupted time to pursue their involvements. In art activities, children need time to experiment, to plan, to create, to revisit, and to evaluate their work. Time for reflection and use of peer verbalizations during art activities have been found to influence the evaluative processes of children (Cocking & Copple, 1979).

When providing choices for children, teachers should take care to provide variety in the art activities. In early childhood settings, a teacher might invite children to choose between drawing from observation, creating a collage, or developing a modeled figure. Although this may be difficult in art instruction in the primary grades, it is advisable to offer young children the opportunity to work in both group and solitary settings. Activities should be offered repeatedly for those children who want to practice or refine skills and for those who want to revisit a piece of art work to add to or complete the work.

H. Multicultural and nonsexist experiences, materials, and equipment should be provided for children of all ages.

Teachers, with the help of school and district administrators, should provide a wide variety of culturally diverse and nonstereotypical educational materials that are developmentally appropriate for young children. Textbooks, picture books, art reproductions, filmstrips and other materials should meet standards for cultural diversity and gender equity. Further, the curriculum should strive to enhance the self-esteem and self-confidence of every child. It should support the integrity of the child's family, strengthening ties between home and school. The curriculum should extend children's experiences to include the ways of others, particularly the ways of people in the community, and present these differences with respectful acceptance and appreciation of the similarities and differences of all people (Bredekamp, 1987). Reproductions of works of art are effective in introducing children to the images and ideas of people from a variety of ethnic origins, as is the study of the work of local artists, architects, craftspersons, and designers.

Summary

Young children need meaningful, developmentally appropriate, playful, and engaging visual arts experiences that address the arts in substantive ways. Teachers need not try to teach every lesson in the curriculum guide, nor do they need to use every medium and art reproduction available. A select group of well developed, appropriate experiences with time available for children to return to their work if needed and time to discuss, reflect, and enjoy the work created will provide more opportunities for personal meaning and will invite children to develop a lifelong interest in the visual arts.

Teachers of the visual arts who work with young children need to nurture children's individuality and artistic development in a calm, unhurried, thoughtful, and unobtrusive manner that conveys to children that they are respected and their artistic efforts are valued. Good teachers of young children focus on what children can do, not on their limitations, and plan experiences that meet their capabilities and stretch their visions of what is possible.

References

Almy, M. (1975) *The early childhood educator at work.* New York: McGraw-Hill.

Biber, B. (1984). *Early education and psychological development.* New Haven, CT: Yale University Press.

Bredekamp, S. (1987). *Developmentally appropriate practice in early childhood programs serving children from birth through age 8.* Washington DC: National Association for the Education of Young Children.

Cocking, R. R., & Copple, C. E. (1979). Change through exposure to others: A study of children's verbalizations as they draw. In M. Poulsen & G. Luben (Eds.), *Piagetian theory and its implications for the helping professions* (pp. 124-132). Los Angeles: University of Southern California.

Colbert, C. (1984). The relationship of language and drawing in description and memory tasks. *Studies in Art Education, 24*(1), 84-91.

Colbert. C. & Taunton, M. (1990). *Discover art: Kindergarten.* Worcester, MA: Davis Publications.

Elkind, D. (1987). *Miseducation: Preschoolers at risk.* New York: Knopf.

Evans, E. D. (1984). Children's aesthetics. In L. G. Katz (Ed.), *Current topics in early childhood education* (pp. 5, 73-104). Norwood, NJ: Ablex.

Forman, G. & Kuschner, D. (1983). *The child's construction of knowledge: Piaget for teaching children.* Washington, DC: National Association for the Education of Young Children.

Frostig, M. (1961). *Developmental test of visual perception.* Palo Alto, CA: Consulting Psychology Press.

Golomb, C. (1974). *Young children's sculpture and drawing.* Cambridge, MA: Harvard University.

Goodnow, J. (1977). *Children drawing.* Cambridge, MA: Harvard University.

Kamii, C. (1985). Leading primary education towards excellence: Beyond worksheets and drill. *Young Children, 40* (6), 3-9.

Kellogg, R. (1969). *Analyzing children's art.* Palo Alto, CA: Mayfield.

Kline, L. W. (1985). *Learning to read, teaching to read.* Newark, DE: LWK Enterprises.

Litt, L. (1977). Naming the parts: How children describe and how children draw common objects. In G. Butterworth (Ed.), *The child's representation of the world* (pp. 73-80). New York: Plenum Press.

Lowenfeld, V. (1947). *Creative and mental growth.* New York: The MacMillan Company.

Piaget, J. (1972). *Science of education and the psychology of the child* (rev. ed.). New York: Viking. (Original work published 1965).

Salome, R. A. (1968). Perceptual training in reading readiness and implications for art education. *Studies in Art Education, 10,* 58-67.

Schickendanz, J. A. (1986). *More than the ABC's: The early stages of reading and writing.* Washington, DC: National Association for the Education of Young Children.

Seefeldt, C. (1986). The visual arts. In C. Seefeldt (Ed.), *The early childhood curriculum: A review of current research* (pp. 183-210). New York: Teachers College Press.

Smith, F. (1985). *Reading without nonsense* (2nd ed.). New York: Teachers College Press.

Taunton, M. (1983). Ways to talk and what to say: A study of art conversations among young children and adults in preschool settings. *Conference Proceedings of the Arts and Learning Special Interest Group.* Annual Meeting of the American Educational Research Association.

Taunton, M. & Colbert, C. (1984). Artistic and aesthetic development: Considerations for early childhood educators. *Childhood Education, 61*(1), 55-63.

Weber, E. (1984). *Ideas influencing early childhood education: A theoretical analysis.* New York: Teachers College Press.

Willats, J. (1977). How children learn to represent three-dimensional space in drawings. In G. Butterworth (Ed.) *The child's representation of the world* (pp. 189-202). New York: Plenum.

Chapter 8
A Portrait of an Early Childhood Art Teacher

Elizabeth Smith Cole
University of Toledo

" I just love little children!"

This enthusiastic response is often given as the reason for wanting to be involved in early childhood art instruction. While such affection and enthusiasm is certainly important for teacher-student rapport, it is naive to equate liking young children to being effective as their teacher. The nurturing factor is only one basic attitude necessary for good art instruction: Many skills and much practical experience must be developed through professional training.

The purpose of this chapter is to examine the instructional and attitudinal qualities of an art educator who has been highly successful in her work with young children. Mrs. S, as she will be called, has had extensive experience in developing innovative early childhood educational programs for a Midwestern museum. Her unique combination of early childhood and art education training provides an interesting profile for teacher effectiveness assessment.

Traditionally, art experiences in early childhood settings are associated almost exclusively with manipulation of materials for self-expression: children are exposed to numerous art media with minimal motivation and discussion. The interactive approach observed in Mrs. S's teaching involves questioning and extending the discoveries children make as they learn, and serves as a model for alternative strategies.

Method

Feeny and Chun (1985) note that although the characteristics important for effective teaching are intuitively known, demonstrating their impact on the quality of children's experiences is more difficult. However, intuition will never fully convince those who seek well defined, well documented research on teaching behaviors. In order to describe Mrs. S's teaching in a concrete and systematic way, her attitudinal and instructional behaviors were studied using methods of participant observation and interpretation. Videotaping was selected as the primary data collection technique. To augment the body of information used for analysis and interpretation, Mrs. S and her students were asked to respond to a series of questions. Mrs. S prepared a list of written responses concerning her philosophical and instructional beliefs. These statements served as a tool to compare what Mrs. S intended and what actually occurred in her teaching. The 10 children, who volunteered to talk about their teacher, had their comments tape-recorded.

The Conceptual Framework

To specify the characteristics which constitute an ideal early childhood art teacher would be both difficult and professionally naive. In the first place, no one person can encompass the realm of desirable traits generated through research. Secondly, to standardize teaching behaviors would deny the personal qualities and experiences that the individual brings to the profession.

For the purpose of this study, two general categories of teaching behavior, instructional and attitudinal, were designated for observation. Instructional behaviors refer to methods or strategies used (Kohut, 1980). Attitudinal behaviors include teacher personality traits, feelings and actions expressed to the children.

The Observed Program

This study was limited to 10 class sessions based on a theme. The theme focused on France and its many cultural contributions to the art world.

The standard format for each lesson was divided into three general categories: (1) teacher-directed discussions of content, (2) material development in which the children created a product related to the daily lesson, and (3) self-directed exploration in which the children engaged in interactive play via costumes and drama centers.

The Teacher's Instructional Beliefs

Mrs. S believes that teaching is facilitating. She sets the stage for learning by providing stimulating information and experiences, then steps back to let the children absorb the information at their own speed. "Questioning," she explains, "is used to keep children on the right track without telling them specifically how to solve the problem." This approach is reinforced by Down (1987) who aptly points out that teaching is not talking, it is asking questions.

Instructionally, Mrs. S's lessons are planned to appeal to many different learning styles through the use of visual cues, experiences with sound, and lots of movement. She frequently asks the children to act out the lesson because this strategy covers all three approaches. Artists and art history are discussed in story form, which she feels is an appealing method of instruction to use with young children. In regular visits to museum galleries, Mrs. S engaged the children's active participation by discussing and examining great works of art from the children's perspective.

She likes to involve as many children as possible in the motivational dialogue. Mrs. S states, "I am particularly sensitive to involving the quiet children in class conversation to let them know their thoughts are valued."

Finally, her instructional space includes a variety of physical conditions for learning. The room is divided into a conversational area, creative play centers, tables for distribution of materials, and a work area for creating art. Lesson reinforcement is done through related art activities and spontaneous play with props.

The Teacher's Instructional Beliefs Modeled in the Classroom

Mrs. S began each class by gathering the children on a floor area in the front of the classroom. This "listening area" is where the information portion of the lesson was shared. The children sat themselves side-by-side to form a square and Mrs. S positioned herself on a low stool within the group setting. The proximity of a teacher to a child during instructional activities, according to Susi (1988), directly affects the child's level of attentiveness and achievement. Although the reason for this has not been formally substantiated, researchers hypothesize that eye contact is the key factor in the success of communication. Throughout the motivational activity, Mrs. S continually scanned the group, thus providing a high level of direct visual contact.

One particular session began with an auditory activity in which the children listened to the court music of Louis XIV. This music had been part of a previous lesson on the grandeur of French court life. Mrs. S began by encouraging the children to move their hands with the music. She instructed, "Pretend your fingers are people walking. Pretend you are the king and queen moving to the music."

The intent of this opening activity was to provide the children with a concrete link to the primary focus of the lesson, the music and movement of the can-can and the way it was depicted visually by the artist, Toulouse-Lautrec. Using a linking process of learning allows the child to transform information in a progressive fashion (Bruner, 1977). The complex nature of the lesson required Mrs. S to carefully lead the children through a sequenced motivation.

To continue the linking process, Mrs. S shifted the children's attention to the music of the can-can. As the music started, she began moving her fingers and arms to the lively music. The children quickly followed suit, imitating their teacher's gestures while responding to the quickened pace of the music.

Mrs. S: "What kind of dance would you do to this music?"

Child: "A wild one!"

Mrs. S: "Wild ... that's great. Would a king or queen dance like that?" (The children were in agreement that this was not a royal dance.) "This is a French dance called the can-can."

Having provided the transition between the first and second link in the motivation, Mrs. S then began to elaborate on the concept. Holding up Toulouse-Lautrec prints of can-can dancers, she explained that the intent of the dance was to see how high one could kick. Once more she played the music and the children practiced the moves of the dance as a means of interactive learning.

In the final phase of the motivation, the children discussed the cabaret prints of the artist, Toulouse-Lautrec. Mrs. S called attention to his representation of dancer's movements and again referred back to the dance steps that had just been practiced.

To lead into the printing process that the children would be doing during the art production portion of the lesson, Mrs. S explained that Toulouse-Lautrec had to make a living: "Not only was he a painter, he also enjoyed making posters about dancers. These posters were bought by the cabaret owners and placed around town as advertisements. Today we will make poster prints as Toulouse-Lautrec did."

This carefully constructed dialogue moved the children through a large expanse of information. The combination of questions, auditory and kinesthetic activity, visual examples, and connected strands of ideas Mrs. S used provided a rich collage of information that was readily grasped by the children.

After a teacher demonstration and explanation of the printing process, the children moved to individual work areas to complete their projects. At this stage in the lesson, it is common practice for teachers to move from child to child to aid and assist with technical problems that they may have in creating the project. Mrs. S followed this procedure by helping children solve compositional problems:

Child: "I don't know how to draw a cat."

Mrs. S: "What shapes could you use to draw the cat?"

Child: "A circle for the head and body and maybe some triangles for ears."

Mrs. S: "Let's see if it works. Why don't you draw those shapes. Terrific! You solved the problem. Now what else could you add?"

The last question was used repeatedly with the children to encourage them to expand their visual response. Mrs. S labeled this "extended motivation." McTighe and Lyman (1988) refer to this technique as cueing. The net result is that teacher-suggested options can trigger new ideas that the child may not have considered.

According to Porter and Potenza (1983), the more clearly teachers perceive their own values and understand the theoretical basis for their teaching, the greater their likelihood of success in the classroom. An initial question posed in this study required Mrs. S to define her philosophical approach to art instruction. She wrote:

I have a student-centered philosophy, which I interpret to mean the valuing of the individual and what he or she brings to the experience. I try to structure and be sensitive to learning styles, variations in strengths, and abilities within the class. That must come first in order to teach effectively.

She further explained that children should be encouraged to combine the many ideas presented in class creatively rather than to imitate the teacher's example. Finally, Mrs. S feels strongly about modeling behaviors for the parent by showing confidence and respect for the abilities of the young child and displaying enthusiasm for young art and creativity.

Mrs. S's patient manner and continuous verbal interaction with the children was a striking instructional behavior. During the lesson motivation she wanted to establish where can-can dancing might occur. Her sensitivity to the children's level of understanding was evident in the following conversation in which she had to adjust her line of questioning to their level of understanding:

Mrs. S: "If you were in a city and wanted to see some dancers, where would you go?"

Child: "France!" (The term "city" was confused with "country" due to the immature categorization capabilities of the child.)

In an attempt to further clarify the concept, Mrs. S finally queried, "Where would you find swimmers or shoppers?" The children enthusiastically responded to the new line of questioning and revealed their understanding that certain activities are associated with certain places.

Enabling children to make connections among bits of information, rather than simply feeding them information, is a key element in Mrs. S's attitudinal behavior. Her clear understanding that young children need time to sort, process, and store information reflects her philosophical view that learning is "finding out together."

Problem solving is an important component Mrs. S promoted in the classroom. She believes that encouraging creative problem solving and response "enables children to extend their thinking and doing beyond the obvious." One method to effect this, which was continuously observed, was her use of the word "or." By repeatedly generating a variety of options for the children's use of material or possible solutions to problems, Mrs. S avoided closure on ideas. Research in creativity has shown that the more one generates ideas, the more likely one is to come up with new ideas (Renzulli, Hartman, & Callahan, 1971). The open-endedness of Mrs. S's approach enabled the children to take risks in solving artistic problems.

The Children's Perceptions of the Teacher

To complement Mrs. S's responses about her instructional and attitudinal beliefs, a series of questions were posed to a sample of 10 children in the class. During individual, tape-recorded sessions, the interviewer began with general questions about the children's interest in the class and the things they looked forward to with each visit. The four-year-olds all remarked that Mrs. S was a nice lady and that she "makes you feel good." The five-year-olds agreed that she was a nice lady and were impressed with how she helped them. One six-year-old said that she was "like an aunt because she really likes me."

Their responses are evidence that the bonding between teacher and child is central to the child's feeling about the art experience. According to Bacmeister (n.d.), when children recognize that their teacher is a congenial partner in learning and caring, many positive behaviors result.

Implications for Practice

During this investigation, it became apparent that teaching art to young children is incredibly complex and multifaceted. Attending to the child's artistic skills and manipulation of materials is only one aspect of instruction. More importantly, the interactive process between the teacher and children, both during and after the motivation, can have a significant effect on the totality of the instruction. The findings of this study can well serve as a viable model for creative early childhood art instruction. To encourage this creative teaching, the following points should be considered:

1. Understand the artistic, psychological and physiological developmental characteristics of young children. Knowledge of these characteristics helps develop insight into the children's world by enabling teachers to understand the needs, tensions, and deeper meanings expressed by children's behavior.

2. Design the classroom environment to link the children with the knowledge and art experience being taught. Matching, supporting, and then extending these experiences can be accomplished through the objects or material provisions children encounter and by the way they are helped to encounter them.

3. Encourage learning connections between art experiences rather than offering isolated lessons. Linking information allows the knowledge absorbed through this interactive process to be transformed and stored in the imagination of the children.

4. Arrange the children in close proximity to the teacher during instruction. Teaching at close range gives children a sense of belonging in the learning process.

5. Present the subject matter in ways compatible with young children's cognitive capabilities. Young children are like sponges; they absorb a large amount of information.

6. Provide open-ended questioning that will encourage creative thinking behaviors. Fostering children's creative potential can promote spontaneity in thinking and a willingness to take risks.

7. Intervene sensitively when appropriate, so that the children's art experience is not dominated by the teacher nor are children left helpless in the art process.

8. Foster positive self-esteem through encouragement and acknowledgment of effort. This should be specific rather than general in nature, otherwise the message can lose its credibility with children.

9. Include opportunities for children to express their feelings and opinions about forms of beauty. At their young age, they may never have thought about how they feel about art.

10. Learn the art of nonverbal communication. Be aware that your moods and intentions are reflected in your actions. Young children catch the mood of the teacher quite uncannily. They feel a teacher's ability to catch their moods, too. As a result, positive communication outside the verbal level can form a sure basis for valuable rapport between teacher and children.

Conclusion

The importance of the interactive approach of questioning and extending the learning of your children is underscored throughout this chapter. Mrs. S's professed beliefs were consistent with her observed practices. Her conscientious effort to bring meaning to the children's learning, while nurturing a partnership in artistic experience, was deliberate and well thought out. This study clearly demonstrates that teaching art to young children is a multifaceted process that requires carefully planned instructional strategies projected through supportive attitudinal behaviors. While liking little children may not be enough to result in effective teaching, effective teaching always means liking little children.

References

Bacmeister, R.W. (n.d.). Teachers for young children: the person and the skills. Urbana, IL: ERIC Ed. 178 155.

Bruner, J. (1977). The process of education. Cambridge, MA: Harvard University Press.

Down, G. (1987). Art as basic education. In Disciplined-based art education: What form will it take? (pp. 52-53). Los Angeles: The Getty Center for the Arts.

Feeny, S. & Chun, R. (1985). Effective teachers of young children. Young Children, 41(1), 47-52.

Kohut, S., Jr. (1980). Research and the teacher: Teacher effectiveness in early childhood education. In D.G. Range, J. R. Layton, & D.L. Roubinek (Eds.), Aspects of early childhood education: Theory to research to practice. (pp. 143-179). New York: Academic.

McTighe, J. & Lyman, F.T., (1988). Cueing thinking in the classroom: The promise of theory-embedded tools. Educational Leadership, 45(7), 18-25.

Porter, C.J. & Potenza, A. (1983). Alternative methodologies for early childhood research. In S. Kilmer (Ed.) Advances in early education and childcare (Vol 3, pp. 155-186). Greenwich, CT: JAI Press.

Renzulli, J.S., Hartman, R.K., & Callahan, C.M. (1971). Teacher identification of superior students. Exceptional Children, 38, 211-214.

Susi, F. (1988). Environmental perspectives for effective classroom management. Ohio Art Education Journal, 27(2 & 3), 7-12.

Chapter 9
*Liberating Art Experiences for Preschoolers and Their Teachers**

Kathryn Gaspar
Rochester, New York

To introduce art to young children one needs to understand art and young children. Understanding of art occurs through having many art experiences, and deepens and evolves over time.

This chapter is a response to questions about art frequently asked at inservice events for early childhood educators. Because of the wide spectrum of teachers' concerns, this chapter touches on many aspects of art and art education, from the nitty-gritty of process to large issues of art, education, and culture.

In addressing these issues I draw on several aspects of my background. As a practicing artist I offer my insights about the artistic process. As an experienced teacher I relate what has been successful with young children. As a visiting artist and art consultant, I make recommendations for designing art experiences in many environments.

The goal of this chapter is to encourage teachers to consider these ideas and to develop their own. It is hoped that teachers who are interested in sharing art experiences with young children will be inspired to experience art more for themselves.

Parents learn from their children. As it is for parents, so it is for teachers of young children. We are constantly learning, because as teachers we are involved in the joys and frustrations of the process, as well as the excitement of discovery and accomplishment.

If you teach young children, then you already know how to share with them. You may value or even love art, but lack experiences in art. You may want to consider how personal experiences of poetry, theatre, dance, and music enhance your visual art experiences.

What has art meant to you? Think of an art work that made an impression on you, whether it was a work in a gallery, a reproduction, or a student work. Was it the colors that drew you to look? Did the choice of subject or the way it was rendered evoke an emotion? Was the mastery of craftsmanship stunning? Were you moved to search for the reason the artist made it? Like many others, I have been impressed in these ways by children's art. Ask the same of your experiences with the other arts—poetry, theatre, dance, and music.

Our *response* to art is the experience I am addressing. We respond on an intuitive, subconscious level to art's spiritual and universal qualities. As teachers we address these aspects in the lives of our students. Think of media and technique as the shell or vehicle; they are considerations, but not the kernel of art experience.

Many of us grew up with little or no art education; we want things to be better for our children, our students, and our society. In wanting to teach children art, *we are challenged to experience art for ourselves*, as an ongoing and integral part of our lives.

Art experiences can take many forms, from reading and listening, to creating. Art museums, galleries, films, videos, and books as well as dance performances, music concerts, and poetry readings are plentiful, often free or at a low cost. Inservices, workshops, continuing education classes, relationships with mentors, and college courses are formal, structured ways to study the making of art. Keeping a sketch pad journal, exploring different media either at work or home, is another independent approach.

As we continue to experience art in any of these ways, sharing and designing meaningful art experiences with young children will follow naturally.

As I work with teachers, I often sense a lack of confidence with art education that is not apparent in their other teaching and sharing. A day care center director commented to me how timid her staff was during an art

* This chapter is adapted from *Designing Art Experiences for Young Children: An Introduction*, by Kathryn Gaspar, a publication made possible with public funds from the New York State Council on the Arts. In Monroe County, the Decentralization Program is administered by Arts for Greater Rochester. The publication was partially funded by the Memorial Art Gallery. Copyright ©1990 Kathryn Gaspar, all rights reserved.

gallery tour. This included those teachers who were usually confident in new places. People are self conscious when they don't know art history, or cannot express their ideas in critical art language.

It is true that art has its own language and history. However, I can also respond to works about which I know little. Furthermore, many artists feel that successful art speaks for itself, needing no further information. When asked to write about her work, one artist wrote that she found this request ironic, for she spends years making works which speak for themselves.

Collecting, storing, and recalling facts involve *analytical* thinking processes. Creating art and aesthetic response involve *intuitive* thinking processes. In viewing art we sometimes engage in both kinds of thinking. Reading the artists' names, calling to mind information or other works, and questioning a technique are examples of analytical thinking. Being drawn to a work because of its effect on us is an example of intuitive response. Analytical thinking can interfere with intuitive response, and sometimes we need to quiet our analytical mind long enough to feel and respond.

People can be intimidated by theories about who can make "real" art, the concept of talent, and the like. Some widely held misconceptions have the effect of preventing people from developing their artistic vision, as viewers or as creators. Art education helps us sort out myth from reality. Art education can take many forms, from independent, personal pursuit, to apprenticeship or college study.

As a guest artist in schools, I am frequently asked, "How long have you been an artist?" A wonderful discussion always follows. It has to do with embracing one's inclinations and elevating them to the level of identity. I ask the children, "Who likes to draw, play sports, or play music after school, not for an assignment, but for the sheer love and pleasure of it? You can say you are an artist, athlete, or musician when you choose to pursue something for pleasure, to achieve excellence, or to earn a living. *All of these are commitments to yourself."*

This identity question and discussion relates to teachers as well. What is your commitment to yourself and to children regarding art? We are familiar with the notion of self-fulfilled prophesies, and we are careful about what we affirm for our students. But what about for ourselves? At teacher inservices, I hear a litany of "I don't have any art talent...training... background" or I don't really know what I'm doing." Then, added on, is, "but I do it because the kids love it."

Teachers of young children put children's well-being ahead of their own so often that they don't often make time for personal development. *Pursue art for the nourishment of your spirit. Your commitment to developing* a personal relationship to art is the key to teaching art in a way that is meaningful to you and to children.

Approaches to Art Teaching

Sometimes teaching is sharing information or an experience. Demonstrating the use of a tool or a printmaking technique are two examples of directly *relating information.*

Sometimes teaching is a process in which both adults and children are learning together. Here the *teacher is a guide or interpreter.* Nature walks, experimenting with texture rubbings, printmaking, or going to a gallery can be examples of this process.

Part of teaching is providing an environment and materials. As facilitator, the teacher encourages learning by responding in a sensitive way to interactions between children and between the child and the environment. As *facilitator* the teacher looks for the next step in the process in which children are engaged and guides them into new areas.

Children can explore according to their own agendas. An interest center, such as easel painting, is a good example. Children mix, wipe, and push the paint around for their own reasons: They liked it yesterday and want to remember the feeling, they want to see color run down, they want a quiet activity, or the like. Most of the time they cannot articulate their reasons, but we know they are there. Why do some children cover the whole paper and others do not? Why do some want just one color and others want a different color every few minutes? *There are not only individual differences, but each child's needs, intuitive agendas, change constantly during the day.*

Learning also takes place on a subconscious level. *Children relate to adults as models.* By making art with them or bringing works of art to the classroom, sharing what we see in nature, or talking about how a picture makes us feel, we teach children that it is meaningful to look, respond, and create.

Which approach is best? Early childhood specialists and developmental psychologists agree that young children need to explore and discover as active learners. An art class experience can incorporate any of the approaches just outlined. My personal experience with hundreds of children, and feedback from many parents and early childhood education specialists, has led me to develop a mixed program. The crucial criterion is not how directive or nondirective an experience is as much as the engagement and enjoyment of the child. A directed approach requires that the teacher be keenly tuned in to the students. Young children tell us in many ways if an experience is engaging them; they are easier to "read" than adults. By paying close attention to them, teachers can gauge the pace, amount of information or steps, length of an activity, as well as how much direction is needed.

In groups of young children, there is always a range of readiness levels. Encouraging children to try something new not only creates the opportunity for learning to occur but encourages the joy of discovering, "I can do it!"

Children benefit from different teachers' styles and personalities. *Teachers teach best in personalized, individual styles.* Free to express ourselves, we model genuine enthusiasm for art. Young children are very sensitive to the energy and ease of a teacher, and *the affect of this enthusiasm transcends the effect of any specific approach.*

Teachers must be true to themselves. If extra noise or clean-up really bothers you, explain this to the children and ask their cooperation. It makes no sense to push your limits so that they have fewer limits if it makes you dispirited or unable to enjoy the process. If teachers are not comfortable then the children will not be either. *Children need our positive, supportive energy more than they need to be totally unrestricted.*

Aspects of Art Experiences

Understanding the different processes occurring in art experiences helps in developing relevant teaching approaches.

There is the act of *creating an image or form.* Often this is thought of as the only kind of art experience to have, or to teach. Many children come to day care centers having had access to markers, paper, and crayons, as many parents know that art is enjoyable and important for self-expression.

Making art requires children to *solve problems,* sometimes on several levels simultaneously. Children integrate visual, expressive, and sometimes conceptual aspects in art.

Seeing, hearing, and touching can also be aesthetic experiences, that is, experiences of beauty. But identifying sounds, describing textures, or describing a picture are not art experiences. Giving children the opportunity to respond can make it an art experience. Asking, "How does the picture make you feel?" differs from asking, "What do you see in the picture?" Here teachers are guides. Consider guided looking as a process distinct from a hands-on experience.

Carefully guided looking can be one of the richest experiences we have with young children. Looking and discussing what is seen is a process where the adults know by direct feedback and observation the nature of the experience the child is having.

This experience can occur spontaneously outside a structured art time, for example, on the playground with flowers, leaves, bark or other natural objects. It can also occur spontaneously during an art process. Special time can be set aside with work that has been chosen for discussion. The more often teachers do this, the greater the children's visual awareness.

What is worth looking at? At one day care center where I taught weekly classes, I told the children we would have a special looking time. Each week I brought one or two objects from nature, well-made crafts, art work, things from other cultures, or unusual toys.

Here is an outline of the project I developed:

- Once a week I brought in one or two objects; because of the repetition, everyone anticipated this experience.

- I told children it was a special looking time, reminding them that careful seeing is an important part of art time.

- The ideal group size is 6 to 8 children, so that each child has speaking time before the group attention disperses.

- I showed objects and asked questions to guide their discovery.

- I passed objects around.

- I gave additional information.

What is *Not* Art

Early childhood programs are materials-oriented. When does an activity cross the line into art? The "working definition" of art is the making or arrangements of colors, lines, shapes, textures, and so forth, that appeals to the senses and communicates a feeling, idea, experience, or view of the world. In some cases the adult has made the choices of arrangements and the children are asked to copy. Often the adult has not even chosen or made the arrangements but has copied a project sample from a book or another teacher. To fabricate means to make or build by joining parts; to construct. Many "art projects" are really fabrication activities. Children enjoy copying and constructing, and there can be other developmental or educational value as well as their enjoyment. *However, it may be helpful for teachers to clarify which type of experiences they have designed for children in order to understand if their students are getting art experiences or copying and fabrication activities.* Evaluate a past art activity that you have done with children. What was their experience? What choices did they make? What were the major and minor learning objectives?

Sometimes because paint, colored paper, glue, or other "art materials" are used in a project it is considered art. When these materials are used to copy with few or no choices then it is not art.

Some common categories of nonart projects include:

1. Assembling projects, such as gluing a magnet to a craft stick to use on a refrigerator door as a note-holder, stringing macaroni in a given pattern, constructing popsicle stick boxes;

2. Tactile experiences, such pudding "paintings" and shaving cream pictures that have a tactile experience as the focus;

3. Copying projects, such as coloring a ditto like the teacher's model or arranging pre-cut paper face parts like the teacher's model.

It is possible to rework a repertoire of projects to make them into art experiences:

1. Brainstorm what could be made with sticks or show many examples. Stringing things? *Have many choices*, colors, different objects. Macaroni accepts color from water color paints or markers (for bigger things like ziti). Offer beads, buttons, macaroni or more and discuss with children their choices of all one kind of object, all different objects, and alternating objects and/or colors. Show several samples and analyze them. How was this made? What kind of things did this person choose? These questions help develop children's ideas.

2. After a basically tactile experience, allow time to *notice and describe* patterns, colors, size and shape comparisons. Encourage children to invent patterns and images.

3. For children who are too young to make images, *increase their choices* by adding things they can select from and arrange. Painting feet for footprints? After the first and second times of walking back and forth and enjoying the novelty of colored feet, try to plan a pattern with two or more different colored sets of feet, or paint each foot a different color, or paint each foot a combination of colors, or mix colors with feet.

Thinking about art *experiences* instead of art *projects* puts the emphasis on the children's process, instead of the thing to be made. Early childhood educators know that when on a walk, going at a comfortable pace and stopping to notice trees, buds, and animals are as important as getting to the destination. How children cooperate in putting away the blocks is as important as getting the blocks picked up. Process is much more important than product in many activities and experiences, and so it is with art.

A craft is a skill, especially in work done with the hands. The traditional crafts include pottery, weaving, glassblowing, woodworking, knitting, quilting, jewelry making and metal work.

What is not craft? Some children's fabrication projects are mislabeled "arts and crafts." The adult version of fabrication projects include many objects found in "craft fairs," in the form of sea shell animals, dried flowers glued to driftwood, and objects made from kits. These things require time and patience, but little skill.

Artists and crafts people argue about where the line between art and craft is drawn. At one extreme, people argue that functionality defines craft and excludes the object from being considered art: For example, no matter how a bowl is glazed or constructed, bowls are not art objects. Others consider the primary *purpose* of the object, aesthetic or functional: For example, Matisse and Picasso painted vases, but these were done for aesthetic purposes. There are varying degrees of how artistic a functional object can be. For early childhood programs, I distinguish between art experiences involving personal, intuitive vision and/or choices; fabrication or copying activities, providing few choices; and crafts, which allow children to acquire specific skills in the traditional techniques of crafts such as clay modeling methods of pinch, slab, and coil building.

Why Teach Art to Preschoolers?

- *Appreciation and understanding of art is an exciting way to learn about ourselves and other people.*

- *Children will have few opportunities to participate in art experiences when they enter school.* Most classroom teachers for grades K-12 have little, if any, training or experience in making or teaching art. In both independent and public education the classroom teachers have a great deal of required material to cover in class. If a classroom teacher does have an art background, there is usually little opportunity or administrative support to use class time for art. Most children will have time for art once a week, for 45 minutes. Some schools exclude kindergarten from art, and some schools have art for one semester only.

- *Young children are ripe for art experiences.* They are sense-oriented and have few prejudices about what is or is not worth looking at, experimenting with, or discussing.

- Because of all the stimulation in this culture, *children need adults to provide an environment that is conducive to the creative process.* The easel in the corner and the boxes of crayons on "choosing shelves" are

48 important, but not enough. Often there are many things going on in the room at once, and this arrangement asks children to constantly tune out a lot of stimulation. Taking a short walk away from the bigger group to look and discuss what is being seen, stepping into a hallway to draw, or going into a separate room to try a new process gives children a chance to focus, quiet themselves, and be in touch with their creativity.

- *Artists give something special to a community.* Unless an artist works in a day care center or preschool, children may not be aware of artists. By comparison, children are aware of police officers, doctors, bus drivers, and others, as people who do particular things for a community. Teachers can increase the visibility of artists and contribute to the valuing of art and artists.

- *Children learn to appreciate art by ongoing, guided observation and discussion. The teacher asks questions that stimulate careful seeing and teach the language of art.* Children are so bombarded by images in advertisements, television, movies, and the like that more attention needs to be placed on sensitive seeing.

- *Art is needed for humanity to grow in a balanced way.* Engaging in art experiences nourishes a vital part of our being that does not get nourished in intellectual and physical activities. Our spirit needs art, music, poetry, dance, and song.

Chapter 10
Birthdays, Children, and Art:
Museums as Meaningful Places for Young Children

Priscilla Lund and Sandy Osborne
Montana State University

Young children are active learners who experience and respond to art in a unique manner. This chapter chronicles an event planned specifically for young children. The purpose of the event was to assist children to learn how art history and cultural legacies are embodied in their community art museum.

Summer in Fort Dodge is usually hot, humid, and full of activities for children who live in this northwest Iowa community. One of these annual summer activities was sponsored by the Blanden Memorial Art Museum. The Blanden opened on June 5, 1932, as the first permanent art museum structure in the state of Iowa. Charles Granger Blanden provided funds for the museum building and the early collection in memory of his wife, Elizabeth Mills Blanden. Because of its historical importance, the Blanden serves as a center for promoting cultural events.

M. Jessica Rowe, Director of the Blanden at the time, asked the authors to develop a week of related experiences for preschool children. Cheryl A. Parker, former museum educator at the Blanden and now a graduate student at Iowa State University in Ames, joined in the planning. After some discussion, it was decided that the week's events should offer experiences encouraging connections between preschool children's lives and the Blanden's permanent collection. This would also fulfill the museum director's goal of bringing young children into the museum in ways that made sense to them. Although art museums are traditionally considered institutions frequented by adults, more and more enlightened directors and other personnel are coming to recognize young children's potential for experiencing and responding to art. Consequently, programming for this age is expanding (Cole & Schaefer, 1990).

Young children are active learners (DeVries & Kohlberg, 1987). They construct their representation of the greater, larger world from their own egocentric world. It was felt therefore, that paintings with subjects that appeal to children would interest children and contribute to their process of understanding most dramatically (Bruner, 1960; Wolf, 1990).

One event that young children and adults have in common are birthday celebrations. The structure of a ritual, celebration, or party unfolded as the theme for the week. Because the session was scheduled for July, an artist born during this month and represented in the Blanden's collection was selected. Marc Chagall became the guest of honor. His painting, "The Fantastic Horse Cart," was on exhibit in the Blanden, a gift of Ann Smeltzer, a resident of Fort Dodge.

Another Chagall painting that appeals to young children is the work "Birthday." According to Compton (1985), when Chagall painted "Birthday" he was living in Vitesk, Russia, and courting his fiancé, Bella. In her memoirs Bella recalled how she discovered Marc's birth date and set out to celebrate it. She described how she picked flowers from the fields located near Vitesk and brought them to Marc at his apartment. Chagall documented this evening of joy and celebration in this painting.

The Workshop

The session time of 9:30 a.m. to 11:30 a.m. was selected as optimum for both the preschool children and their families. Because the museum's classrooms were being renovated, the sessions were held in a church across the alley. This apparent inconvenience eventually contributed to the final activity for the workshop.

The first session began with greetings and introductions. The instructors then revealed their ages to introduce the idea of birthdays and how they are celebrated. The children were then taken to the museum.

After a brief visit to all the galleries, the children moved to the east gallery where selections from the museum's permanent collection were exhibited. It was explained that these works of art stayed at the museum, whereas some art was here for a short time and then moved to another museum for other people to see. The morning ended with a look at Chagall's painting.

The second session began with a brief description of Chagall's life and his July 7th birth date. Several reproductions of his paintings were shown to the children, concluding with the "Birthday." The previous day's topic of their own birthdays and how they are celebrated was then reintroduced. The children were encouraged to describe activities that usually happen at birthday parties. They were then asked to suggest activities for a celebration of Chagall's birthday. Their ideas included decorations, cards, hats, costumes, gifts, and, of course, a cake.

To create a birthday party atmosphere, the children were allowed to select from a variety of art materials: crepe paper, clay, dough, watercolors, rolls of white paper, felt markers, crayons, scissors, tape, and glue. Easy access to appropriate art materials is critical for young children as they learn best by repeated experience with basic materials (Clemens, 1991). Materials were in an area where the children had convenient access and they were free to choose as they worked, materials that suited their ideas.

In order to maintain several activities simultaneously, the instructors arranged tables according to categories: one for the cake, another for the costumes, and so forth. The children moved from table to table as they made their preparations for the party to be held on the last day of the workshop.

The cake presented an interesting challenge. Because it was desirable to have all of the children participate in the cake decoration, a large sheet of styrofoam coated with several layers of plaster gauze was prepared. The children painted the cake and then used felt markers to complete its decorations. The children made candles, flowers, and tiny animals from clay dough and attached them to the cake's surface.

By the end of Thursday's session, the party decorations, gifts, cards, and costumes were complete (although the humidity kept the cake from drying thoroughly). Friday began with a brief review of the week's preparations, of Chagall's life, and of the much anticipated celebration. Then the decorations were gathered, the costumes completed, and the gifts, cards, and cake carried out of the classroom down the stairs and onto the sidewalk.

The children then paraded around the museum singing happy birthday to Marc Chagall. When they arrived at the museum entrance, the director, members of the museum's staff, and the children's families were waiting to greet them. Together adults and children proceeded into the gallery where Chagall's painting was exhibited. The cake, gifts, and cards were presented to the museum director, who accepted them with a brief speech. The celebration concluded with a final performance of "Happy Birthday," followed by applause.

Analysis

This description of one workshop provides a framework for considering how to structure art experiences in early childhood environments. Reviewing the structure implied in this particular instance can lead to other series of sequential art experiences that nurture young children's deep involvement in learning about their physical and social worlds.

The structure of the birthday party series evolved from four questions that suggest integration of ideas and actions or thinking and doing. The first two questions emphasize the sources of concepts and themes that are the focus of the series.

1. How do the planned experiences address the lives of children?

   Children's interests, ideas, and speculations serve as subject matter for the spontaneous art that they initiate (Lark-Horovitz, Lewis, & Luca, 1973). Because children have established ideas and interests that guide their artistic expression at home, instructors need to consider how to draw upon that knowledge and experience to make the experiences they plan meaningful (Leeds, 1986; Lowenfeld & Brittain, 1987).

   According to Viktor Lowenfeld (in Michael, 1982), children use art materials within the context of their lives as they construct ways to learn about themselves and their community. In the workshop described here, personal birthday celebrations served as a grounding for exploring how the local museum might be a foundation and springboard, a part of children's lives. Connections were then made by studying an artist who lived in a different culture and historical period.

2. How do the planned experiences connect with processes, materials, historical, and contemporary aspects of art?

   A response to this question should include consideration of how children can proceed with art materials that are genuine, appropriate, and representative of the substances that artists use in their work. This question also encourages careful thought about processes as a personal endeavor guided by the idea or interest the children are exploring. Constructing things is a way to understand themes and concepts.

The response described in this chapter included planning on how to bring children to an awareness of artists, their historical and cultural importance, and the role of museums as a place to learn. Furthermore, the children were introduced to how a community participates and constructs a museum's importance in order to begin their awareness of historical legacy in a meaningful way.

Another important aspect of this art experience was that the children made these connections by making and doing things. Birthdays are annual events, so their repetition invites ceremony and ritual. Lippard (1983) described rituals as ways for us to give form to our experience. Young children in our culture discover the ritual of birthday celebrations early in their lives, so it is a familiar form of expression. They enjoy this event and recognize it as an annual, dramatic, and visual experience. Birthday celebrations combine the focus on an individual, a guest of honor, with an awareness of a community's acknowledgment of a rite of passage.

Often when individuals experience a special event they choose to document it in some way. Photographs and videos may be taken during the event, and scrapbooks assembled to document its occurrence. Chagall considered Bella's commemoration of his birthday so joyful and sincere that he chose to paint that expression of their love and affection. Just as Chagall drew from an event in his life, the children reviewed their experience with birthday celebrations. They, thus, made connections with an artist, his art, and an art museum that holds one of his paintings in its permanent collection.

Two more questions emphasize actions and participation. It is important to discuss these questions from the perspective of their relationship to each other.

3. What does the teacher choose and decide about the experiences?

4. What do the children choose and decide about the experiences?

Answers to these questions emerge from a blend and balance between them. Teachers choose and decide themes, focus, time, places, or, in other words, they set up situations that nurture children's choices and decisions that are guided by their personal expressions (Leeds, 1986). Children's choices and decisions are focused by their ideas, intentions, and interests (Donaldson, 1978; Vygotsky, 1962). When teachers set up these situations, they are guided by their knowledge of human development and learning as they coincide with artistic growth

and aesthetic awareness (Lowenfeld & Brittain, 1987).

Conclusion

The week of preparation and participation enabled the young children to move from an awareness of their relationship with their city's art museum to making art and participating in an event meaningful to them.

Young children became personally aware of the art museum in their community and a particular artist whose painting was in its permanent collection. The potential to view Chagall's painting again in the future was an important goal of the week. During the workshop young children visited the museum daily and explored its physical structure and the nature of its purpose and contents. They explored a variety of art materials and processes as well as the concept of ritual as a human endeavor. They generated categories that guided the activity and chose how to proceed with the materials. They had time to inquire and reflect, wonder, and think about their ideas and how they connected with the theme. They utilized their previous experience in order to acquire new knowledge and connected their ideas about the concept of ritual through their personal expression with art materials (National Association for the Education of Young Children, 1991). These children integrated ideas and actions in order to learn about how art history and cultural legacies are embodied in their art museum.

References

Bruner, J. S. (1960). *The process of education*. Cambridge, MA: Harvard University Press.

Clemens, S. G. (1991). Art in the classroom: Making every day special. *Young Children, 46*(2), 4-11.

Cole, E. S., & Schaefer, C. (1990). Can young children be art critics? *Young Children, 45*(2), 33-38.

Compton, S. (1985). *Chagall*. New York: Harry N. Abrams.

DeVries, R., & Kohlberg, L. (1987). *Constructivist early education: Overview and comparison with other programs*. Washington, DC: National Association for the Education of Young Children.

Donaldson, M. (1978). *Children's minds*. New York: W. W. Norton.

Lark-Horovitz, B., Lewis, H., & Luca, M. (1973). *Understanding children's art for better teaching* (2nd ed.). Columbus, OH: Charles E. Merrill.

Leeds, J. A. (1986). Teaching and the reasons for making art. *Art Education, 39*(7), 17-21.

Lippard, L. (1983). *Overlay: Contemporary art and the art of prehistory*. New York: Pantheon.

Lowenfeld, V., & Brittain, W. L. (1987). *Creative and mental growth* (8th Ed.). New York: Macmillan.

Michael, J. A. (Ed.) (1982). *Lowenfeld lectures*. University Park: Pennsylvania State University Press.

National Association for the Education of Young Children, & National Association of Early Childhood Specialists in State Departments of Education. (1991). Guidelines for appropriate curriculum content and assessment in programs serving children ages 3 through 8. *Young Children, 46*(3), 21-38.

Vygotsky, L. S. (1962). *Thought and language*. Cambridge, MA: MIT Press.

Wolf, A. D. (1990). Art postcards—Another aspect of your aesthetics program. *Young Children, 45*(2), 39-43.

Chapter 11
The Picture Museum: Creating a Photography Museum With Children

Suzanne Kolodziej
The University of Illinois - Graduate Program in Art Museum Studies

Dear Family and Friends,
We are making a Picture Museum. We will open our museum on Monday, February 11, 1991, at 4:00 and you can come in. It will be a big museum, a giant one like Godzilla. The pictures are going to be like a big Eastman House. It is going to be nice.
Sincerely,
The Children of the Dinosaur Room
St. Paul's Day Care Center

The Picture Museum pithily but eloquently described above was developed as a previsit experience for George Eastman House—International Museum of Photography and Film. Especially designed for preschoolers and kindergartners, the Picture Museum involved children personally in the creation of a classroom museum, featuring images they selected, described, and prepared for display. This chapter describes Picture Museums created by preschoolers at two area day care centers in Rochester, New York, and suggests certain features of this activity which might be replicated in other settings.

Creating the Exhibition

The first goal of the Picture Museum was to introduce children to the concept of a museum as a place where art, photographs, artifacts, or objects are collected, studied, preserved, and displayed. Each child was asked to select a photograph of himself or herself that had special significance in his or her life. These photographs became part of an exhibition in their museum under the theme, "My Favorite Photograph of Myself." Having the children choose a favorite photograph was intended to convey the idea that their museum was a collection of photographs most valued by themselves and their friends.

To expand on the idea that museums are places where valuable objects are housed, each child was asked

individually: "What is special about your picture?" and/or, "What would you like to tell me about your picture?" The children's responses reflected their experiences, observations, and existing knowledge of their world. The children shared their opinions, ideas, thoughts, and impressions about a photograph that had meaning in their lives.

After each child's response to his or her photograph was transcribed, each was asked to give the photograph a title. This was the introduction to the second goal of the Picture Museum: understanding the purpose of a museum label. The label created for each child's photograph included a title, the year the photograph was taken, the name of the photographer, and the name of the person who owns the photograph. Many children chose concrete titles, describing the content of their photograph. For example, Becky's photograph titled "Me Loving Benny" shows her smiling as her cat Benson contentedly rests wrapped in her arms. There was a spontaneity to the children's titles, which captured the spirit of their photographs as well as their descriptive content. When a child chose not to title a photograph, it became "Untitled."

Creating titles can readily lead to discussions about one of the choices artists have: to describe their photographs with words or numbers or to rely on the image to convey its meaning without the aid of a title. The process of creating titles for photographs is an activity that can be used easily during a visit to the museum. Because children are perceptually aware of colors, shapes, and lines as well as images, it is provocative to ask them how they would title certain photographs. This encourages observation and reflection, and initiates dialogue among the children.

The third goal of the Picture Museum was to teach children the purpose of a catalog. The Picture Museum catalog, produced on a personal computer, included photocopies of the photographs, their titles, the children's descriptive responses, and labels. Each child received a catalog. While the museum exhibition was ephemeral, installed only temporarily, the catalog preserved the collaborative experience of forming a collection as a group. It reinforced the concept that collections are created from varied sources with many parts becoming a whole. The catalog covers were personalized with the children's scribbles, drawings, or designs which emphasized the fact that the museum catalog was indeed the children's creation.

The children's discussion of their photographs encouraged close observation of an image for an extended period of time and in a manner requiring their active participation. Sustained viewing in which one is actively engaged with an image is the foundation of visual literacy. Too often in our culture diluted images are designed to engage the child passively. The majority of images children perceive from television and other technological sources do not evoke a desire to respond. Teachers can develop in children a capacity for responsive behavior by providing occasions for response. An aesthetic response "includes those responses in which the qualities and meanings of objects and artistic intentions are the major focus" (Taunton, 1982). The responses initiated by the children's photographs encompassed what could be defined as an aesthetic response: The children created their own meanings. Enabling children to create and articulate the meanings of photographs that they value may assist them in discovering meanings in other works of art, photographs, or everyday objects they will encounter later. Children learn the syntax of images prior to learning the syntax of spoken and printed words (Feldman, 1981). Children can verbally respond to the arrangement of elements that form a photograph. Unlike printed words, artistic images—even complex ones—can be shared with young children. The logic Harry used as he responded "Daddy took the picture because you see Mommy in it" demonstrates that he read the image. The ability to search and extend to create meanings and confidently communicate those meanings is the goal of an aesthetic response and an end in itself.

The Picture Museum, like all truly collaborative learning experiences, provides a participatory situation in which children formulate and express their own concerns as they learn to interpret and understand their own images. "Any activity that stimulates young children's natural curiosity about artworks has possibilities as a first step in their aesthetic growth towards perceiving aesthetic characteristics" (Stokrocki, 1984, p. 13). The Picture Museum provides an age-appropriate foundation for viewing photographs and encouraging children to recognize, value, and express their preferences. The process of choosing a meaningful photograph can begin to develop in children the potential for aesthetic capabilities. For children, the aesthetic is multisensory.

In their responses, children not only perceived what was imaged, but became involved in explanations of numerous sensory experiences. The children spoke of sounds heard, textures felt, and images seen. In Libby's photograph she hugs her dog and exclaims, "I love Nellie because she is nice and soft and cuddly. I love everyone in my family."

Whether the image is of oneself, or a photograph in a museum, our aesthetic choices are complicated and are a reflection of our personal viewpoint. "We see things not as they are," the educational philosopher Neil Postman once wrote "but as we are." The Picture Museum creates a necessary reference for preschoolers to encounter a photography museum or exhibition with confidence and interest and provides them with a means to relate the photography museum or exhibition to their previous learning experience. Finally, the Picture Museum allows the children's life at home to become part of their daily environment in their places of learning, which is vital whether the setting is day care, preschool, or elementary school. When children assign value to a photograph in a positive manner, which is then shared with peers, teachers, and family, it can serve as a link between their home and various learning situations. Among the several goals of the Picture Museum, the most important was to empower the child. By acknowledging the validity of children's responses, we affirm in them a sense of self.

Providing occasions for children to respond aesthetically, the children's photographs created a basis for elaborate storytelling. Each child embellished the photograph by revealing his or her own story. The words not only described what was pictorially represented but also what was remembered, experienced, and felt. It was only through the children's words that I entered their world, reaching beyond the perimeters of the photograph to share the details of their discoveries.

Developing the Project

Developing the idea for the Picture Museum began with personal requests to nieces and nephews to share their favorite photographs. The results were illuminating. My four-year-old niece Whitney-Ann sent a picture of herself seated by her birthday cake, which she had decorated with small plastic toys. It was titled "Happy Birthday". When asked why her photograph was special her reply was "Because it's my birthday. And my Aunt came. I like myself and I like my cake." Ruben, who is four and a half years old, is fond of animals. He chose a photograph of himself with a cat. He replied "I like it because it has a cat. I called it 'Friend the Cat.' He loves me because I was friendly to him." In "Chelsea Doing A Jig," Chelsea declares how happy she is and then gives an inventory of all the objects in the photograph. My nephews, Garrett, who is two and a half years old, and Kyler, who is eight years old, responded to their photographs with the appropriate interest, enthusiasm, and language one would expect from children their age. This provided evidence that the Picture Museum is developmentally sound for a wide age range, from children just beginning to express themselves verbally to children learning to express themselves through the written word.

These children are part of my life; I am familiar with their personalities, temperaments, and moods. Through sharing their favorite photograph I realized the intensity of descriptive language. For teachers in new learning situations this type of interaction can be enlightening. By providing paths to understanding children in an affective sense, it affirms that certain aspects of being remain unmeasurable and must be understood in ways which are more akin to the understanding of art.

"Paul and Miss Kimberly" 1990
Photographer — Uncle Craig
Collection of the Maves Family

"Well, I was holding her when I was having my picture taken at my Mom's friends' house, Chris and Craig. And I got to hold her at Chris's Mom's house. She came to my house. My brother Casey was sitting next to me and we each got a turn to hold her. And her name is Miss Kimberly. I like my picture so much I always open my picture book and look at it. And I like Harry's picture that he brought in. It is so beautiful, isn't it? And he is riding a camel. At the circus I got to ride an elephant. Chris and Craig brought me a present. It was tiny Legos, well—one was a motorcycle, one was a car, one was a wagon, and one was a person. I like Miss Kimberly, she is so beautiful. She was born and has a dog and her name is Isis."

Paul Maves

Although I did not know four-year-old Paul prior to the creation of the Picture Museum (see Figure 11.1), through this work I quickly gained a sense of this child. His fondness for the newborn child Miss Kimberly, evident visually, was expressed verbally. I felt his excitement about the birth of Miss Kimberly, his pride in holding her, as well as his pleasure in receiving a new toy! As Paul described his "treasuring" of his picture, he also found an opportunity to convey his appreciation for his classmate Harry's

Figure 1. *An entry in the Picture Museum complete with title and description.*

photograph. Harry's photograph which he entitled "Ride," depicts Harry with his mother riding a camel at the Toronto Zoo. Children invariably learn from one another as they communicate meaning and share experiences. "Ride" became a point of departure for Paul to share his adventure of riding an elephant at the circus. Paul responded, understanding those features of his photograph, and his friend's, as they related to his priorities and interest.

Educational Implications

The Picture Museum can be integrated into numerous learning situations. The concept of museums, collections, or photography can be explored. To understand the children's interpretation of museums I asked, "What do you think museums do?" Stewart replied, "They have things. You can put things there and they will protect them. They make dinosaur bones. One day we saw an elephant's trunk in there." Bethany answered concisely, "They set things up so you can see them." Caroline decided that "They make things like statues. Sometimes museums are made out of rectangles and wood." Other questions included, "What type of objects do you collect?" "Do you keep the objects you collect in a special place?" "Can you describe that special place?" "Are there any objects that you collect which are also found in a museum?" "Can you describe those objects?"

Asking children what they collect, value, and preserve can initiate an exploration of the idea of collections. The process of deciding what to collect is also the process of searching for a common source of value which binds our human identity, and acknowledging that each selection to the museum collection adds something unique and diverse. Thus, in exchanging and sharing treasured objects, explaining their origins, and describing the reasons these objects are cherished, children can also begin to learn to respect cultural differences.

Activities such as this, which elicit verbal response to meaningful objects, or images and experiences, foster the development of thought and language. Wells (1986) suggests that as children "narrate those experiences to others they are perhaps for the first time discovering their significance for themselves. These are the conditions that foster language development: when one has something important to say, and other people are interested in hearing it. It is then that language and thinking most fully interpenetrate in the struggle to make meaning that captures what one has observed and understood and communicates that understanding to others" (p. 107).

Being child-centered, the Picture Museum allows children to explore their interests while building self-esteem through shared language experiences. In the area of whole language learning the Picture Museum provides for divergent responses, natural language, and speaking to facilitate thinking while the teacher listens. We can teach children more effectively by listening, and, if we listen, they will listen. We can delight in their discoveries, we can learn their interests, we can grasp how children perceive. We can provide children opportunities by which they enable us to be insightful teachers. We can honor the process of learning as one of reciprocity.

The Picture Museum can create a setting in which children develop their thoughts as well as their language, experience those thoughts as words in print, and realize the strength gained by sharing that which they value. We can combine their words with their images in a manner that contributes to their growth, to the recognition of the qualities of their inner selves. We can teach children that their written words convey meanings, ideas, and imaginative possibilities.

As an art medium, photography has the potential to teach children the differences between the creation of an image to convey an idea versus an image whose sole purpose is commercialism. Photographic images permeate our culture, yet these images are not always conducive to human development. Photographs as artistic images, ones of quality and content, can be experienced by children in a meaningful and positive way. Engagements with art, as the educational philosopher Maxine Greene (1981) has written, can serve as a vehicle to break through the petrified world:

To be petrified is to be granite-like, susceptible to neither learning nor change. If the artistic-aesthetic can open up the petrified world, provide new standpoints on what is taken for granted, those who are empowered by their teachers to engage in the arts may find themselves posing questions never thought of before. They may find themselves posing questions from their own locations in the world and in light of what they themselves are living, what they themselves are discovering to be warranted, to be true. This is because engagements with works of art—aware, informed engagements—make individuals present to what is given to them, personally present, no longer lulled by the natural attitude. And it is those who can ask their own questions, ask them in person, who are the ones most ready to learn how to learn (p. 141).

The Picture Museum can be understood as a contribution to those collaborative learning experiences aimed at making children confident of the worth of their own vantage point, and thus "ready to learn how to learn." Yet, like all collaborative learning experiences, it requires the teacher to be open to the child's interpretation of his or her world; it requires that teachers also be willing to break through the petrified world.

As adults we need to take time to listen. We need to attend to children's responses, for their words encompass their feelings, thoughts, wishes, dreams, hopes, and fears. We need to ask children questions to which we do not know the answers; our intentions need to have purpose so their replies are valid. Too often as teachers we come to a situation with nothing ourselves to learn, only a procedure, or a technique, or a set of instructions to hand out. Through appropriate questioning strategies we can move beyond the general assessment of known replies to begin to understand the intricacy of the children we are responsible for educating. It is through that understanding we can celebrate together what has worth, significance, and meaning in each other's lives not only inside our museums, but also in our daily encounters with children in their places of learning.

References

Feldman, E. (1981). Art is for reading: Pictures make a difference. *Teachers College Record, 82*(4), 649-660.

Greene, M. (1981). Aesthetic literacy in general education. In J. F. Soltis (Ed.), *Philosophy and education* (pp. 115-141). Chicago: The University of Chicago Press.

Stokrocki, M. (1984). The meaning of aesthetic awareness for preschoolers in a museum class. *Art Education, 37* (2), 12-16.

Taunton, M. (1982). Aesthetic responses of young children to the visual arts: A review of literature. *The Journal of Aesthetic Education,* (3), 93-109.

Wells, G. (1986). *The meaning makers: Children learning language and using language to learn.* Portsmouth, NH: Heinemann Educational Books, Inc.

Chapter 12
A Bunch of Naked Ladies and a Tiger: Children's Responses to Adult Works of Art

Marianne S. Kerlavage
Millersville University

A friend, her five-year-old son Adam, and I recently visited the Metropolitan Museum of Art in New York. Adam's mother is an artist and teacher and it has been her mission to instill in her offspring a love and appreciation for all the arts. To that end Adam visits the museum and galleries and has been taught to look at art works, to discuss his feelings about them, and to hunt for artistic merit. He is a little boy who seems quite at home among the representative examples of the visual arts. Adam and his mother went off to see some new works being exhibited in the 17th-and 18th-century European collection while I spent considerable time in another part of the museum at a Pre-Columbian exhibit.

Later, over lunch, my friend and I discussed what we had seen. As adults will do, we spent considerable time on our own reflections. In an attempt to include Adam in our discussion, I asked him what he had seen. After giving the matter considerable thought he replied: "Oh, a bunch of naked ladies and a tiger!"

Adam's comment caused me to give serious thought to children, especially young children, and their responses to works of adult art. There is no doubt that all of us involved in the arts are, like my friend, desirous of instilling a love for the arts in all children. To that end the current trend in art education places children, at a very young age, in formal situations involving works of art (Art Image, 1992; Colbert & Taunton, 1988; Herberholz & Hanson, 1990; Milwaukee Public Schools, 1991; Morris, 1991; Sharp, 1976; Smith, 1982). We take children to museums, we show them reproductions of works of art, we ask them to analyze and critique. We hope that this exposure initiates an interest and an understanding of art works which will develop into a lifelong love and involvement with the arts. Many believe such interaction with works of art will increase cognitive skills and encourage creative thinking (Herberholz & Herberholz, 1990; Sharp, 1976). All of these are admirable goals, from an adult perspective. But Adam's response to his day at the museum put me in mind of another kindergartner who,

when asked what her favorite thing at the museum was, responded: "The big moving stairs! No! No! I know, the fancy water fountain with a stool to climb on." These responses raise the question: "What are children learning from their interaction with adult works of art?

What the Research Shows

Art appreciation was introduced into American elementary schools in the 1880s. Since that time there has been a constant debate among art educators as to how or if art works should be used with children (Kerlavage, 1992a). Henry Bailey (1910) asked much the same questions that continue to puzzle art educators today:

> Are these the best with which our children are to be made familiar? We placed before them the things that appealed to us as being the greatest and the best, the things that are supreme from the adult point of view, not the things that would appeal to children from their point of view (p. 17-18).

Throughout their history (Colby, 1907) art educators have asserted that, in order to develop curricula which use adult works of art, it is necessary to understand how children perceive and respond to art objects. Researchers, beginning around 1910, designed studies to determine which works of art children prefer, which factors influence those preferences, and what understanding children gain from art works. This desire to understand children's interaction with art works has inspired many studies asking children to look at art works, order them by preference, and defend their choices.

Research on Preference and Response to Art Works

A primary finding supported by numerous investigations is that children's preferences rely on two main stimuli, subject matter and color (Baker, 1989; Feeney,

Fennel & Moravcik, 1987; Gardner, 1970, 1973; Katz, 1944; Lark-Horovitz, 1937; Machotka, 1966; Marschalek, 1983; Pintner, 1918, Rosensteil, Morison, Silverman, & Gardner, 1978; Steinberg & DeLoache, 1986; Taunton, 1982, 1984; Williams, 1924).

Another tendency frequently observed in studies of children's art work preferences is an attraction for realism which seems to increase with age (Coffey, 1968; Gardner, 1972; Gardner, et. al., 1975; Hardiman & Zernich, 1977; Mendenhall & Mendenhall, 1933; Moore, 1973; Rosario & Collazo, 1981; Russell, 1988; Taunton, 1980, 1982, 1984; Williams, 1924). In other studies it is reported that preference for complexity of composition also increases with age (Arnold, 1987; Clark, 1973; Feinstein, 1984; Hardiman & Zernich, 1982; Lucio & Mead, 1939; Marschalek, 1986b; Morrison, 1935; Rosario & Collazo, 1981; Silverman, Winner, & Gardner, 1976; Taunton, 1980, 1983, 1984).

Research also indicates that as children age they become increasingly sensitive to individual artistic style, media use, and artistic principles (Clark, 1973; Frechtling & Davidson, 1970; Gardner & Gardner, 1970; Gardner, 1970, 1972, 1974; Gardner, et. al., 1975; Hardiman & Zernich, 1982, 1985; Lark-Horovitz, 1938; Steinberg & DeLoache, 1986; Turner, 1983; Van der Mark, 1929).

Interest in multicultural, non-gender-biased curricula has generated several attempts to ascertain whether ethnicity, race, or gender influences children's preferences for particular works of art (Baker, 1989; Barone, 1986; Child, Hanson, & Hornbeck, 1968; Child, 1970; Curtis, 1988; Turner, 1990).

A related area of investigation, greatly influenced by the work of Rudolf Arnheim (1954), focuses on picture perception. A number of investigators have studied the child's ability to perceive images and define factors involved in the recognition of images (Braine, 1972; Mackworth & Bruner, 1970; Marschalek, 1986a; Silverman, Winner, & Gardner, 1976; Spitz & Borland, 1971). The child's ability to perceive depth cues in flat images has also been the subject of perception research (Carothers & Gardner, 1979; Jahoda & McGurk, 1974; Yonas & Hagen, 1973).

This response, preference, and perception research has identified some very clear patterns in children's ways of interacting with works of art (see Figure 12.1).

The research shows that children in the early childhood years react positively to art works that depict

---

Figure 1. Summary of factors, culled from research literature, which influence children's responses to art works.

- Young children respond primarily to subject matter and color in reproductions.
- Children respond to the sensory qualities of art works, such things as color, shape, and movement.
- Children are strongly attracted to bright intense color and tend to dislike muted or dark tones.
- Young children respond positively to patterned and nonobjective pieces which are brightly colored more frequently than they do to dark-toned realistic works.
- Young children explain image choices in realistic narrative based on familiar objects and scenes.
- Children invent stories about the shapes, colors, and images found in the art works, whether realistic or abstract.
- Children identify content in both abstract and realistic works and base their discussion of content on their immediate world.
- Children under age eight prefer (a) still life over figure groups and portraits and (b) low realism with few objects in the image.
- Young children give limited attention to the style of the painting.
- Children tend to group paintings by subject matter even when asked to order by style or artist.
- Young children's preferences relate more to what is pictured than how it is portrayed.
- Younger children have difficulty relating parts within a complex painting. They respond to part of a work without giving much attention to the whole work.
- Children do not consistently choose abstract or realistic pictures as their favorite. Their choices seem to depend on perceived themes.
- When children are asked to repeat a preference task, they seldom respond with the same order. Their reasons for choice, however, do not change.
- Children frequently do not differentiate between reproductions and photographs when making choices.
- Children are seldom able to identify whether an image is a photograph of an object or a reproduction of an art work.
- Children frequently have difficulty verbalizing exact reasons for choice.
- Children under eight have difficulty perceiving contours of shapes and patterns within shapes.
- Children perceive more detail about a shape in the art work when the shape is isolated from competing surroundings.
- Choice in the early childhood years does not appear to be influenced by race or gender.
- Age and maturation are the deciding factors for changes in response and perception.

favorite or familiar subject matter; present a clear image; contain bright, highly saturated, and contrasting colors; are simple in composition; and contain unambiguous spatial relations.

Research on Cognitive Processing and Developmental Stages

In addition to explaining how children perceive and respond to works of art some researchers have attempted to establish developmental sequences of responses. Early work of this nature was influenced by the work of G. Stanley Hall (1893, 1901, 1907) and Edward Thorndike (1916, 1917), who inspired researchers such as Earl Barnes (1908), Rudolph Pintner (1918), and Parthenia Van der Mark (1929) to attempt to establish patterns of aesthetic growth. Other early researchers, Anna Berliner (1918) and Gilbert Brighouse (1939), attempted to establish cognitive growth patterns which influenced children's responses to art works.

A number of contemporary researchers (Arnold, 1987; Burkett, 1977, 1986; Coffey, 1968; Cole, 1985; Gardner, 1978; Hardiman & Zernich, 1980, 1985; Housen, 1983; Housen, Miller, & Yenawine, 1991; Parsons, Johnston, & Durham, 1978; Parsons, 1987) posit that preference, perception, and response to art works can be explained by cognitive changes, similar to those described to Piaget (1951, 1952; Piaget & Inhelder, 1969). These researchers suggest that as children move through the various stages of development their ideas about art, picture preference, reason for preference, concept of style, and verbal responses all undergo change. The investigations attempt to show that as children age and mature their artistic and aesthetic understanding go through well defined stages, influenced and controlled by cognitive changes. Children in the early childhood years travel through three progressive and sequential stages. Based on information gleaned from the various studies, the stages will be referred to as the sensorial, concrete, and expressive.

The youngest children, those in the sensorial stage, frequently select images that are nonobjective in nature as their first choice while older children tend to choose more realistic images. The developmental research indicates that the younger children react more positively toward the abstract image because of their lack of a complete definition of symbols. Because children of this age are extremely curious, egocentric, open to new experiences, unable to think abstractly, and react to the moment, they respond to images kinetically and viscerally. They intuitively respond to works which please the senses. Therefore, color and pattern are the dominant influences on young children's preference for images.

As children develop their own sense of symbol they enter the concrete stage and become less sensorial in their choices and more reliant on subject matter or theme. For children in this stage subject matter and symbol identification gradually become the dominant reason for choice. Color and pattern continue to pay a role in picture choice, but are now contributing factors rather than dominant influences. Children move from an immediate response to color and pattern toward choice based on reality of the image portrayed. Young viewers develop a tendency to "like" paintings that are about themes and subject matter with which they can relate, represented in a realistic manner. This stage is marked by judgments based on theme, realism, and the beauty of the image. Children rely on concrete information for preference and response.

Toward the end of the early childhood years children enter the expressive stage. They begin to develop the ability to think abstractly. This influences their response to art works in that they are willing to perceive and appreciate the expressive and stylistic aspects of the works. The children still tend to prefer realistic images but they become more interested in subtle colors, complicated compositions, and expressive messages. Because they are less egocentric and now able to evaluate another's point of view, viewers of this age also develop the ability to identify artistic styles. Children begin to recognize and appreciate the different media used, the expressive differences, and varying theme interpretation of various artists and periods of art. Realism becomes one of several ways to express an idea or feeling.

Preference for subject matter, color, and artistic style travel gradually through the three stages. Children move from a total reliance on the senses to a place where they can make judgments based on expressive and abstract information. These stages are also apparent when discussing children's verbalized reasons for choice and their ability to respond about their choices.

Children in the sensorial stage will choose an image but may be unable to define a reason for choice. A shrug of the shoulders and a pointing finger will mark early interactions with art works. When children begin to verbalize reasons for preference it is almost always in terms of content. Even when children choose abstract or nonobjective art works, they relate the content to real images and experiences. While their initial reactions are immediate and sensorial they define those actions in terms of symbols and content. Children explain their preference for choice based on an assumed reality and relate the image to their known world. When asked to define the purpose of an art work or to explain the reason for the artist's creation they are seldom able to do so.

Additionally, children at this age have a tendency to focus on a single feature of an object or event at the expense of other relevant factors in an artwork. Thus, the child will see only the "horse" in an artwork and will not define other characteristics, shapes, or colors appearing in the work. Frequently children will be unable to distinguish between a photograph of a horse, a painting of a horse, and a two- or three-dimensional reproduction of a horse.

Children in the concrete stage define their reasons for choice very clearly and always in terms of the concrete information provided by the art work. They base their choices on themes and subject matter with which they can relate. The "story" of the painting is most relevant. The purpose of an art work, for these children, is to represent something, to record a "real" person, place, or object. They seldom make choices based on expression or artistic principles.

At this concrete stage, children demonstrate an ability to construct and manipulate class hierarchies. This allows them to sort a set of objects into subcategories, making it possible for them to place the representation of the "horse" into the separate categories of picture, painting, and reproduction.

Time also begins to have relevance for the child in this stage. No longer controlled by immediate reaction the child develops a limited sense of history. Terms such as "long ago" and "in the future" can be used successfully to define time and place. However, an exact concept of time has yet to be established.

In the expressive stage, the children begin to define their reasons for choice based on expressive and artistic factors found in the art work. Children now perceive the purpose of a painting as a way to express an idea or a feeling, and not just to record reality. Children will defend their choices in terms of artistic style, expressive qualities, and artistic principles.

The children are also able to distinguish between a picture, a painting, and a reproduction, and begin to recognize style and media. They can describe how various artists might begin to interpret the "horse" in different ways and with different media. Critical and aesthetic analysis becomes possible at this stage.

Time, in the abstract, is also becoming comprehensible. Children will now be able to place events and situations in proper historical time. Additionally they will be able to distinguish and classify time periods.

Interaction With Art Works Meaningful for Kids

The research shows that students in the early childhood years are basically sensorial in their responses to works of art, are seldom able to analyze works as artistic pieces, and have a limited concept of time. This brings into question the developmental appropriateness of many current curricula which base methodologies on aesthetic interpretation, critical analysis, and historic time lines. Children who are seldom able to relate to subject matter beyond themselves and their immediate world cannot be expected to "look at and talk about" works of art with any true artistic and aesthetic understanding.

The research also suggests that children advance through several stages of aesthetic and artistic understanding. They begin with little ability to express views on works of art and limited understanding of their meaning. They eventually become able to think abstractly and view the world from another's point of view. This enables them to examine and explain artworks, artistic styles, and various media techniques. Developmental research also points out that children do not develop true appreciation without some training in analysis and criticism.

Children observed in preschool and kindergarten classes (Kerlavage, 1992b) joyfully engaged in discussions about works of art, but their responses and choices tended to be based on sensory responses. Therefore, to develop programs that allow children to move beyond their initial sensorial responses, educators need to consider meeting the children's developmental needs. If programs that include young children's interaction with works of art are to be educationally, developmentally, and artistically meaningful they must:

- Be based on the child's interest and knowledge of the world.

- Provide opportunities for the child to engage the works from an individual point of view.

- Make art works a part of the child's everyday world.

- Be based on the child's natural inclination to learn through play.

Children may learn about the process of artistic creation and the techniques for producing art by acting out the artists' role. They learn how sculptors feel and produce through their own modeling activities. They become painters through painting. However, these studio experiences need to be more than manipulation of materials and opportunities for self-expression. Art works and media should serve as the raw materials for developing an understanding of the creation of art. Children, through their own production activities, may begin to look at art works and reproductions and discuss artistic creation from their own knowledge of the process. Thus, media opportunities should always include examples of art works for inspiration and comparison. Preschool children who worked in media centers that included a variety of examples of adult art works freely discussed their own work and the work of the artists represented (Kerlavage, 1992b). Additionally, their conversations were in greater depth and showed greater understanding of artistic process than a formal adult-led discussion on media and process.

Research discussed earlier also indicates that art works and young children's interactions with them need to be considered from the standpoint of total sensory involvement. Interaction needs to involve not just the sense of sight but all the senses. Young children will learn most about art works if they not only look at the works and discuss them in their own language and from their own point of view, but also relate them to what they know about the world. Their involvement needs to include investigating how images might feel, smell, and taste. This allows the children an opportunity to enter into the world of the work which may in many respects be alien to them. Involving all the senses allows children to develop an understanding of how art works relate to their world.

For example, young children would gain greater understanding of Van Gough's painting "The Sunflowers" if they looked at, touched, smelled, drew, and painted real flowers, than they would in formally discussing the style, technique, and formal artistic qualities of the artist's work. Neither formal discussion of the painting nor creatively rendering a flower would, by themselves, increase the children's knowledge of art or artists. However, combining information gained from sensory involvement with objects, artistic involvement with media, and discussion about artists' works would help children grow in their ability to produce, perceive, and respond to art.

Young children need to have opportunities to construct artistic encounters to fit their needs. At a young age, children should encounter art works informally. The art works could be displayed in media centers, as imagery for bulletin board displays, or as stimulation for narrative discussion or art production. Children at this level should be given as much opportunity as possible to "talk about art works." Use of formal art criticism, aesthetics, and art history inquiries is inappropriate for young children with little knowledge of time and the world. For these components to become viable in later life, they must be integrated into daily routines and general experiences. Children process information in a holistic manner; therefore, teachers need to structure programs which enhance and increase children's knowledge and skill at making art, perceiving art, and reflecting on art rather than depending on formal discussion and analysis.

Art and education programs for young children which include art works must also take into consideration the children's ability to define the images they see. It is vital that any use of art works and reproductions gives attention to children's literal translation of images and ideas. Children in the early childhood years are not able to understand that a reproduction represents a work of art and is not in fact the work of art itself. Thus a component of appropriate curriculum must be a discussion of what a reproduction is. Additionally, whenever possible real examples of painting, sculpture, and other media should be provided. Showing children a "real" art work and a reproduction would be the ideal approach. This would not have to be a masterwork, but an artist's work and a photograph of it would aid children in understanding that they are not discussing "the real thing" when looking at a reproduction.

Prints and reproductions in books should also take care to explain to children the size, the dimensions, and the media of images produced. Most reproduced images are shown in similar size. This leads children to assume incorrectly that art works are all the same size. Also, all reproductions are flat photographic images. This does not allow the children to understand the difference between a two-dimensional and three-dimensional work. Nor does it provide information on the differences between a tapestry, a drawing, a painting, or the like. Teachers, commercial programs, books, and other resources therefore need to provide this type of information so that children gain an understanding of the true materials and dimensions of art works.

Art works should be an important part of all young children's education experience. However, their use must (a) be based on developmental and perceptual issues affecting the children's ability to interact with art works; (b) include consideration of the fact that children learn in a holistic, integrated manner; and (c) allow for informal interaction and involvement with the works. When art works are approached in this manner they become a natural part of the children's world. By providing opportunities for informal, self-initiated interaction with the works and by allowing children to learn through doing, adults can lead children to increase their natural love of pictures and watch art works become as familiar to the children as Snoopy and the Ninja Turtles. If young children grow up with art as a part of the world and if they can approach works from their own level of understanding and extend their artistic understanding through play, sensorial responses such as Adam's "A bunch of naked ladies and a tiger" may develop into deeper insights and a greater appreciation of art works.

Arnheim, R. (1954). *Art and visual perception*. Berkeley: University of California Press.

Arnold, M. (1987). *Responding patterns of naive children and adults to artistic styles in painting*. Unpublished doctoral dissertation, University of Illinois at Urbana-Champaign.

Art Image. (1992). *Imagine and me*. Champlain, NY: Art Image Publications, Inc.

Bailey, H.T. (1910). Editorial notes. *School Arts Book, 10*(1), 17-19.

Baker, D.W. (1989). [Preferred images: 3-8 year old children's preferences for art reproduction]. Unpublished raw data.

Barnes, E. (1908). Child study in relation to elementary art education. In James Haney (Ed.), *Art education in the public schools of the United States* (pp. 101-132). New York: American Art Annual.

Barone, T. (1987). On equality, visibility, and the arts. *Curriculum Inquiry, 17*(3), 421-426.

Berliner, A. (1918). Aesthetic judgement of children. *Journal of Applied Psychology, 2*, 229-242.

Braine, L. (1972). A developmental analysis of the effects of stimulus orientation on recognition. *American Journal of Psychology, 85*, 157-188.

Brighouse, G. (1939). A study of aesthetic appreciation. *Psychological Monographs, 51*(5), 1-22.

Burkett, M. (1977). *Concepts of art as verbally expressed by children aged 5 through 15 years*. Unpublished doctoral dissertation, The Pennsylvania State University, University Park.

Burkett, M. (1986). Developmental stages of children's concepts of art and educational implications. In E. Kern (Ed.), *Collected papers: Pennsylvania's symposium on art education, aesthetics, and criticism*. Harrisburg: Pennsylvania Department of Education.

Carothers, T., & Gardner, H. (1979). When children's drawings become art: The emergence of aesthetic production and perception. *Developmental Psychology, 15*(5), 570-580.

Child, I. (1970). Aesthetic judgements in children. *Transaction, 7*, 45-51.

Child, I. Hanson, J., & Hornbeck, F. (1968). Age and sex differences in children's color preferences. *Child Development, 39*(1), 237-247.

Clark, G.A. (1973). Analyzing iconic learning in the visual arts. *Studies in Art Education, 14*, 37-47.

Coffey, A., (1968). *A developmental study of aesthetic preferences for realistic and non-objective paintings*. Unpublished doctoral dissertation, University of Massachusetts, Boston.

Colbert, C., & Taunton, M. (1988). *Discover art: Kindergarten*. Worcester, MA: Davis Publications, Inc.

Colby, E. (1907). The aims of art education in the public schools. *National Education Association Journal of Proceedings and Addresses of the Forty-sixth Annual Meeting* (pp. 822-825). New York: National Education Association.

Cole, E. (1985). *The effect of a cognitively oriented aesthetic curriculum on the aesthetic judgement and responses of 4, 6, and 8 year olds enrolled in an art museum program*. Unpublished doctoral dissertation, University of Toledo.

Curtis, M. (1988). Understanding the black aesthetic experience. *Music Educators Journal, 75*(20), 23-26.

Feeney, S., & Moravcik, E. (1987). A thing of beauty: Aesthetic development in young children. *Young Children, 42*(6), 7-15.

Feinstein, H. (1984). The metaphoric interpretation of paintings: Effects of the clustering strategy and relaxed attention exercises. *Studies in Art Education, 25*(2), 77-83.

Frechtling, J. & Davidson, P. (1970). The development of the concept of artistic style: Classification study. *Psychomonic Science, 18*, 77-81.

Gardner, H. (1970). Children's sensitivity to painting styles. *Child Development, 41*(2), 813-821.

Gardner, H. (1972). The development of sensitivity to figural and stylistic aspects of painting. *British Journal of Psychology, 63*, 605-615.

Gardner, H. (1973). The contribution of color and texture to the detection of painting styles. *Studies in Art Education, 15*(2), 57-62.

Gardner, H. (1974). Developmental trends in sensitivity to form and subject matter in paintings. *Studies in Art Education, 14*(2), 52-56.

Gardner, H. & Gardner, J. (1970). Developmental trends to sensitivity to painting style and subject matter. *Studies in Art Education, 12*(1), 11-16.

Gardner, H. (1978). Critical judgement: A developmental study. *Journal of Aesthetic Education, 9*(2), 60-77.

Gardner, H., Winner, E., & Kircher, M. (1975). Children's conceptions of art. *Journal of Aesthetic Education, 9*(3), 60-77.

Hall, G. (1893). *The contents of children's minds on entering school*. Boston: Ginn & Company.

Hall, G. (1901). The ideal school based on child study. *National Education Association Journal of Proceedings and Addresses of the Fortieth Annual Meeting*. (pp. 475-488) New York: National Education Association.

Hall, G. (1907). *Aspects of child life and education*. Boston: The Athenaum Press.

Hardiman, G. & Zernich, T. (1977). Influence of style and subject matter on the development of children's art preferences. *Studies in Art Education, 19*(2), 29-35.

Hardiman, G. & Zernich, T. (1980). Some considerations of Piaget's cognitive-structuralist theory and children's artistic development. *Studies in Art Education, 21*(3), 10-18.

Hardiman, G. & Zernich, T. (1982). The relative influence of parts and wholes in shaping preference responses to painting. *Studies in Art Education, 23*(3), 31-38.

Hardiman, G. & Zernich, T. (1985). Discrimination of styles in painting: A developmental study. *Studies in Art Education, 26*(3), 157-162.

Herberholz, B. & Hanson, L. (1990). *Early childhood art* (4th ed.). Dubuque, IA: Wm. C. Brown Publishers.

Herberholz, D. & Herberholz, B. (1990). *Artworks for elementary teachers: Developing artistic and perceptual awareness*. Dubuque, IA: Wm. C. Brown Publishers.

Housen, A. (1983). *The eye of the beholder: Measuring aesthetic development*. Unpublished doctoral dissertation, Harvard Graduate School of Education, Boston.

Housen, A., Miller, N., & Yenawine, P. (1991). *MoMA research and evaluation study: Preliminary report*. New York: Museum of Modern Art.

Jahoda, G. & McGurk, H. (1974). Pictorial depth perception: A developmental study. *British Journal of Psychology, 65*, 141-149.

Katz, E. (1944). *Children's preferences for traditional and modern paintings*. New York: Teachers College Press.

Kerlavage, M. (1992a). *Artworks and young children: An historical analysis of the paradigm governing the use of art appreciation in early childhood*. Unpublished doctoral dissertation, University of Wisconsin/Milwaukee.

Kerlavage, M. (1992b). [Living with works of art: Image responses of pre-school children after continuous exposure to artworks]. Unpublished raw data.

Lark-Horovitz, B. (1937). On art appreciation of children. I: Preferences for picture subjects in general. *Journal of Educational Research, 31*, 118-137.

Lark-Horovitz, B. (1938). On art appreciation of children. II: *Journal of Educational Research, 31*, 572-598.

Lucio, W. & Mead, C. (1939). An investigation of children's preferences for modern pictures. *Elementary School Journal 39*(5), 678-689.

Machotka, P. (1966). Aesthetic criteria in childhood: Justifications of preference. *Child Development, 37*(8), 877-885.

Mackworth, N. & Bruner, J. (1970). How adults and children search and recognize pictures. *Human Development, 13,* 149-177.

Marschalek, D. (1983). The influence of viewing time upon the recognition of color and subject matter placement in paintings for elementary and high school students. *Studies in Art Education, 25*(1), 58-65.

Marschalek, D. (1986a). What eye movement research tells us about perceptual behavior of children and adults: Implications for the visual arts. *Studies in Art Education, 27*(3), 123-130.

Marschalek, D. (1986b). Attention to contour and interior pattern of shapes in color drawings. *Studies in Art Education, 28*(1), 30-36.

Mendenhall, J. & Mendenhall, M. (1933). *The influence of familiarity upon children's preferences for pictures and poems.* New York: Columbia University Press.

Milwaukee Public Schools. (1991). *Milwaukee public schools K-12 art curriculum.* Milwaukee, WI: Milwaukee Public Schools.

Moore, B. (1973). A description of children's verbal responses to works of art in selected grades one through twelve. *Studies in Art Education, 14*(3), 27-34.

Morris, J. (1991, October). Reading works of art. *Teaching Pre K-8,* pp. 64-66.

Morrison, J. (1935). *Children's preferences for pictures commonly used in art appreciation classes.* Chicago, IL: The University of Chicago Press.

Parsons, M. (1987). *How we understand art: A cognitive developmental account of aesthetic experience.* New York: Cambridge University Press.

Parsons, M., Johnston, M., & Durham, R. (1978). Developmental stages in children's aesthetic responses. *Journal of Aesthetic Education, 12*(1), 84-104.

Piaget, J. (1951). *Play, dreams, and imitation in childhood.* (C. Gaitegno and F.N. Hodgeson, Trans.). New York: Basic Books.

Piaget, J. (1952). *The origins of intelligence in children* (M. Cook, Trans.). New York: International Universities Press.

Piaget, J. & Inhelder, B. (1969). *The psychology of the child* (H. Weaver, Trans.). New York: Basic Books, Inc.

Pintner, R. (1918). Aesthetic appreciation of pictures by children. *Pedagogical Seminar and Journal of Genetic Psychology, 25,* 216-218.

Rosario, J. & Collazo, E. (1981). Aesthetic codes in context: An exploration in two preschool classrooms. *Journal of Aesthetic Education, 15*(1), 71-82.

Rosensteil, A., Morison, P., Silverman, J., & Gardner, H. (1978). Critical judgments: A developmental study. *Journal of Aesthetic Education, 12*(2), 95-107.

Russell, R. (1988). Children's philosophical inquiry into defining art: A quasi-experimental study of aesthetics in the elementary classroom. *Studies in Art Education, 29*(3), 282-291.

Sharp, P. (1976). Aesthetic responses in early education. *Art Education, 29*(5), 25-29.

Silverman, J., Winner, E., & Gardner, H. (1976). On going beyond the literal: The development of sensitivity to artistic symbols. *Perception, 4,* 373-384.

Smith, N. (1982). The visual arts in early childhood education: Development and the creation of meaning. In B. Spodek (Ed.), *Handbook of research in early childhood education* (pp. 295-317) New York: The Free Press.

Spitz, H. & Borland, M. (1971). Redundancy in line drawings of familiar objects: Effects of age and intelligence. *Cognitive Psychology, 2,* 196-205.

Steinberg, D. & DeLoache, J. (1986). Preschool children's sensitivity to artistic style in paintings. *Visual Arts Research, 12*(2), 1-10.

Taunton, M. (1980). The influence of age on preference for subject matter, realism, and spatial depth in painting. *Studies in Art Education, 21*(3), 40-53.

Taunton, M. (1982). Aesthetic responses of young children to the visual arts: A review of the literature. *Journal of Aesthetic Education, 16*(3), 93-109.

Taunton, M. (1983). Questioning strategies to encourage young children to talk about art. *Art Education, 36*(4), 40-43.

Taunton, M. (1984). Four-year old children's recognition of expressive qualities in painting reproductions. *Journal of Research and Development in Education, 17*(4), 36-42.

Thorndike, E. (1916). Tests of aesthetic appreciation. *Journal of Educational Psychology, 7,* 509-523.

Thorndike, E. (1917). Individual differences in judgment of the beauty of simple forms. *Psychological Review, 24,* 147-153.

Turner, P. (1983). Children's responses to art: Interpretation and criticism. *Journal of Art and Design Education, 2,* 36-42.

Turner, R.M. (1990). Gender-related considerations for developing the text of art instructional materials. *Studies in Art Education, 32*(1), 56-64.

Van der Mark, P. (1929). *An experimental study of what types of pictures children are most interested and why.* Unpublished master's thesis, Teachers College, Columbia University, New York.

Williams, F. (1924). An investigation of children's preferences for pictures. *Elementary School Journal, 25*(2), 119-126.

Yonas, A. & Hagan, S. (1973). Effects of static and kinetic depth information on the perception of size in children and adults. *Journal of Experimental Child Psychology, 15,* 254-265.

Chapter 13
Art Historical Understanding in Early Childhood

Mary Erickson
Arizona State University

This chapter examines traditional wisdom on the developmental appropriateness of art history instruction in early childhood, then presents some challenges to that tradition. Following that is a report on a pilot study of second graders' art historical understanding with conclusions and implications for further study.

Traditional Wisdom

An analysis of recent curriculum development efforts and instructional resource publications in art education reveals increased attention to art history throughout the grade levels. According to a 1990 *School Arts* survey by Laura Chapman and Connie Newton, teaching art history has become more common since 1979; art history is now reported to be the second most frequently taught art discipline after art production (Chapman & Newton, 1990). When art content is distributed throughout grade levels, however, art history content is usually delayed at least until after the primary grades (Chapman, 1985; Hubbard, 1987). Gilbert Clark, Michael Day, and Dwaine Greer (1987) recommend that primary students be engaged in "relatively simple art criticism experiences" while "knowledge of cultural-historical contexts" can be introduced in the intermediate grades (p. 171). Eugene Kleinbauer (1987) claims that "in secondary school, students can acquire the rudiments of art history" (p. 210). He reserves art historical methods for 10th and 11th grade, and argues against comprehensive art history surveys in high school, reserving such surveys for college (pp. 210-211). Somewhere between Clark, Day, and Greer's recommendation to introduce art history in the intermediate grades and Kleinbauer's proposals for high school and college can be found the recommendations of Ralph Smith. In his four-phase aesthetic learning curriculum, Smith (1989) advocates the introduction of art history content in the junior high grades (pp. 137-140).

As the preceding paragraph indicates, some art educators seem to assume that art history is developmentally inappropriate for early childhood. Many social studies educators have reached a similar conclusion. In social studies, recommendations for delayed introduction of history often rely on studies of historical learning conducted by Roy Hallam in the 1960s. In his studies Hallam concluded that historical understanding does not keep pace with Piaget's stages. According to his findings, in history, young people's concrete operations stage starts from 12:4 to 13:2 years, and formal operations do not begin until 16:8 to 18:2 years (1972, p. 342). Hallam (1971) reported that "if the pupils do not have the ability to reason near the concrete or formal levels then they will either ignore or reject the material" (p. 172). Martin Sleeper (1975) cites evidence that children do not grasp chronological dates until about the age of eleven and do not "understand interpretation and hypothesis in history" until adolescence (p. 97).

Although the development of art historical understanding has not been the subject of direct investigation by art educators, some developmental studies in art education can be seen as related to the issue of teaching art history in early childhood. The work of Michael Parsons (1987), for example, has contributed to art educators' beliefs about developmentally appropriate art activities. In interviews with scores of young people, Parsons found that aesthetic responses clustered into five stages. Although Parsons does not intend to tie his five stages to particular ages he does propose that the five stages occur in sequence. Parsons does not identify historical context as significant in young people's response to art until stage four (1987, p. 110). Such findings tend to support the traditional assumption that art history instruction is developmentally inappropriate for early childhood.

Howard Gardner's (1990) early studies suggest that style recognition, though not a "natural tendency," is possible in early childhood (p. 14). When Modernist ideas prevailed in art education, some art educators considered the ability to recognize historical styles to be the essential art historical skill. When historical-cultural context is seen as incidental and formal-expressive qualities are seen as central, then projects emulating historical styles (Sharer, 1990) can be seen as significant art historical learning appropriate for all ages including early childhood. As we move into a Post-Modern world, style emulation may diminish as the predominant art history activity at all levels of art education. Instruction may focus more on higher level art historical processes such as historical narrative and cultural interpretation.

Challenges to Traditional Wisdom

In spite of the tradition of delaying art history instruction until after the early childhood years, a number of art teachers across the nation have introduced art history content in the primary grades.

Theoretical analysis and empirical studies on teaching history have been reported and may provide some guidance to thinking about teaching art history in early childhood. John Poster (1973) advocates a more careful look at the different senses of "time" which may be required for historical understanding (p. 588). For example, children's personal sense of time may differ from the sense they understand in stories or the type of calibrated time measured by a clock. Lorraine Harner's (1981) study provides evidence that children from 3 to 7 years old can use past and future tenses appropriately (p. 503). Robert Craig's (1981) research suggests that children between the ages of four and eight "hold quite specific concepts of time" (p. 37). He found that they can order actions in sequence and relate sequences in a temporal fashion.

Several scholars have considered the development of historical understanding from a cognitive point of view. Martin Hoffman (1976) has looked at the development of role-taking abilities, abilities which presumably are necessary for historical understanding. He challenges Piagetian studies as having assessed advanced cognitive or verbal operations rather than role-taking abilities (p. 129). Kerry Kennedy (1983) challenges the Piaget-Hallam model as flawed for undervaluing or omitting the influence of information-processing capacity on historical understanding (p. 1-22). Jerry Moore, James Alouf, and Janie Needham (1984) propose four levels of historical reasoning skills which take into account more than oral and written language. These levels represent thought, first through sensori-motor actions, then through symbols and images, then through signs and words, and finally through logical

thought (p. 56). If Moore, Alouf, and Needham's levels are correct, then the physicality of art works as well has their imagic nature seem to support an argument that art historical understanding might be developmentally more appropriate for early childhood than traditional history which is centered on events rather than objects or images.

Perhaps the researcher whose work has most potential insight for guiding the study of art historical understanding is Linda Levstik. She argues that:

- Conclusions about development may not apply similarly across domains (1988).

- Narrative may play a significant role in children's historical understanding (Levstik, 1981; Levstik & Pappas, 1987, p. 14).

- "If...early learning does not occur, the optimal teaching time for some concepts [such as attitudes toward different racial and ethnic groups] may pass" (1988, p. 10).

Levstik argues that "there is reason to think that missing these crucial opportunities to build interest, to develop social perspectives and civic understanding, to introduce concepts from history and the social sciences, may make it more difficult for citizens of the 21st century to cope with their future" (1988, p. 16).

A Pilot Study

This writer recently conducted a pilot study of children's art historical understanding in a large suburban school district in the American Southwest. For the purposes of this study, art historical understanding is defined as the ability to interpret art works in their own historical-cultural contexts. Two classes each of second-, fourth-, and sixth-grade students were subjects in the study. This chapter reports only on the data collected on the 60-second-grade students. On two occasions, 2 weeks apart, this writer led three 45-minute discussions with one second-grade class and 2 45-minute discussions with the other. In each class, reproductions of three art works (a prehistoric cave painting, an Egyptian tomb painting, and a portion of Michelangelo's Sistine ceiling) were distributed to each child. The age of each work was explained to the children in terms which they might understand. For example, dates and well-known historical events can be used with older students, while grandparents' ages are more easily understood by younger children. Then children were asked three questions about each work:

1. How life was different then from now.

2. How life back then made a difference in the way the painting looked.

3. What question they could ask to help them better understand the painting.

Questions were paraphrased and restated to focus the discussion. Student and teacher comments were recorded and transcribed for analysis. (Concurrent pilot testing of two short instructional videos is not reported here.)

Several weeks later one of the classes was shown 100-year-old works made by three different Native American tribes from three different geographic areas: a Navajo cliff painting, an Ojibway beaded bag, and a Tlingit carved board. The earlier discussion of prehistoric, Egyptian, and Renaissance paintings was reviewed. Children were oriented to how long ago 100 years is and to major geographic differences of the three Native American tribal homelands. A discussion of the same series of three questions followed. Transcripts of the second-grade students' responses have been analyzed and compared with Parsons' stages of aesthetic experience.

Children's responses exhibited little of Parsons' stage-one understanding. Children did not focus on favorites or on colors. A few remarks might be characterized as what Parsons' (1987) calls "freewheeling associative responses to subject matter" (p. 22). One student compared stylized bear paws on the Tlingit carving with wheels on a car. Another student likened the Egyptian tomb painting to the interior of a restaurant. A number of students spoke of Egyptian buried treasure or secret doors. Another student compared fringes on the Ojibway beaded bag with today's popular woven bracelets.

Parsons identified attention to subject matter as characteristic of stage two. A number of second graders in this study focused their attention on making sense of subject matter. Students commented on the depiction of fighting in the Navajo painting and noted battle details such as the use of horses and spears instead of tanks, helicopters, and guns. The Egyptian tomb painting was described as a depiction of family members or stories from the life of the king. Students asked questions aimed at identifying subject matter references in the Egyptian and Navajo paintings. About the Michelangelo painting students asked who the figure is reaching to; why one man has clothes while the smaller people are naked; why they are floating; and what that "shell" is behind them. Parsons found stage-two understanding focusing on beauty and realism as well as on technical skill and difficulty. In this study children did not comment on beauty or realism but seemed quite interested in difficulty and skill. They asked about how Michelangelo painted on the ceiling. They proposed materials cave painters might have used ("Did they burn a stick and then write with it?"). One student

speculated that the Navajo painter might have hung from a rope to paint on the side of the cliff.

Parsons describes stage-three understanding of subject matter as more general. According to Parsons instead of being a transparent "window" through which one can see the world, a painting can represent an idea or have a theme. Some children's responses in this study described subject matter as more than direct depiction. One student suggested "Maybe they painted it so they could remember their king." Another proposed that the Ojibway beaded bag showed flowers and plants because, in contrast with the Navajos, the Ojibway live where there are lots of trees and flowers. Another student explained the cave painting by speculating that maybe "the animal got killed and they painted it because they were sorry." Another student proposed, "They probably wanted to be strong as that animal." One student suggested that the cave painter may have been poor and wanted to make money by painting. Without adult prompting, a classmate brought this speculation back to its appropriate historical context by asking whether people back then had money.

Parsons (1987) describes persons exhibiting stage-three response as being more open minded and willing to search for meaning beyond the obvious (p. 99). Comments like the ones noted above suggest that some second graders in this study were "willing to keep looking" and hypothesizing. Parsons' examples illustrate searching for expressive meaning through extended looking at the work. Second graders in this study were asked to search for meaning by considering the times and cultures within which the works were produced.

It is not until stage four, according to Parsons, that historical-cultural context plays a role in understanding art. At this stage persons become aware of a community of viewers. Although some second graders seem to understand that artists of other times and places might have purposes different from their own, no second graders in this study spoke explicitly about social purposes for art. It may be interesting to note that a number of fourth graders did. They explained paintings by referring to education of the young, celebration, group pride, ceremonies, and religion.

No second graders' response in this study exhibited any of the self-awareness or autonomy with which Parsons characterizes stage-five understanding.

Conclusions and Implications

An analysis of second graders' art historical understanding reveals responses dominantly from Parsons' stages two and three. In addition, a few students made stage one responses, exhibiting historically inappropriate free associations. A number of students exhibited some understanding of cultural-historical influences on art works, awareness which Parsons reserves for his stage four.

It must be noted that Parsons' subjects were asked about their preferences and judgments of paintings, nor about their cultural-historical understandings. Children in this pilot study seem to have exhibited more advanced understanding than subjects cited in Parsons' study. Two approaches might be used to attempt to explain this apparent developmental discrepancy. First, one might reexamine Parsons' stage theory from a Post-Modern perspective. His stages tend to describe more advanced aesthetic understanding as more Modernist understanding, that is, understanding focused less on subject matter and more on form and expression. If aesthetic understanding were redefined to include more focus on cultural-historical purpose and meaning, different questions might be asked of children that might lead to modifications of Parsons' stages. Second, one might investigate whether focus on subjective response to art works masks a more developed capacity for art historical understanding. If the questions adults pose to children focused on historical-cultural understanding rather than on subjective response, we might discover a faster pace of developmental understanding.

A number of important variables could be studied more carefully in an attempt to describe art historical understanding in early childhood. Some of those variables are the significance of teacher questions (Farrar, 1986; Stokrocki, 1991); the role of narrative, myth, and romance (Levstik, 1981; Levstik & Pappas, 1987); the role of increased background knowledge (Levstik & Downey, 1988); and the influences of cultural diversity on art historical understanding (Young, 1991). Extended planning of carefully prepared questions, art historical narratives, or presentations of background knowledge must be achieved before research on such variables can be undertaken. Developmental studies can tell us more than what children do now; more sophisticated developmental studies can tell us what children can do when offered appropriate educational intervention (Feldman, 1987). Sophisticated studies require the cooperation of teachers and curriculum developers as well as researchers.

More research is necessary to guide attempts to plan developmentally appropriate art history instruction for early childhood. This pilot study, as well as recent theory and research in children's historical understanding, suggests that educators may have underestimated primary school children's capacities for art historical understanding.

References

Chapman, L. H. (1985). *Discover art*. Worchester, MA: Davis Publications.

Chapman, L. H., & Newton, C. (1990). Teacher viewpoint survey. *School Arts, 90*(1), 41-45.

Clark, G. A., Day, M. D. & Greer, W. D. (1987). Discipline-based art education: Becoming students of art. *Journal of Aesthetic Education, 21*(2), 130-193.

Craig, R. P. (1981). The child's construction of space and time. *Science and Children, 19*(3), 36-37.

Farrar, M. T. (1986). Teacher questions: The complexity of the cognitively simple. *Instructional Science, 15*, 89-107.

Feldman, D. (1987). Developmental psychology and art education: Two fields at the crossroads. *Journal of Aesthetic Education, 21*(2), 243-258.

Gardner, H. (1990). *Art education and human development*. Los Angeles: The J. Paul Getty Trust.

Hallam, R. N. (1971). Piaget and thinking in history. In M. Ballard (Ed.), *New movements in the study and teaching of history* (pp. 162-178). Bloomington: Indiana University Press.

Hallam, R. N. (1972). Thinking and learning in history. *Teaching History, 2*, 337-346.

Harner, L. (1981). Children talk about the time and aspect of actions. *Child Development, 52*, 498-506.

Hoffman, M. L. (1976). Empathy, role taking, guilt, and development of altruistic motives. In T. Lickona (Ed.), *Moral development and behavior: Theory, research, and social issues* (pp. 124-143). New York: Holt, Rinehart and Winston.

Hubbard, G. (1987). *Art in action*. San Diego: Coronado Publishers.

Kennedy, K. J. (1983). Assessing the relationship between information processing capacity and historical understanding. *Theory and Research in Social Education, 11*(2), 1-22.

Kleinbauer, W. E. (1987). Art history in discipline-based art education. *Journal of Aesthetic Education, 21*(2), 205-215.

Levstik, L. S. (1981). Historical narrative and the young learner. *Theory into Practice , 28*(1), 114-119.

Levstik, L. S. & Pappas, C. C. (1987). Exploring the development of historical understanding. *Journal of Research and Development in Education, 21*(1), 1-15.

Levstik, L. S. (1988, March). *Conceptual development in social studies*. Paper presented at the Association of American Publishers Conference, Palm Beach, FL.

Levstik, L. S. & Downey, M. T. (1988). Teaching and learning history: the research base. *Social Education, 52*(5), 336-342.

Moore, J. R., Alouf, J. L., & Needham, J. (1984). Cognitive development and historical reasoning in social studies curriculum. *Theory and Research in Social Education, 12*(2), 49-64.

Parsons, M. J. (1987). *How we understand art: A cognitive developmental account of aesthetic experience*. Cambridge, England: Cambridge University Press.

Poster, J. B. (1973). The birth of the past: Children's perception of historical time. *History Teacher, 6*, 587-598.

Sharer, J. W. (1990, April). *Integrating art history into the art curriculum*. Panel presentation with M. Erickson, D. Ebitz, G. Geahigan, E. Katter, & M. Stewart at the Annual Convention of the National Art Education Association, Kansas City, MO.

Sleeper, M. E. (1975). A developmental framework for history education in adolescence. *School Review, 84*, 91-107.

Smith, R. A. (1989). *The sense of art: A study in aesthetic education*. New York: Routledge.

Stokrocki, M. (1991, March). *Instructional resources: Springboards for collaborative curriculum development and research*. Panel presentation with M. Erickson, J. Sharer, E. Shipp, & B. Young, at the Annual Convention of the National Art Education Association, Atlanta, GA.

Young, B. (1991, March). *Instructional resources: Springboards for collaborative curriculum development and research*. Panel presentation with M. Erickson, J. Sharer, E. Shipp, & M. Stokrocki, at the Annual Convention of the National Art Education Association, Atlanta, GA.

Chapter 14
Understanding Young Children's Ways of Interpreting Their Experiences Through Participant Observation

Mary Stokrocki
Arizona State University

"Planets, shooting stars," "Moons and mountains," "A village," "Circles, triangles, swirls in the sky," "He painted how he felt," "It's Halloween," "Yeh, and he's in jail." (See Figure 1.)

These comments were made by six-year-olds in response to Van Gogh's painting, *The Starry Night*. They describe subject matter and art elements fluently. They also show evidence of the children's ability to understand artistic style and to interpret artistic meanings. Many things can be discovered about young children and their art abilities through participant observation of their ordinary experiences and interactions in the classroom. This chapter describes, analyzes, and interprets the performance of a class of six-year-olds as they interpret Van Gogh's painting *The Starry Night* visually and verbally. The emphasis of this study is on the children's experience—their interaction with Van Gogh's artwork, with their teacher, with each other, and with their own painting imitations. As these experiences are presented, the visual and verbal interpretive abilities of young children are disclosed.

Through participant observation inquiry, teachers can analyze young children's artistic behavior, interactions, and interpretations in the classroom. Parsons (1976) describes young children's aesthetic level of appreciation as "aesthetic confusion"—they respond to

artworks based on their own interests and experiences. Parsons mainly concentrates on the children's verbal responses to selected artworks in a clinical situation. This study reinforces Parson's claim that young children respond to familiar subject matter, art elements, and feelings, but suggests that they rely on other forms of verbal and visual interpretation as well:

- Conventional and expressive forms.

- Repetition and patterning of skills.
- Some early representational frustration.
- Outlining and painting from the bottom-up.
- Identification of style and contrasting moods.

The sharing of social meaning, "reading-off," and romancing—that is, the

Figure 1.

development of metaphors and the interpretive realm of thinking—are also apparent. Such classroom-based research describes what actually happens in classrooms when teachers attend to unusual child behavior and hidden and taken-for-granted behavior.

What is Interpretation?

Interpretation is the process of social understanding, which is present from the beginning but expanded with new knowledge. Heidegger (1962) maintains that pre-understanding is a necessary pre-condition to

68 knowing or understanding. Even though Heidegger had little to say about young children, others have applied his ideas on interpretation to the study of young children. Young children base their interpretations on their own experiences. Bleicher (1980) suggests that "understanding is the recognition and reconstruction of meaning through language" (p. 57). Vandenburg (1971) suggests that when young children learn the norms of language they also become aware of the conditions for interpreting them, since language is functionally flexible.

What is Participant Observation?

Participant observation is the intense documentation, analysis, and interpretation of an everyday setting (Pohland, 1972). Classroom art teachers as researchers can employ participant observation to understand their own young students better by collecting data, analyzing it, and comparing it with other studies.

1. Data Collection. Start with an audio or video recorder and document yourself teaching a class to collect responses for future use. When the children speak so softly that the tape cannot pick up their voices, repeat what they say loudly or take notes to form a diary. 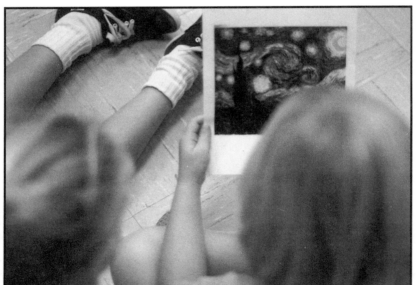 Photograph children working and their final art works as supplementary analytical documents. Invite another teacher, college student, even a parent to assist in documentation.

2. Content Analysis. Photocopy your notes or transcripts and analyze them by color-coding the notes in the margins of your paper. Use borrowed concepts initially, as I borrowed from Parsons' (1976) ideas on aesthetics. In my initial analysis, I looked for students' verbal responses (VR) to The Starry Night; their art-making abilities(AM); their visual imitations (VI) of Van Gogh's *The Starry Night*; and

their verbal responses to child art (VRCA) —their own art work.

3. Comparative Analysis. Interrelate your findings about child behaviors with results from other early child researchers to form insights or conclusions. Conclusions are good guesses initially that your young students show evidence of certain abilities. If you repeat a lesson at least 3 times on different occasions and compare the results, then you can support or refute your initial findings.

An unexpected finding may emerge that has no scientific label and it can then be labelled temporarily. For example, I discovered two young Asian children imitating Van Gogh's artwork by starting their own painting from the bottom up. I called this interpretive behavior "bottom-up" painting. I later supported this finding by looking at literature on Asian teaching methods and found nothing. I stumbled across a filmstrip which informed me that Asian people start to read scroll paintings at the bottom and continue upward. This behavior may be true of the painting behaviors of young

Figure 2.

Asian children as well, so my new conjecture is now partially supported.

The aim of this research is to find aspects of education that may be overlooked, hidden, or persistent. This research generates ideas about education, but does not generalize them to all cases. The findings may be true for this particular case, but not for others. Several related participant research case studies build or strengthen findings.

Context and Participants

This 1-hour class of six-year-olds, taught by a student teacher, was part of a 10-week, fall Children's Saturday Art Program at Arizona State University. The racially mixed 12-member class consisted of seven girls and five boys.

69

Figures 3 & 4.

Verbal Responses to Van Gogh's *The Starry Night*

The student teacher was inspired by a lesson suggested by Chapman (1989). At the beginning of class, the teacher assembled students on the floor in a circle. Van Gogh's painting, *The Starry Night*, was color photocopied for each child to discuss (see Figure 2). The teacher directed students to tell her what was happening in the picture—to describe what they saw. Children reacted to the subject matter—moons and planets and shooting stars— with which they were familiar. "The first level of appreciation is descriptive in which children take an inventory of what they've seen: noting objects, colors, etc., as relates to their prior experience" (Parsons, 1987, p. 482). Children identified art elements—"circles, triangles, swirls in the sky"— and reacted to the artist's feeling. The interpretation, "It's Halloween," was inspired by the forthcoming holiday.

Visual Imitations

Conventional and expressive forms:

Following the introduction, the teacher invited the class to paint their own "starry nights" and provided the students with white chalk and their choice of colored paper to plan their ideas. She demonstrated and directed, "Start drawing the sky and planets and

I'll show you how to draw the village later." Students were excited and one little boy exclaimed, "Looks like a big face. I can make swirls like Van Gogh."

Two boys enthusiastically talked while drawing. One child lined up his planets in a row and counted 10 of them. Then he added snowflake-shaped stars and showed his neighbor how to make stars by criss-crossing. Figure 3 shows student influence and copying of such conventional forms. Figure 4 also shows the five-pointed star schema.

Repetition and patterning of skill:

The teacher then distributed tempera paints, primary colors plus white in muffin tins, and asked students to mix new colors to paint their starry night drawings. She demonstrated how to mix green, "Add little daubs of blue and yellow." White was then added to make the mixture lighter.

One little boy began painting by outlining his large house and spent a great deal of time filling in the sky with vertical strokes. He seemed intrigued with the repetitious task of pushing the luscious paint. Repetition is a fundamental aesthetic response (Zurmuehlen, 1983). The teacher asked him if he wanted to add swirls in his sky. The child responded that he didn't know how. While he was painting, she grabbed his brush and guided his stroke to make a swirl pattern (See Figure 5). Later, she encouraged him to make more swirls by himself. Such repetitive patterning of action is common in teaching beginners new physical skills (Stokrocki, 1986), though seldom mentioned in art education literature.

Unusual Child Art-Making Results

Early representational frustration:

One little girl looked at Van Gogh's work (to her right), continued painting, and interpreted, "This is a mountain [really a cypress tree], this is the wind [she begins to swirl her paint], and these are the houses [unpainted in the foreground]." (This magnificent beginning attempt is shown in Figure 4.) Later, I noticed that she had stopped painting, despite the teacher's encouragement to continue or to try another. She explained her disappointment, "I didn't get it right." Such frustration over realistic portrayal at a young age is unusual. Three possible findings can be interpreted from this experience:

- The lesson and semi-realistic masterpiece might be too advanced for the child.

- The child needs more demonstration or guidance on how to proceed painting step-by-step.

- The child needs another masterpiece as a guide.

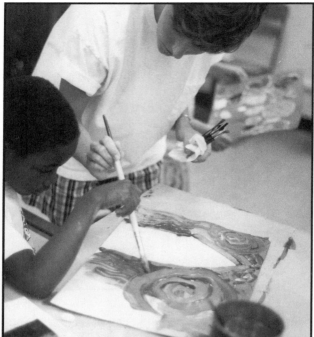

Figure 5, Figure 6, and Figure 7.

Painting from the bottom up:

Besides outlining forms, some young children seem to build their painting from the bottom up. Two Asian children seemed to proceed in this manner. One girl started by brushing in the water at the bottom of the page with horizontal strokes. She next overlapped the top edge of the water with vertical strokes in a row, which she called grass. Mountains were added in the middle of the page with horizontal and vertical strokes, paint was scrubbed into the paper for sky in different directions, and two criss-crossed stars were added. Later, she went back and painted a darker color in the sky. Also notice the unusual way she holds her brush in Figure 7. Scroll paintings in Asian cultures are read traditionally by starting at the bottom and then moving upward.

Verbal Responses to Their Own Paintings

Identification of style:

When the children seemed finished with their paintings, the teacher pinned them to the wall and asked students to sit together again and share their results. In the first example, a shy little girl pointed out the

tree and sun in her painting. A boy pointed out the "swirly lines" used by the girl as "sign language." The teacher then pointed out the swirling lines and asked what the swirling signs meant (see Figure 8). The little boy cried, "A sunburst!"

Next, the same boy named the individual elements of subject matter, painted in a row, in his painting (see Figure 9). He also pointed out a face he had painted and called "the man in the moon." When the teacher asked why he painted so many moons and stars, another student interpreted, "You mean falling stars."

Identification of color mood:

The teacher then asked what new colors were mixed in the painting. A third student answered, "light green made with yellow and blue and white." The instructor then praised the student and asked how the colors made him feel—

cool or warm. He answered that the suns made him hot and the sky made him cold. The directive question enabled the young child to note the color mood or contrasts in Van Gogh's work and in his own.

"Reading-off" and romancing:

Finally, a little girl explained the story which she had written on her painting, "One day, I had to stop the stars from coming out" (see Figure 10.) Two huge swirling masses were separated by a lighter curved one in the middle of her painting. Then the teacher asked her what she meant or why she had to stop the stars. The child answered, "So they don't run into each other." Some young children prefer to complete their visual interpreta-

tions with verbal or oral ones. In this case, the child perceives the meaning in her work through a process called "reading off." Golomb (1974) explains this as a phase in which no intentional image is formed, but an unexpected outcome determines the meaning of the finished piece. These cryptic interpretations can also occur as children tell stories when pressed by an adult to account for their scribbles or the meaning of their work. Golomb (1974) calls this tendency romancing, stressing that "the interpretation is not yet tied to a perceptual likeness" (p. 5).

Conclusions and Recommendations

The following recommendations for promoting young children's visual/verbal interpretations are offered: 1) Arrange young children in small groups or in pairs to discuss a work of art and encourage them to share ideas and stories. In this case, the young children shared interpretations as well as identifications. Use small color prints for the students to share, because young children tend to be near-sighted (Wolfe, 1988) and learning is then more social and intimate.

2) Pattern manipulative skills, if necessary, when children are painting by directing their hands in how to hold a brush and in what direction to paint. Patterning is the direct guidance of a person's physical and mental activity through manipulation or demonstration (Stokrocki, 1986). Patterning applies to basic skills such as scissor-cutting, using a paper punch, making a rubbing (Stokrocki, 1984), and even finger-painting. The patterning of painting skills can also include the demonstration of repetitive parallel or swirling lines with a brush and the change of

Figure 10.

directions. Pattern young children's ability to mix colors in a methodical way through demonstration. Colbert and Taunton (1990) suggest a controlled system for mixing color in their teacher's guide, *Discover Art, Kindergarten*.

Rarely do children of this age become frustrated when they are painting spontaneously. However, many children do not receive art training at home and evidence shows that some children are beginning to develop artistic dissonance at earlier ages. If children become frustrated because they cannot literally copy a work the way they expect, this may be alleviated somewhat through the skill patterning.

3) Because young children naturally copy each other's work, a form of social learning (Wilson & Wilson, 1982), encourage young children to imitate the style of master artists. Young children can learn to master a simple configuration, then proceed to more advanced ones. Wilson, Hurwitz, and Wilson (1987) described their experiments with young children mastering such expressive conventions as the use of parallel lines in Munch's art work, *The Cry*. The observed case adds credence to their views, because young children showed evidence of imitating Van Gogh's swirls and spirals as well. Take care, however, in over-directing them to work realistically, because this prodding may lead to frustration. When individual students need help with images they choose to reproduce, then the teacher may illustrate simply on a scrap piece of paper, for example, how to paint a simple house or tree. This becomes a pattern for the child to imitate. Educators must not overlook the importance of repetition of skill and simple images in aesthetic development.

4) Develop children's metaphoric thinking, usually considered an advanced form of cognition. A metaphor is a speech device used to describe a new meaning by substituting another word or phrase, denoting something else, establishing a similarity and a form of condensed language. While young children are learning to master conventional skills, configurations, and rules, they are also learning to interpret them. They simply lack the vocabulary, so they develop metaphorical descriptions for their images or experiences, for example, "the man in the moon" or "I had to stop the stars." Encourage young children to describe and interpret their own work, and the work of their classmates, as

well as artists. Ask them "what their work is like." Children as young as three and four are capable of such metaphoric interpretation (Stokrocki, 1984).

7) Adopt participant observation methods (documentation, analysis, and interpretation) in order to understand the interpretive abilities of your own students. Participant observation research by teachers is extremely important in translating theory into practice, and also in revising understanding.

References

Bleicher, J. (1980). *Contemporary hermeneutics: Hermeneutics as method, philosophy, and critique*. Boston: Routledge and Kegan Paul.

Chapman, L. (1989). *Teaching Art: 1-3*. Worcester, MA: Davis.

Colbert, C., & Taunton, M. (1990). *Discover art: Kindergarten*. Worcester, MA: Davis.

Golomb, C. (1974). *Young children's sculpture and drawings: A study in representational development*. Cambridge, MA: Harvard University.

Heidegger, M. (1962). *Being and time* (J. Macquarrie & E. Robinson, Trans.). New York: Harper & Row.

Parsons, M. (1976). A suggestion concerning the development of aesthetic experience in children. *Journal of Aesthetics and Art Criticism, 34*, 305-314.

Parsons, M. (1987). *How we understand art: A cognitive developmental account of aesthetic experience*. New York: Cambridge University Press.

Pohland, P. (1972). Participant observation as a research methodology. *Studies in Art Education, 13* (3), 4-23.

Stokrocki, M. (1984). The meaning of aesthetic awareness for preschoolers in a museum class. *Art Education, 37* (2), 12-16.

Stokrocki, M. (1986). Patterning as an important strategy in fostering artistic development. *Journal of Art & Design Education, 5* (3), 225-237.

Vandenburg, D. (1971). *Being and education*. Englewood Cliffs, NJ: Prentice-Hall.

Wilson, B., & Wilson, M. (1982). *Teaching children to draw*. Englewood Cliffs, NJ: Prentice Hall.

Wilson, B., Hurwitz, A., & Wilson, M. (1987). *Teaching drawing from art*. Worcester, MA: Davis.

Wolfe, D. (1988). Child development and different cognitive styles. In *Issues in discipline-based art education: Strengthening the stance, extending the horizons* (Proceedings from the 1987 Seminar in Cincinnati, OH) (3-23). Los Angeles, CA: The Getty Center for Education in the Arts.

Zurmuehlen, M. (1983). Form as metaphor: A comparison of aesthetic structure in young children's pictures and stories. *Studies in Art Education 24*, 111-117.

Chapter 15
Art Criticism with Young Children Experiencing Developmental Delays

Karen M. Kakas
Bowling Green State University

How feasible is art criticism with young children experiencing developmental delays in language and cognitive development, delays caused by mental retardation, neurological disorders, family deprivation, or other unknown factors? An exploratory study conducted with a readiness class of children with significant developmental delays convinced this author that response activities with works of art are educationally beneficial and meaningful to this student population.

Some educators would argue that conversations with young children about art should not be labeled "criticism" because these youngsters are unable to make informed judgments about the comparative merits of art works. According to Barrett (1990), the act of criticism includes description, interpretation, evaluation, and theory, but criticism can be primarily descriptive or interpretive. Judging or evaluating is not a necessary part of the criticism process. Because art discussions with the children in this study were primarily descriptive, the art lessons I conducted with the readiness class might be labeled criticism, pre-criticism, or response activities.[1]

Traditionally, art lessons for young children experiencing physical disabilities or developmental delays have been studio based and often laden with nonart objectives intended to promote development of motor skills, self-esteem, and awareness of self (e.g., Anderson, 1978; Clements & Clements, 1983; Insights, 1976; Uhlin & De Chiara, 1984). Special education teachers seem to concur with the interest in nonart objectives. A survey of a large number of special educators revealed that they mentioned aesthetic/artistic benefits least often as rationales for art education (Kearns, 1989). Instead, they believed that art activities should nurture cognitive, social, physical, and emotional growth. Art lessons that reflect this nonart orientation are designed to help students compensate for their disabilities rather than to help them learn more about art (Blandy, 1989, 1991).

However, some art educators advocate that the art curricula for children experiencing physical disabilities or developmental delays be no different than for children who are not disabled (Blandy, 1989; Kearns,

1989). This view is reflected in Hurwitz and Day's (1991) chapter devoted to children with special needs. They recommend museum visits and art-postcard sorting tasks and suggest that "simple perceptual and verbal activities, such as aesthetic scanning, can be adapted for slow learners" (p. 114). Nevertheless, specific adaptation suggestions and documentation of art criticism with young children experiencing developmental delays do not appear in this text or in other sources. This void in the art education literature led to the criticism project with the readiness group described in this chapter.

Subjects

For one school year I conducted a study in Mrs. C.'s readiness class of six- and seven-year-olds at a rural elementary school in northwest Ohio. For funding purposes her class is labeled DH, developmentally handicapped. Children attend this class because of significant developmental delays in language, cognition, and social skills. According to Mrs. C., her students have little ability to attend, to follow a sequence, to remember instructions, or to recall steps in a procedure. In general, they have problems with auditory processing of language and they are inconsistent in their retention of information. Her students also tend to be distractible and experience difficulty in focusing or discerning what is important and what is extraneous in both the verbal and visual information they receive. Although a number of her students later attend regular elementary classes, the majority remain in special education programs.

Mrs. C.'s students function in the late preoperational and early concrete operations stages of cognitive development (Wadsworth, 1984), and learn best when they act on their environment, that is, when they "construct" or "discover" concepts. Direct experiences with concrete materials are critical to their learning.

Mrs. C. highly values art experiences for her students and welcomed my visits. She was especially curious about how art criticism lessons would affect her students' language development, one of her major program goals.

Project Objectives

While my goal was to nurture the children's understanding and appreciation of art, I sought to answer such questions as: What do young children with developmental delays notice and respond to in art works? What kinds of activities and questioning strategies will engage them in dialogue about art? In addition, the teaching of specific art concepts was included. For example, plans were made to teach art vocabulary such as painting, drawing, sculpture, photograph, and portrait. The children were expected to learn the difference between two-dimensional and three-dimensional art and that some art works look more or less real. They would be able to describe subject matter, media, line, shape, and color in individual art works, as well as compare these qualities in two or more works. In addition, it was intended that the children would learn to discern facial expressions and other feelings evoked by works of art.

Essentially, the point of the study was to discover if I could guide the children to respond more fully to art works and to perceive them more accurately. In what ways could their readiness for seeing and interpreting their visual world be enhanced?

Art Objects

Large and small reproductions, art postcards, photographs, and actual art objects were used during the sessions. A wide variety of art works reflected differences in (a) time periods and artists from the Renaissance through the 20th century; (b) gender and race of the artist; (c) origin, including Europe, America, Mexico, Guatemala, Canada, and China; (d) art forms—paintings, drawings, sculptures, photographs, toys, puppets, and dolls; (e) levels of abstractions from realism to nonobjective; and (f) subject matter, including animals, landscapes, seascapes, urban scenes, portraits, and adults and children involved in a variety of activities.

Lesson Procedures and Activities

I visited the class on a biweekly basis for 30 to 45 minutes. The seven children sat in a semicircle on the floor, Mrs. C. and her assistant sat behind them, and I sat on a low chair in front of the group. When three-dimensional works were shown, they were removed one-by-one from a bag. Likewise, reproductions were not revealed until they were shown to the group to be discussed. Being

hidden from view contributed to curiosity and heightened anticipation among the children.

Typically, one object at a time was discussed. After all the objects were talked about individually, comparisons were made, and favorites were picked. In order to ensure regular participation by all the group, I often asked the children questions in the order they sat in the semicircle. Questions were also directed to the entire class for a group response or to individual students who raised their hands. Throughout each session, everyone's participation was monitored, and if some children seemed less involved in the unison responses or did not raise their hands, questions were directed specifically to them.

Discussions about the art works were primarily descriptive, focusing on subject matter, media, size, line, color, shape, and texture. References were also made in selected figurative works to feelings that seemed to be evoked by a scene or an individual. In addition, we discussed processes, tools, and techniques, deciding, for example, what size paintbrush an artist used for certain parts of a painting.

Another procedure used with reproductions was to group three or four of them (usually representing similar subjects or themes) and pose questions that required the class to decide which work depicted a particular object or quality: "Which painting contains a boat...cloud...a smiling girl...is not a portrait?" A similar activity was conducted with each child holding an assortment of art postcards and being asked to sort through them to find one that illustrated a request: "Find the sculpture among your art postcards." "Which postcard contains an animal?" The children were asked to verify each other's selections.

From time to time they were asked to act out what they saw in a reproduction, such as poses of figures and facial expressions: "Can you make your face look like the the girl's face in this painting? Is she smiling? Is she frowning?" The group would evaluate each other's attempts as well as look in a large mirror to compare their facial expressions to the reproduction. I also found it helpful to bring in props (e.g., hats, a guitar, or a watering can).

Speculating about sounds in paintings also took place: "If you were in this painting, what sounds would you hear?" "Is the wind blowing and making the trees noisy?" "Are there any animal sounds you might hear?" Another type of speculative question asked them: "If you were in this painting, who would you be (an animal, a person), where would you be, what would you be doing?"

Questioning Strategies

My previous experience with children with learning disabilities and developmental delays had made me aware of the importance of using concise, clear language; of monitoring word choices and the speed of my voice; and of repeating information, requests, and questions. These behaviors were necessary to maintain attention, to enhance acquisition of knowledge and skills, and to reinforce retention of information (Sedlak & Sedlak, 1985). According to Mrs. C., her students often did not express their lack of understanding. Therefore, it was necessary to regularly check for understanding. When questions were asked or new vocabulary or information introduced, I observed their facial expressions, noted their ability to respond, and assessed the content of their responses. Unfamiliar words were explained and related to their experiences and, when necessary, questions were repeated and rephrased.

Because some children had more difficulty attending than others, I regularly checked that all were paying attention, were listening, and had heard what was said, either by me or someone else. At times, questions were directed toward an inattentive child to draw her back into the conversation. With 20 years of teaching experience in special education programs, Mrs. C. served as an excellent model as I used her word choices, repeated her ways of getting children's attention and giving directions, and so forth.

Because of the marked differences among the children's developmental levels and verbal skills, I continually varied the types of questions and the content within those questions in order to engage all the children in dialogue about the art works. A continuum of questions and requests from open ended to highly specific were used throughout the response activities. Attending to the way questions were constructed to ensure full participation by everyone was a form of "cue hierarchy" (Blandy, Pancsofar, & Mockensturm, 1988).[2]

A conversation usually began with general questions about an art work: "Tell me about this painting." "What do you see in this painting?" I favored starting with open-ended questions in order to learn the nature of the children's spontaneous responses. These generally referred to subject matter (e.g., a girl, dog, boat, flowers) and details of objects and activities taking place in a scene ("He's feeding the horse.").

After initial remarks by the group, increasingly specific questions were asked. The next level of question specificity referred to particular aspects of an art work: "What colors can you find in the painting?" "How do you think she is feeling?" "Where are these people?"

And even more specific: "What color is the horse's saddle?" "What is the girl holding in her left hand?"

Another type of question asked for additional information about a particular topic: "What other animals do you see?" "Can you think of other words to tell how she feels?" At times an "either/or" question that contained the answer was useful. The children were to choose from two possible answers and explain their choice: "Does this painting take place in the daytime or nighttime?" "Is this summer or winter?" "Is she happy or sad?"

At times rhetorical questions were used that stated information as a question, to review what children had already pointed out or to explain something they did not perceive: "She looks sad, doesn't she?" "He's far away, isn't he?" Such questions were followed by discussion about why that was so. Hewett and Rush (1987) described similar approaches in their discussion of constructing questions for aesthetic scanning.

Initially, less verbal youngsters were asked questions that required shorter answers, yet they were also guided to lengthen their responses. They often preferred to point to parts of a reproduction. When this happened, they were asked to "use words" to tell about the painting. Others whose cognitive development was more delayed were asked questions about simpler aspects of the art works. Questions about color, for example, were easier to answer than questions about space or feelings.

Patience was needed with children who were slow to answer or whose speech was difficult to understand. If other children interrupted and tried to answer for their peer, they were told, "It's Don's turn." Children were asked to repeat unclear responses, and at times, Mrs. C. understood what was said and acted as interpreter.

Wrong answers were not overlooked. The children were urged to look again or were told, "Let's check if Bill is right." If two children gave conflicting answers, the child who answered correctly was asked to explain her response: "How did you know that? Tell us why you think she is sad." I also commented about why a student may have misread something in the art work: "I see why you thought those clouds looked like smoke, since they are gray and in the sky, and smoke is gray and might be in the sky, too." "That long, skinny shape does look a bit like an airplane, doesn't it? But this painting was made a long time ago, before we knew how to build airplanes." Even when children responded correctly, they were not always able to explain their perceptions.

The group's perceptions seemed to exceed their ability to organize those perceptions with verbal statements about what they saw. For example, when asked which horses among a displayed group looked more or less real, the children pointed to parts of a horse that they could easily recognize. However, they had difficulty articulating an explanation of the differences by saying that one was more detailed than another or more accurate in the depiction of the head. I helped them articulate those perceptions by using such phrases as "You mean…?", clearly stating what I assumed the child meant. To reinforce this verbal information, it was useful to return to that observation and see if the child could independently restate the perception she had been helped to articulate.

Whenever I talked about the art works or visual aspects in their classroom (e.g., a portrait displayed on the bulletin board or how the blue in Todd's shirt matched the blue in the painting being discussed), I used vivid, descriptive language. My verbalization about what I saw was a way to model for the group how language could be used to talk about visual and expressive qualities in art and the environment (Colbert & Taunton, 1990).

The following section describes the first session in the study when the difference between two- and three-dimensional art forms was explained.

Learning How Sculptures Differ From Paintings

The study began in a concrete manner with actual art objects instead of reproductions of paintings. A selection of small horse sculptures were discussed—a Chinese straw horse, a Guatemalan wooden horse puppet, and several plastic toy horses. These horses varied in color, medium, size, and posture. After the abstract straw horse was easily identified as "horse," I asked, "What can you tell me about this horse?" This elicited statements about parts of the horse: "That's his tail…ears…eye." I probed for other kinds of information: "What is this horse made of?" "What colors do you see on him?" "What is he doing?" And more specific: "Where do you see red on the horse?" "What is this red part (pointing to the saddle on his back)?" The horses were passed among the children so they could feel their textures, gain further understanding of the materials, note their weight and sizes, and perhaps discover characteristics they had not previously noticed.

After they were discussed individually, the horses were lined up in front of the group and the children were asked which one was the smallest, the largest, was mainly white, was made of wood, had a saddle, had painted decorations, was jumping, and so forth. They were also asked to identify the one which looked most like a real horse. I explained that these objects were called sculptures—a new word—and that artists had made and planned them. I demonstrated that when we

look at a sculpture we can see the front, the back, the top, and the bottom (of these horses).

Next the children viewed a painting reproduction, Velasquez's *Prince Balthazar Carlos and His Pony*, I pointed out that we could only see the horse in the painting from one side. We could not see the back or the other side of the horse; there was no way to change which part of the horse we saw. We also talked about what "flat" meant and how the painting was flat and the sculptures were not. To relate the concept of three-dimensional horses to their previous experiences, I asked if anyone had ridden or owned a real horse or had horse sculptures at home. If so, what did they look like? Had anyone ridden a horse sculpture? When I showed a photograph of a carousel horse, Mrs. C. reminded the children about riding the merry-go-round during their trip to the zoo. After this explanation of the differences between two- and three-dimensional art forms, they were asked to look for animal sculptures at home and bring them for our next session.

Several lessons focused on animal sculptures and then shifted to animal paintings. Repeated comparisons were made between the sculptures and the paintings to reinforce the distinctions between two-dimensional and three-dimensional art forms. Throughout these discussions, attention was on the animals: what they were doing, where they were located, what people were doing on or near them, what else was in the scene, which colors were in the painting, and other characteristics of the environment. In addition, the children explained which paintings appeared more or less real looking.

Feelings in Art

The sessions on animal sculptures and paintings and landscapes were followed by discussions of figurative paintings. More attention was given to eliciting responses about feelings perceived in works of art. After initial conversations about Wyeth's *Christina's World* and Picasso's *The Tragedy* elicited perceptive responses to the feelings evoked in them, more reproductions were introduced for additional talk about feelings: a loving *Madonna and Child* by Raphael; Lee-Smith's *Boy With a Tire* depicting a lonely or sad child; and Renoir's , a "happy" scene. This time, however, the group gave mixed responses. Although several children were highly perceptive of the feelings, others had difficulty discerning expressive qualities and either guessed or quickly imitated an answer someone else provided.

These varied responses prompted me to devote several sessions to looking at photographs of adults and children whose faces expressed obvious emotions— happy, sad, mad, and surprised. As they identified the emotions, the children acted out the facial expressions and body language they saw in the photograph. The children looked at each other to assess the imitations and also viewed themselves in a large mirror to compare their expressions. Their comprehension of facial expressions was determined by displaying several photographs and asking them to pick the one that looked "sad"…"happy"…and so forth. These activities appeared to increase their understanding of facial expressions and make them more attentive to people's faces in the reproductions.

Making Distinctions Among Art Forms

Although the students were able to correctly label the sculptures and painting reproductions brought to class, they were confused by photographs of sculptures. Moreover, they were also inconsistent in their understanding of photographs as different from paintings. Attempting to eliminate this confusion with a demonstration, one day I brought drawing and painting materials, clay, and a Polaroid camera to class. As I photographed one of the students, I talked about the "camera" I was using to make a "photograph" of Jane. Next, I told them I was making a "drawing" of Jane. I began the drawing of one eye, then the other eye, and asked the group to tell me what to draw next as I moved down her facial features to her jaw, then to her ears, and finally her hair. At times I asked what was missing in the "drawing" of Jane. "This is a drawing of Jane," I repeated. This was followed by a watercolor "painting" of Jane. We reviewed the name "watercolors," the reason for that name, and that I was making a "painting" of Jane. Again, I began with the eyes and asked for suggestions as I painted. Next, I used clay to complete a small "sculpture" of Jane's head, and I repeated the word "sculpture" as I worked. Finally, I took a photograph of the sculpture with the Polaroid. We then compared the art works I had created, repeated the words I had used to label them, and contrasted the photograph of the sculpture to the actual sculpture.

Using the same subject and creating the works in front of them helped the group make connections between the finished work, the process, and the art terms. This demonstration contributed to their increased understanding of the different art forms and the appropriate vocabulary for labeling them. I was highly impressed with how absorbed and attentive they were throughout this 60-minute session. Their excitement about what took place that day made it clear that they all wanted to be photographed, drawn, painted, and sculpted. To reinforce learning of the vocabulary and the distinctions among the art forms, the same process was repeated the following week with another

child. During my absence, Mrs. C. displayed the art works and reviewed the art terms with them.

These sessions were followed by discussions of portraits that comprised several weeks of looking at and talking about portraits in the history of art.[3] During my last meeting with the children, they picked their favorite paintings from a selection of reproductions talked about during my visits. The children's explanations of their selections reflected preferences for particular subject matter or colors.

Results and Discussion

Analysis of audiotapes and field notes and discussions with Mrs. C. allowed me to make qualitative judgments about the effects of the criticism sessions on her students. She and I agreed that her students learned to:

1. Distinguish two- and three-dimensional art forms and to label drawings, paintings, sculptures, and photographs correctly much of the time.

2. More adequately identify colors, shapes, and types of lines.

3. Notice more in art works and to describe what they saw, including the subject matter, art processes, and what was happening in scenes depicted.

4. Identify and explain emotions expressed by people in paintings and photographs (some children were more successful at this than others).

5. More skillfully find similarities and differences among two or more art works.

6. Understand the concept of portrait and to identify "portraits" among a variety of subject matter.[4]

In general, growth occurred in language development, both in the use of art vocabulary and other words, such as adjectives that referred to subject matter, and in the children's perception of their environment and verbalization about what they saw.

In addition, the children were learning to listen to each other and were more able to participate in conversations about art and to take turns in conversations. We were both impressed with how attentive they were during the art discussions, how avidly they wanted to talk about the objects, and how they grasped the new words and meanings. Mrs. C. was pleased that her students were introduced to aspects of art and to art works that "they may well never be introduced to otherwise." It was apparent that this project not only nurtured their language development and knowledge of art, but also enhanced their openness to art and developed their curiosity and desire to talk about art.

Like other young children whose perceptions of art works have been studied (Parsons, 1987), Mrs. C.'s students delighted in all the art works shown to them. They enjoyed varying levels of abstraction, different styles, and types of subject matter. They tended to view the works more in parts than in wholes. For example, when describing a painting, they were satisfied with naming or itemizing the objects throughout the composition. And the children also explained activities of individual figures or of groups within a painting. When viewing art, this group of children responded in ways similar to youngsters without developmental delays. Both student populations respond to questions and tasks that ask them to describe, compare, sort, and speculate, and they point out similar aspects of works of art.

While other young children tend to make associative responses to subject, for example, talking about their pet dog if they see a dog in a painting (Parsons, 1987), it was necessary to ask questions to elicit such responses from these children. At times, Mrs. C. reminded the children of something they had done or seen that related to some aspect of the art work. Such associations helped to nurture the students' visual recall.

Because of these students' poor recall, much repetition and review of new words and concepts was required. A limited number of new words could be introduced in a session, and Mrs. C.'s review of new terms and concepts between visits helped them retain new learning.

It was necessary to repeat questions and requests often because of students' inability to attend. Their lack of attention in general seemed to result in responses unrelated to a question posed to them, although it is possible that they may have been so absorbed in looking at the reproduction that they did not hear the question. Such responses were always acknowledged and the initial question repeated.

The students' language delays required careful monitoring of the phrasing of questions and comments and revision of them when necessary. This "cue hierarchy" of types of questions enabled all the children to respond to the art works.

Some kinds of "why" questions that sought explanations were difficult for children to answer, but I was unable to determine if that inability was due to their state of cognitive development, language or perceptual delays, or all three factors. Regardless of the causes, strategies were employed to assist the children in articulating such answers.

Understanding of perceptions, concepts, and vocabulary was enhanced by referring to their previous experiences or to concrete objects in the classroom. Multisensory activities as well contributed to full participation.

Conclusion

By looking and talking about art, young children experiencing developmental delays can acquire greater understanding of art. Moreover, their lives can be enriched by these encounters. Such experiences can be enhanced if the art teacher seeks guidance from special education teachers regarding communication strategies they use with their students, for greater success can be achieved through collaborative efforts. It is also helpful to develop a particular routine or art viewing "frame," for this will result in student expectations to talk about art during art lessons (Elkind, 1979). It is vital that all students, regardless of their developmental levels, participate fully in conversations about art.

There is a body of literature that reports on young children's aesthetic responses to the visual arts (see Parsons, 1987; Taunton, 1982). However, art educators need to conduct, in collaboration with special education teachers, criticism research with young children experiencing developmental delays to learn the effects of teaching on their ability to respond to and understand art. We underestimate the capabilities of young children with developmental delays by focusing on their perceived disabilities rather than on devising ways to ensure full participation in art lessons meant for all students (Blandy, 1991). By expanding art criticism research with this student population we will gain insight about how to more skillfully guide them toward rich and meaningful experiences with their visual world.

References

Anderson, F.E. (1978). Art for all the children: A creative sourcebook for the impaired child. Springfield, IL: Charles C. Thomas Publishers

Barrett, T. (1990). Criticizing photographs. Mountain View, CA: Mayfield Publishing Company.

Blandy, D. (1989). Ecological and normalizing approaches to disabled students and art education. Art Education, 42(3), 7-11.

Blandy, D. (1991). Conceptions of disability: Toward a sociopolitical orientation to disability for art education. Studies in Art Education, 32,(3), 131-144.

Blandy, D., Pancsofar, E., & Mockensturm, T. (1988). Guidelines for teaching art to children and youth experiencing significant mental/physical challenges. Art Education, 41(1), 60-67.

Chapman, L. (1987). Discover art: Art print guides, 1-3. Worcester, MA: Davis Publications, Inc.

Clements, C.B., & Clements, R.D. (1983). Art and mainstreaming: Art instruction for exceptional children in regular school classes. Springfield, IL: Charles C. Thomas Publishers.

Colbert, C .B., & Taunton, M. (1990). Discover art: Kindergarten. Worcester, MA: Davis Publications, Inc.

Elkind, D. (1979). The child and society. New York: Oxford University Press.

Feldman, E.B. (1981). Varieties of visual experience. Englewood Cliffs, NJ: Harry N. Abrams

Hewett, G.J., & Rush, J.C. (1987). Finding buried treasures: Aesthetic scanning with children. Art Education, 40(1), 41-43.

Hurwitz, A., & Day, M. (1991). Children and their art (4th ed.). New York: Harcourt, Brace, Jovanovich, Inc.

Staff Insights: *Art in special education*. (1976). Milburn, NJ: Art Educators of New Jersey.

Kearns, L.H. (1989). Making and beyond: Implementing a balanced, sequential art education. In *Collected Papers: Pennsylvania's Symposium III on the Role of Studio in Art Education* (pp. 87-94). Harrisburg: Pennsylvania Department of Education.

Parsons, M. J. (1987). *How we understand art*. New York: Cambridge University Press.

Sedlak, R.A., & Sedlak, D.M. (1985). *Teaching the educable mentally retarded*. Albany, NY: State University of New York Press.

Taunton, M. (1982). Aesthetic response of young children to the visual arts: A review of the literature. *Journal of Aesthetic Education*, 16(3), 93-109.

Uhlin, D.M., & De Chiara, E. (1984). *Art for exceptional children* (3rd ed.). Dubuque, IA: Wm. C. Brown Publishers.

Wadsworth, B.J. (1984). *Piaget's theory of cognitive and affective development* (3rd ed.). New York: Longman.

Notes

[1] Barrett's delineation of the content of criticism differs somewhat from the popular Feldman model that comprises description, formal analysis, interpretation, and judgment. Readers are encouraged to compare these two approaches (Barrett, 1990; Feldman, 1981).

[2] For an explanation of how cue hierarchies are used in a studio context, the reader can refer to Blandy et al. (1988).

[3] In this latter part of the study a series of studio activities was integrated with the portrait response activities.

[4] The above observations were made during an interview with Mrs. C. at the end of the school year.

Chapter 16
Language and Learning About Art

Connie Newton
University of North Texas

Language is a major component of learning in art. If children are to learn about art, then language is essential. It is necessary for children to possess a language about art in order to communicate their perceptions, responses, and knowledge about art. The development of an adequate language should go beyond knowledge about elements and principles or the standard idea of an "art vocabulary." The goal of language development should include a language rich in adjectives, adverbs, verbs, and nouns which children may use to describe, discuss, and interpret works of art. The language available to children should be adequate to communicate their thoughts, ideas, feelings, and meanings about art.

How Children Acquire Language

Most children learn language in a relatively short time, and certainly before they enter any formal schooling experience. Goodman (1986) suggests that children are naturally compelled to learn language because of their need to communicate, to express themselves, and to understand others. Children become language users through interaction with people and their environment, and they learn oral language as a functional system, that is, as a system in use. In fact, the function of language for young children is the motivating factor and the form of the language is gradually acquired and refined through interaction.

Research suggests that young children first acquire connotative meaning while denotative meaning is still confused (Ervin & Foster, 1969). Connotative meaning refers to the emotive or affective aspects of speech which are built upon association and personal experiences in contrast to denotive meaning which is literal and agreed upon by mature language users. The meaning of particular words or phrases is less consistent with younger children and changes as the child matures. By age 8, children have relatively consistent semantic meanings (Maltz, 1963). Often younger children will treat adjectives such as good, pretty, and happy as interchangeable (Ervin & Foster, 1969). For example, kindergarten children understand that skinny and thin are synonyms, but they do not understand what distinguishes a skinny person from a thin one (Genishi & Dyson, 1985).

Preschool children are able to use figurative language and produce similes and metaphors in speech (Gardner, Kircher, Winner, & Perkins, 1975), and 6- and 7-year-olds have a limited capacity to interpret metaphoric statements (Winner, Rosenstiel, & Gardner, 1976). This description of children's connotative, semantic, and metaphoric development is consistent with Taunton's (1984) research, which indicated that 4-year-olds were able to match word clues to expressive qualities of works of art.

Kindergarten and first-grade students acquire concepts about shape, quantity, space, number, and time such as more/less, same/different, high/low, above/below, before/after, greater/fewer, big/small, and between, and behind. Because of the importance of these concepts in learning, Genishi and Dyson (1985) refer to them as cognitive codes.

When children play, they often use language in a more adult-like manner. In trying to sound like adults, children stretch both the forms and the functions of their language (Genishi & Dyson, 1985). During play, children use more adverbs and adjectives and produce longer utterances (Hutt, 1979). If play situations are free from anxiety, observers or evaluators may witness children using their most competent language.

Whole Language Philosophy

No discussion about language would be complete without mention of the whole language philosophy. Central to the whole language theory are the notions that learning in school should go from whole to part, just as spoken language is learned, and that language and literacy are best developed through functional use

(Goodman, 1986). Children must actively pursue and own their learning (Watson, 1989). Thus, they take significant responsibility for learning within whole language classrooms. Both teachers and children must be learners, risk takers, and decision makers.

Of particular significance for preschool children is the large portion of learning which occurs through social interaction, involving a collaborative effort with small groups of students. This productive interaction among children is based upon the idea that children learn a great deal about language from each other, when they are involved in sharing ideas and responsibilities.

In dealing with emergent reading and writing, teachers recognize the manner in which children's oral language develops (Fountas & Hannigan, 1989). The focus is on the active functional process rather than correctness. Some classroom time is obviously spent in direct teaching, but a large portion of children's time is spent actively involved in verbalizing and exploring ideas. School-age children spend most of their time reading materials about subjects in which they already have an interest and in writing about these subjects.

Another important characteristic of whole language is the idea of holistic or integrated curriculum (Goodman, 1989). The curriculum is not prepackaged but evolves as teachers and children explore topics and themes. Curriculum is holistically organized with thematic units or topics and is multidisciplinary rather than fragmented and linear. Teachers and children explore themes and generate new interests from these. Language is acquired and developed across disciplines, and this requires more communication between the various teachers that children may have.

Language and Imagery

Relating words to visual images is a powerful educational tool. Broudy (1987) stressed the importance of the relationship between visual images and language. Visual images embedded in memory can assist in remembering and clarifying the meanings of words and phrases. Art images combined with verbalization are embedded in memory both visually and semantically. Ideas and concepts are not isolated in memory but are organized and associated with the natural language that students utilize and the situations they have encountered in the past.

Works of art can be utilized as stimuli to assist in language acquisition and development. Many of the strategies and games discussed in this chapter present wonderful opportunities for students to acquire and use language.

Adapting Language Strategies To Learning About Art

Because children learn language through interaction, it is important to provide opportunities for all children to verbalize and talk about art. Genishi and Dyson (1985) recommend collaborative talk to facilitate verbalization and language development. Placing children in small groups provides more opportunities for each child to verbalize and communicate ideas. Children should be grouped according to their interests and not in terms of their ability levels (Hiebert & Fisher, 1990). All children should take turns rather than just high-ability-level students.

Children learn from each other as they talk and listen. Interacting with their classmates, children hear others using different but similar adjectives, and acquire a much richer art language. They also learn other ways to think about art which clarify their own thinking as they find ways to express themselves.

Kinesthetic Movement

When children utilize body movements in responding to works of art, the acquisition and use of descriptive words is increased. Werner and Burton (1979) explored the effectiveness of teaching young children a variety of subjects using interrelationships with movement, and found that teaching art elements with movement was particularly successful. For example, young children can move their bodies to represent a specific line or shape in a painting. Children can place their bodies in a position similar to a particular line in a work of art, move their bodies in the direction of the line, or move the way they think that line would move.

As children move their bodies to represent actual lines, shapes, movement, texture, and rhythm found in reproductions of art works, they should be encouraged to describe the position of their body, the way it moved, and the quality of the particular art element. If children have positioned their bodies to represent a particular vertical line in Mondrian's *Broadway Boogie Woogie*, for example, the teacher should accept the wide range of words such as tall, straight, and strong that children might offer to describe what they have done.

Young children can perceive aspects of works of art before they can verbally describe them. Teachers can watch children engaged in kinesthetic body movements to determine if indeed they are responding to certain qualities in works of art. Movements can be directional or shaping. Other concepts to explore are near/far, still/moving, thick/thin, straight/curved, warm/cool colors, ordered/chaotic, high/low, and wide/narrow.

Play Strategies for Intensifying Involvement With Art

Strategies designed to increase children's empathy or involvement with works of art are excellent ways of learning language through play and interaction. Empathy involves the projection of one's own personality into a situation or personification of the situation (Chapman, 1978). Although these subjective strategies should eventually be balanced by some objectivity, they are excellent ways to initiate more intense involvement with works of art.

There are many ways to facilitate such involvement. Children can be asked to find one spot in a painting or print and to imagine that they are there. Landscapes, seascapes, and some interiors are applicable for this approach. Appropriate questions dealing with sensory impressions and expressive qualities might be: What do you hear? Is it warm or cold? How do you feel? Is the wind blowing? What do you see? Do you feel safe? Questions can be extended to include: What are you doing? How did you get there? What do you think might happen next? These questions could lead to role playing, creative drama, or extended play.

Works of art can be utilized as settings or backgrounds for children's invented stories. Art works which depict adventure or drama work well. Questions centering around the action could initiate the story-telling: What is happening? What happened just before? What might happen next or later? After the teacher or a student has told a story, the children should enact and then retell the story. Older children could then write stories about the work of art.

It is important to encourage intense involvement with works of art. Significant dimensions of children's aesthetic responses are familiarity and degree of interest, factors which are related to how long children are willing to look at art (Newton, 1989). There is evidence that exposure to and involvement with some works of art increase children's receptivity to other, similar works.

Developing Language to Describe Literal and Expressive Qualities

Expressive language can be encouraged by using visual images. Taunton (1984) found that 4-year-olds could respond to subtle and expressive qualities in art. Taunton further suggested that when teachers use language rich with elaborate description and metaphor, they model the process of responding to these qualities in works of art.

Activities which involve sensory descriptions matching expressive labels to works of art foster attention to expressive as well as literal qualities. Combining music with art works encourages the use of a rich language. Comparing two art works with opposite qualities works well because it is often easier for young children to discern differences than similarities.

It is important to remember that the teacher should be accepting of all responses. The precise, correct art vocabulary is not as important as encouraging children to talk about art and develop a rich language which enables each child to communicate observations and ideas. Young children do not need to know the word 'horizontal' in order to describe a particular line. Words such as "lying down", "an asleep line", "across", "wide", "lazy", and "flat" are adequate descriptors and help build connotative meanings. A diagonal line might be "leaning", "falling over", or "not straight". Vertical lines might be described as "up and down", "tall", or "standing up". The teacher's acceptance of this wide range of appropriate responses facilitates language development.

Teaching vocabulary is not done in phonetic groups but by means of semantic clusters of conceptually related words. Many art activities are particularly applicable to this approach. As children observe and describe qualities in reproductions of works of art, they might describe a particular line, shape, or texture. Rather than describing one particular line, children might also describe the qualities of all the lines in a work of art and generate a word list containing "long", "straight", and "strong". With this process the selected works of art generate the semantically clustered word list. This process can be reversed and semantically grouped word lists generated in other areas can be matched to works of art. For example, a word list from a story might include "family", "child", "mother", "father", "love", "happy", and others. These words could be matched to reproductions including paintings and pastels by Mary Cassat, sculpture by Henry Moore, or multiculturally with African sculpture and Japanese woodcuts. Children could find characteristics and qualities in works of art which match a previously generated word list.

Works of art can be effectively utilized to help children acquire cognitive codes about concepts involving time, number, space, and shape. As they describe qualities in art, children can also describe where each quality is located in the work of art. Concepts such as "above", "below", "under", "over", "on", "beside", "up", "down", "next to", "around", and "in" could be further developed in this manner. Children will also need to use concepts such as more/less, greater/fewer, same/different, before/after, big/small, and the like in describing and talking about art. The meanings of these cognitive codes develop over time as children encounter them in different situations.

Art Games

Art games and game-like strategies present wonderful opportunities for students to acquire and use language. Young children can match reproductions of art works to verbal labels containing connotative meanings and both literal and expressive qualities. Small reproductions could be sorted according to similarity, and children could then name or label the categories. Kindergarten and first-grade children can write their own labels and learn ways to encode their own messages. As children attempt to match or sort reproductions, they should give reasons for their choices.

Many art games could include manipulatives which acknowledge the natural inclination of children to learn through play. With art games, children manipulate small reproductions or other playing pieces and engage in behaviors such as matching, sorting, categorizing, comparing, contrasting, and reasoning.

Summary

The strategies discussed in this chapter are beneficial in the acquisition and development of language for young children. Visual images provide a powerful tool which encourages the development of descriptors for both literal and expressive qualities, metaphor, and cognitive codes. Through collaborative talk about art, children can acquire a much richer art language. This language enables young children to describe their perception and responses to art and also to more fully communicate ideas and meanings about art.

References

Broudy, H.S. (1987). *The role of imagery in learning.* Los Angeles: The Getty Center for Education in the Arts.

Chapman, L. H. (1978). *Approaches to art in education.* New York: Harcourt Brace Jovanovich, Inc.

Ervin, S. M. & Foster, G. (1969). The development of childrens' terms. In J.G. Snider & C.E. Osgood (Eds.), *Semantic differential technique.* (pp. 335-338). Chicago: Aldine Publishing Co.

Fountas, I. C. & Hannigan, I. L. (1989). Making sense of whole language: The pursuit of informed teaching. *Childhood Education,* Spring, 133-137.

Gardner, H., Kircher, M., Winner, E., & Perkins, D. (1975). Children's metaphoric productions and preferences. *Journal of Child Language,* 2, 125-141.

Genishi, G. & Dyson, A. H. (1985). *Language assessment in the early years.* Norwood, NJ: Ablex Publishing Corporation.

Goodman, K.G. (1986). *What's whole in whole language.* Portsmouth, NH: Heinemann Educational Books.

Goodman, Y.M. (1989). Roots of the whole-language movement. *The Elementary School Journal,* 90(2), 113-127.

Hiebert, E.H. & Fisher, C. W. (1990). Whole language: Three themes for the future. *Educational Leadership,* March, 62-64.

Hutt, C. (1979). Exploration and play. In B. Sutton-Smith (Ed.), *Play and learning* (pp. 175-194). New York: Gardner Press.

Maltz, H. E. (1963). Ontogenetic changes in the meaning of concepts as measured by the semantic differential. *Child Development,* 34, 667-664.

Newton, C. (1989). A developmental study of aesthetic response using both verbal and nonverbal measures. *Visual Arts Research,* 15(1), 76-85.

Taunton, M. (1984). Four-year-old children's recognition of expressive qualities in painting reproductions. *Journal of Research and Development in Education,* 17(4), 36-42.

Watson, D. (1989). Defining and describing whole language. *Elementary School Journal,* 90, 129-141.

Werner, J., & Burton, E.C. (1979). *Learning through movement: Teaching cognitive content through physical activities.* St. Louis: C.V. Mosby (ERIC Document Reproduction Service No. ED 173 333).

Winner, E., Rosenstiel, A. K., & Gardner, H. (1976) The development of metaphoric understanding. *Developmental Psychology,* 12(2), 289-297.

Chapter 17
Art Education and Children's Literature: An Interdisciplinary Approach for Preschool Children

Florence S. Mitchell
Mercer University, Atlanta

The integration of art education and children's literature is not a new idea. References in the literature of both disciplines encourage integrating the two fields (Criscuolo, 1985; Norton 1983). However, most proponents of this integration are reading specialists who advocate using art in activities referred to as "book stretching" (Cox, 1981, p. 9). The art activities described as "book stretching" often do not reflect the style and mood of the illustrations and are only loosely related to the books through the books' subject or theme. Generally, the outcome of such methods of integration is to use art in an instrumental way. The objectives include little or no art learning and the aesthetic quality of the art objects produced is not considered.

This chapter describes ways in which children's literature can be used to teach art to young children, 3- to 5-years-old, so that substantial learning about art can take place. A basic assumption underlying this goal is the importance of discipline-based learning in art, even for the young child. The component parts of a discipline-based curriculum—knowledge of art history, criticism, and aesthetics as well as production of art (Eisner, 1987)—should all be included in art programs for young children.

Using Children's Literature in the Classroom

Using children's literature to teach young children about art has an advantage over other strategies used to teach older students about art history, criticism, and aesthetics. Early in their lives children begin looking at books and talking with adults about the text and the pictures in them. Most children are familiar with this process through home exposure or are introduced to it as a part of their preschool training. Observing and discussing art content contained in books can be a natural extension of this well established teaching-learning strategy.

Even teachers with limited training in art, especially in art history, criticism and aesthetics, can feel comfortable reading and discussing picture books with children. Concepts to be learned are presented in a format familiar to both teacher and student. Also, when necessary, the teacher can become a co-learner with the child (Goodman, 1989) through exploration of the text.

We know that children's literature is used in elementary and secondary classrooms to aid in concept development (Lehman, 1989). Social science teachers, for example, have found that children's literature can be a "valuable vehicle for teaching about history and human relations" (Connet, 1988), writing about the value of children's literature in the classroom, provides guidelines applicable when selecting books for teaching art concepts. She found that learning can take place "if the literature selected contains significant content, concepts and generalizations that are the building blocks of that content area" (p. 50).

Although most examples of integration of art and literature do not support discipline-based objectives, some educators have described how children's literature can be used to reach such goals. The title of Kiefer's (1988) paper, "Picture Books as Contexts for Literary, Aesthetic, and Real World Understandings," states succinctly that artistic knowledge can be gained from the study of this literature. Art educators have described how children's literature can be used to teach art history (Mitchell, 1990), and how this literature can provide experiences that may lead to an appreciation for art (Szekely, 1990).

When books are used in a classroom situation, they should be presented in a relaxed but enthusiastic manner. Guidelines published by the International Reading Association recommend that preschool children be encouraged to look at the illustrations and listen, speak, and reflect on the reading (Early Childhood and Literacy Development Committee, 1986). With these guidelines in mind, the following books are suggested for use in teaching young children about art.

Some Books to Consider

The best books for use with young children are those with large pictures and uncomplicated illustrations: the type of book classified in children's literature as a picture book. In a picture book, the illustrations either carry the entire story line or are a significant part of its expression. Various styles and media are used to illustrate picture books and this variety makes identifying exceptional books enjoyable.

As children get older, the text can become longer and more involved. Books whose text may be too long and complicated for a child of three, can be talked about, summarized, or excerpted. In this case, teachers may encourage children to look at and discuss the illustrations and bring into the discussion information that would be appropriate.

The following books have been selected to show the range and variety of children's literature that can be used in art education with young children. The age range assigned to each book should be considered only as a suggestion. The development and the experience level of the children should always be the prime consideration in selecting a book.

Books About Portraits and the Artists Who Make Them

Benjamin's Portrait by Alan Baker is the story of a hamster who, after attending a portrait exhibit of animals, attempts to paint a portrait. When Benjamin is unsuccessful in his attempts, he ends by making a photographic portrait. This is a true picture book whose format is similar to others of its kind. Age range 3 to 4.

Angus and the Mona Lisa by Jacqueline Cooper is the story of a cat who saves the *Mona Lisa* from being stolen from the Louvre Museum in Paris. The frontispiece shows Angus looking at the *Mona Lisa*. This and the other illustrations in the book are watercolor paintings presented in the format of a picture book. Age range 3 to 5.

Da Vinci by Mike Venezia is the story of Leonardo da Vinci's life. It is illustrated with reproductions of Leonardo's paintings, drawings and other works. Venezia's humorous cartoon-style drawings are used to interpret some of the events in Leonardo's life. The reproductions are a quarter- to a half-page in size and the text is appropriate for children. The book could be looked at and talked about with children 3 to 4 and read to older children. This author has written and illustrated books about other artists including Picasso. Venezia's books are a cross between a picture book and an informational book. Age range 3 to 5.

Some art historical concepts and generalizations that can be drawn from these books include:

- Artists in the past and present have made portraits.
- Artists help us know what people look like, even those who lived long ago.
- Some portraits become very famous.
- One such portrait, the *Mona Lisa* was stolen but recovered.

Venezia's book contains more detailed historical information about the artist Leonardo da Vinci and his portrait of *Mona Lisa*. It presents different kinds of art, such as Leonardo's drawings, paintings, sculpture, and architecture as well as his inventions.

Aesthetic and critical concepts, such as the idea that in a portrait an artist pays attention to the way someone looks and dresses, can be presented with these books. Other concepts are associated with the use and selection of media. For example:

- Portraits can be made using different media—paint, crayon, clay, or photographic film.
- Portraits executed in different media will look different from each other when compared.
- Artists may have specific reasons for choosing a particular medium for a portrait.

Other concepts related to an artist's style can be found in these books. Venezia identifies an artist's style as a special way of painting and describes Leonardo's style as making objects look real and emphasizing the background in his paintings. Some people consider the *Mona Lisa* an important painting because of the way Leonardo painted his subject — for example, her expression, and the subtle shading used in the painting.

Auxiliary materials help expand the context in which art concepts are presented and further integrate art learning with general knowledge. A globe and map of the world allow students to locate their home and the homes of artists and paintings, in this case, France and Italy. A time-line chart will allow older students to visualize and locate on a scale Leonardo's dates, 1452- 1519. (Although not mentioned in *Angus and the Mona Lisa*, 1911 is the date the *Mona Lisa* was actually stolen.)

Large reproductions of Leonardo's paintings allow for further looking and discussion. Additional books on the same topic provide other insights into the subject and support greater depth of understanding. An appealing book, *Leonardo da Vinci* by Alice and Martin Provensen, emphasizes Leonardo's inventions. It is a pop-up book in which the inventions move when manipulated.

Classroom exhibits of portraits, of and by students, engage students with the art concepts on a different level. The exhibit might include portraits in different media of animals or of famous people selected by the students. An exhibit allows student and teacher to review and elaborate on the concepts under study.

Books About Museums

Curious George and the Dinosaur is part of a series of books about the popular monkey character, George. In this book George visits a museum with dinosaurs on exhibit and embarks on a series of adventures in the city with one of the dinosaurs before it must return to the museum. Age range 3 to 4.

The Child's Play Museum by Peter Adams is a play book about museums that exhibit dinosaur bones, Stone Age objects, armor, coins and medals. Double-page illustrations show children visiting the exhibits. The succeeding double-page illustration shows the objects exhibited in the museum as they might have been used or as they might have appeared in their native habitat. Age range 3 to 5.

A B C: The Alef-Bet Book, The Israel Museum, Jerusalem; A B C: Egyptian Art From the Brooklyn Museum; A B C: Museum of Fine Arts, Boston; and A B C: Museum of Modern Art, New York—all by Florence Mayers—are typical of books organized around the alphabet with each letter represented by an object from a museum's collection. Such books are useful in showing children what kind of objects are housed in museums. In this series each object is photographically reproduced. Age range 3 to 5.

Visiting the Art Museum by Laurene and Marc Brown is a story of a family visiting a museum. The illustrations include both reproductions of art and drawn illustrations used together in a double-page format. The works and periods of art are identified as the family progresses through the museum. The text is contained in the type of dialogue boxes used by some cartoonists. Age range 4 to 5.

Art historical generalizations about museums that can be drawn from these texts or stories include:

* Museums are places in which old and important objects are kept.
* Objects from long ago help us know about the past.
* There are different kinds of museums categorized by what they contain.

Works of art can be categorized in different ways, such as how they look (style or art form), when they were made, or how they are used. Critical concepts and

generalizations that can be drawn from these books include the idea that museum visitors pay attention to how colors, shapes and textures are used in art works.

Auxiliary materials that can enhance learning with these books include adult books illustrating art in specific museums. These books will give students an idea of the range of materials in museums. As with the books on portraits, a time-line chart with relevant dates, maps, and a globe of the world will help place a given museum and its art in a specific time and place.

Children can be engaged in establishing a collection by developing a classroom museum. Prized objects of all kinds or art works can be assembled, categorized, labeled and displayed.

Books About Collage

Children's literature can also be used to teach concepts and generalizations about techniques and materials used in art, such as collage. Used in this manner, illustrations can be exemplars for the children's own art, as well as visual examples of the concept being taught. Further learning about the history and the fine art use of the technique can evolve from the experience with the picture book.

Kanahena, A Cherokee Story by Susan Roth uses different kinds of materials, fabrics, leaves, and paper to interpret this traditional Cherokee fable. The tactile qualities of the materials used in the original collages are obvious in each illustration. Leo Lionni is another author (see reference list) who combines various textures in his illustrations and whose books are appropriate for this age group. Age range 3 to 5.

Jungle Sounds by Rebecca Emberley is wordless except for the sounds made by the animals depicted. The written sound becomes part of the design of each illustration. The illustrations are double-page, colorful collages made of solid colored, cut paper. A similar use of cut paper can be found in a new book by Leo Lionni, *Matthew's Dream*, the story of a mouse who wants to be an artist. Age range 3 to 4.

Do You Want to be My Friend? by Eric Carle is wordless, except for the title question and final answer. In this book, a mouse looks for a friend. The illustrations are simple and cut from paper which has been painted with patterns and textures. Carle uses this technique to illustrate all his books, most of which are suitable for children of this age. Age range 3 to 5.

Art historical concepts and generalizations about collage that can be drawn from the text or associated with the content and illustration of these stories include:

- Collage is a technique used by artists in which different kinds of materials are used to make works of art.
- In 1913 Picasso became the first artist to use different kinds of materials in the collage technique.
- Other artists, such as Matisse, made collages using materials different from those used by Picasso.
- Some artists such as Matisse, Carle and Lionni use painted papers to make collages.

Aesthetic and critical generalizations to be drawn from these books include:

- It is important to pay attention to the materials used in a collage or illustration.
- The materials used in a collage make a difference in the way a collage looks.
- Different sizes, shapes, colors and textures can be used to construct objects in a collage.

Auxiliary materials to use with these books are similar to the materials suggested for the other books. Original collages rather than reproductions will be valuable in demonstrating the tactile quality of some collages. Here again the use of a time-line marked with the first use of collage, identified as 1913, helps students place collage in a chronological time frame with other art.

A collection of materials, such as paper painted with finger paint, and other colored papers are important to gather for use in future collages. Useful in discussing papers with the children is the book, *Meet Matisse* by Nelly Munthe. It includes examples of Matisse's cut-outs as well as an explanation of how he made his papers.

Conclusion

Children's literature contains a wealth of material that can be used for teaching children about the making of art, art history, aesthetics, and criticism. However, authors such as Kiefer (1991), Marantz (1977), and Szekely (1990) remind us to pay attention to the special quality and character of picture books, especially when using this literature as a tool for teaching about art. It is important not to fall into the trap of thinking of this very special art form only in an instrumental way. Take time to enjoy the layout and the illustrations in each book. Notice how the illustrations contribute to the overall aesthetic quality of the book, not just the story line. Paying attention to these qualities in books will encourage the same kind of appreciation in children.

References

Connet, D. (1988). When using literature in your history-social science program, don't forget to include history-science! *Social Science Review, 28*, 41-51.

Cox, V. (1981). The literature curriculum. In L. L. Lamme (Ed.), *Learning to love literature* (pp. 1-11). Urbana, IL: National Council of Teachers of English.

Criscuolo, N. (1985). Creative approaches to teaching reading through art. *Art Education, 38*, 13-16.

Early Childhood and Literacy Development Committee of the International Reading Association (1986). Joint statement on literacy developmental pre-first grade. *The Reading Teacher, 39*, 819-821.

Eisner, E. (1987). The role of discipline-based art education in America's schools. *Art Education, 40*, 6-45.

Goodman, Y. (1989). Roots of the whole-language movement. *The Elementary School Journal, 90*, 113-127.

Kiefer, B. (1988). Picture books as contexts for literary, aesthetic, and real world understandings. *Language Arts, 65*, 260-271.

Kiefer, B. (1991). Accent on art. *The Reading Teacher, 44*, 406-414.

Lehman, B. A. (1989). Content reading, trade books and students: Learning about the Constitution through nonfiction. *Reading Improvement, 26*, 50-57.

Marantz, K. (1977). The picture book as an art object: A call for balanced reviewing. *Wilson Library Bulletin*, March, 148-151.

Mitchell, F. (1990). Introducing art history to young children through children's literature. *Language Arts, 67*, 839-846.

Norton, D. (1983). *Through the eyes of a child: An introduction to children's literature.* Columbus: Charles E. Merrill.

Szekely, G. (1990). An introduction to art: Children's books. *Childhood Education, 66*, 132-138.

Children's Books

Adams, P. (1979). *The child's play museum.* New York: Child's Play (International) Ltd.

Baker, A. (1986). *Benjamin's portrait.* New York: Lothrop, Lee & Shepard.

Brown, L. & M. (1986). *Visiting the art museum.* New York: E. P. Dutton.

Carle, E. (1971). *Do you want to be my friend?* New York: Thomas Y. Crowell Company.

Cooper, J. (1981). *Angus and the Mona Lisa.* New York: Lothrop, Lee & Chepart Books.

Emberley, R. (1989). *Jungle sounds.* Boston: Little, Brown and Company

Lionni, L. (1991). *Matthew's dream.* New York: Knopf.

Mayers, F. C. (1986). *A B C: Museum of Modern Art, New York.* New York: Harry N. Abrams.

Mayers, F. C. (1988). *A B C: Egyptian art from the Brooklyn Museum.* New York: Harry N. Abrams.

Mayers, F. C. (1988). *A B C: Museum of Fine Arts, Boston.* New York: Harry N. Abrams.

Mayers, F. C. (1989). *A B C: The alef-bet book, The Israel Museum, Jerusalem.* New York: Harry N. Abrams.

Munthe, N. (1983). *Meet Matisse.* Boston: Little, Brown and Company.

Provensen, A. & Provensen M. (1984). *Leonardo da Vinci.* New York: Viking Press.

Rey, M. & Shalleck, A. J. (Eds.). (1989). *Curious George and the dinosaur.* New York: Houghton Mifflin.

Roth, S. (1988). *Kanahena, A Cherokee story.* New York: St. Martin's Press.

Venezia, M. (1988). *Picasso.* Chicago: Children's Press.

Venezia, M. (1989). *Da Vinci.* Chicago: Children's Press.

Chapter 18
Early Education in Geography and Art: A Focus on Spatial Ability and Visual Skill

Joanne K. Guilfoil
Eastern Kentucky University

Map Making Versus Map Understanding

Over the last ten years writers have identified a pervasive lack of cultural literacy in American society, targeting several specific academic disciplines. Surveys reporting children's geographic ignorance at all levels have fueled such remedial responses as awareness celebrations and the development of K-12 geographic curriculum guidelines (Natoli et. al., 1984). Already geographic learning is being narrowly equated with an ability to locate places on a map (Downs & Liben, 1990). In the near future teachers will ask children to demonstrate their geographic knowledge by producing maps which will be used to assess how well they have acquired facts about places. Thus maps, place learning and geography will be forever linked in the curriculum and in the children's minds (Liben & Downs, 1989a, 1989b).

This rather myopic view of geographic knowledge and map understanding could become reality if Goal #3 of U.S. national school goals takes effect. It states, "By the year 2000 American students will leave grades 4, 8 and 12 having demonstrated competency in challenging subject matter, including English, mathematics, science, history and geography; and every school in America will ensure that all students learn to use their minds well, so that they may be prepared for responsible citizenship, further learning, and productive employment in our modern economy" (Darling-Hammond, 1990, p. 286).

Since the early 1970s several art educators, such as Neperud (1978) and McFee and Degge (1977), have been quite concerned with the notion of "responsible citizenship" as developed through environmental education as part of art education. Although the professional interests of art educators are increasingly diverse, some art educators continue this environmental concern with a strong social/cultural bias and the social/political commitment needed to engage environmental issues (Neperud, 1991).

If art education curricula with a focus on environmental design are to be developed and implemented, the social/cultural contexts of art and the social/aesthetic concerns of environmental experiences must be addressed. The goal is to have students develop "responsible citizenship" through a more sympathetic view of their surroundings. This must start with the involvement of very young children and their understanding of how their surroundings affect them and how they affect their surroundings (Neperud, 1991). Young children are most readily able to develop environmental responsibility when they are supported in their efforts to know and understand various environments.

Art educators concerned with children's early education should also consider children's map understanding as a basis for visual and spatial performance (Guilfoil, 1986; McFee & Degge, 1977), rather than accepting it as a measure of a child's factual knowledge about a place. The drawing or map a child produces is not just a convenient tool for knowledge assessment but also an important part of geographic understanding (Kurz, 1983). Maps are complex, symbolic representations (Downs & Liben, 1988) and map skills develop slowly with age and experience (Liben & Downs, 1989c). Thus, a theoretical approach to map understanding is essential for geography and art educators alike.

Children's Spatial Concepts

Young children's abilities to use maps and related graphic representations rely on the mastery of two spatial concepts. First, the child must realize that the map is a "spatial transformation" of an object or world, real or imaginary (Downs & Liben, 1990, p. 16). Next the child must understand the "spatial relations" among self, map, and the represented object or world (Downs & Liben, 1990, p. 16).

Piaget and Inhelder (1956) produced the "most relevant and best articulated" (Downs & Liben, 1990, p.

16) psychological theory of the development of spatial concepts. Downs and Liben use the Piagetian analysis of projective spatial concepts to suggest theories of maps and mapping supported by data from their study of 3- to 8-year-olds performing mapping tasks.

The Piagetian position is that children slowly develop increasingly complex spatial concepts through their interactions with the environment. First young children master topological spatial concepts by which they understand qualitative relations between objects including proximity, order, and separation. Later children construct projective spatial concepts which help them understand the relative importance of viewpoint concerning spatial relations between objects. And finally older children develop Euclidean concepts which involve the use of a stable reference system (horizontal and vertical axes) to represent locations and extensions in space. This conceptual system continues to be criticized (Kurz, 1983; McFee & Degge, 1977) and modified (Newcombe, 1989) but it is useful for "organizing the study of children's abilities to produce and interpret graphic representations of spatial environments" (Downs & Liben, 1990, p. 17).

Downs and Liben use the Piagetian model to analyze young children's spatial operations and to design visual tasks aimed at map understanding. The model of projective space was particularly helpful for examining the development of children's map understanding. Central to the Piagetian model of projective space and map use is the realization that viewers at different viewpoints have differing views of space. This means children can identify and locate the views and coordinate them. When children understand the ways in which views change from different viewing angles and distances, then they can compute bearings on graphic representations of space. According to Piaget, this understanding of projective space occurs in children during early to middle school years.

Downs and Liben (1990) present two types of data supporting this position. They found that children (3- to 6-years-old) had difficulty on mapping tasks requiring an understanding of point of view. An interview study (using an aerial photograph and a road map) and a series of classroom activities were used to assess and expand their map understanding.

Conclusions and Implications

Overhead Viewpoints

Findings from one set of interviews and classroom activities with 3- to 6-year-olds were used to suggest that some children have difficulty in interpreting or recognizing aerial photos and producing a drawing of a bird's eye view of an environment. Downs and Liben

conclude that the ability to recognize and use an overhead viewing point develops gradually. They noted that the young children "did not fail" to draw overhead views, but instead they were "unable to avoid" drawing the elevation of a building (Downs & Liben, 1990, p. 19).

They argue that most young children have not directly experienced overhead viewpoints except in limited instances such as observation platforms or airplane windows. However children are indirectly exposed to such bird's eye views through video, television, movies, and print media. Other geographers (Blaut & Stea, 1971; Hart, 1979) argue that these experiences along with toy play with scale models of environments are crucial to developing young children's understanding of the mapping process. These direct and indirect experiences with overhead viewpoints require and further develop spatial ability and visual skills in young children.

Implications for educators are clear. Young children need an appreciation of alternative and especially hypothetical views of space. We need to ask young children to imagine they are birds or ants, and then ask them what the world would look like. We need to make sure they encounter maps and other graphic representations (photos, video, drawings) that vary the viewing angle. They should produce a variety of map forms and display and discuss this graphic work as confidently as they do their other artwork (Guilfoil, 1986; Kurz, 1983).

In this way, young children can use visual and spatial skills to develop a map understanding that is flexible and unrestricted.

View Coordination

Findings from a second set of tasks were used to suggest that even school children do not yet have an integrated flexible understanding of space as seen from many viewpoints. When asked to coordinate views by identifying direction of view on more than one representation of the same space (photos, maps, computer graphics) their performance was low. Downs and Liben (1990) conclude that the children's projective spatial concepts are just being developed at this time and that they will master these later in life, as first suggested by Piaget and Inhelder (1956). Work in progress with fifth through seventh graders on these same tasks already indicates a higher level of performance (Downs & Liben, 1990).

Educators must realize that young school children have difficulty employing spatial concepts requiring a projective model of space (Kurz, 1983). Young children should be exposed to a variety of graphic representations of the same space from different angles. Adults can then help them translate from one graphic representation of the world to another and develop the visual and spatial skill needed in school and out of school.

Place Location

Findings from the last task were used to suggest that school children also have difficulty in matching locations on representations from different viewpoints of the same space. Children were asked to locate points using two depictions of local topography (a contour map and a three-dimensional relief model) which involved different viewpoints, graphic form, and scales. The children's performance was relatively low; however, individual differences in mapping strategies were notable! Work in progress with individual children is aimed at examining strategy choice and identifying the relative influences of age, task difficulty, and other factors (Downs & Liben, 1990).

Educators must recognize the individual differences in performance by children on these and other spatial tasks (McFee & Degge, 1977). As a group, children have difficulty matching locations (and bearings) on representations based on different viewpoints and as a group they will improve with age. However, individual differences in task performance and strategies used are striking! All young children need exposure to a variety of graphic representations from differing points of view. Geography and art educators need to employ a less restricted view of map forms and map functions (Kurz, 1983). Educators must also recognize and appreciate children's various levels of mapping strategies, as they unfold (Guilfoil, 1986).

Summary

Two issues emerge relative to the Downs and Liben (1990) study as it relates to early education in geography and art: (a) the need to establish a theoretical perspective on children's map understanding and (b) the practical value of adopting such a theoretical position.

First, this study was not used to test Piagetian theory but instead to identify operations necessary for map understanding in young children. Piaget's model of projective space was employed to identify spatial concepts within a developmental framework and to generate specific tasks for map understanding. For the 3- to 8-year-olds in this study the interaction between viewpoint and graphic form was central to their map understanding. Young children's ability to adopt and control hypothetical viewpoints develops slowly and is hampered by the graphic similarly between representations.

Second, with the probable linkage between maps and geographic education fueled by well meaning interdisciplinary visual art instruction, educators must ensure that maps are used appropriately with young children. This means that children need exposure to multiple representations of the same place, not a canonical view of the world; and to different viewpoints of spatial relationships, not rote learning of shapes and patterns. Children need to be allowed to master these spatial concepts at different rates with different strategies, and not be pressured to conform to age norms for performance standards for drawing ability or map use (Guilfoil, 1986; Kurz, 1983; McFee & Degge, 1977). The idea here is to encourage children to move toward a more flexible use of ideas for problem solving (Bloom, 1956; Bloom, 1987), but not through inflexible rote learning. Young children need to learn early that each form of a map is but one of many possible realizations of space. Then they are equipped with a "powerful and flexible tool" (Downs & Liben, 1990) for expressing spatial knowledge, their ideas and themselves.

Note: This article is dedicated to the memory of Kevin Lynch who died April 25, 1985. He had a strong concern for children and the place of environment in their development. He encouraged and supported others to do the same.

References

Blaut, J. M., & Stea, D. (1971). Studies of geographic learning. *Annals of the Association of American Geographics*, 61, 387-393.

Bloom, A. (1987). *The closing of the American mind*. New York: Simon and Schuster.

Bloom, B. S. (Ed). (1956). *Taxonomy of educational objectives: Cognitive domain*. New York: McKay.

Darling-Hammond, L. (1990, December). Achieving our goals: Superficial or structural reforms? Phi Delta Kappan, 286-295.

Downs, R. M., & Liben, L. S. (1988). Through a map darkly: Understanding maps as representations. The Genetic Epistomologist, 16, 11-18.

Downs, R. M., & Liben, L. S. (1990). Getting a bearing on maps: The role of projective spatial concepts in map understanding by children. *Children's Environments Quarterly*, 7(1), 15-25.

Gauvin, M. (Ed.) (1985). To Kevin Lynch. *Children's Environments Quarterly*, 2(3), 2-3.

Guilfoil, J. K. (1986, March). Techniques for art educators in architectural design research and evaluation. *Art Education*, 10-12.

Hart, R. (1979). *Children's experience of place*. New York: Irvington.

Kurz, J. (1983). *Classroom spaces: A descriptive study of a one room school in Alaska*. Unpublished doctoral dissertation, University of Oregon, Eugene.

Liben, L. S., & Downs, R. M. (1989a). Educating with maps: Part I the place of maps. *Teaching Thinking and Problem Solving*, 11(1), 6-9.

Liben, L. S., & Downs, R. M. (1989b). Educating with maps: Part II the place of children. *Teaching Thinking and Problem Solving*, 11(2), 1-4.

Liben, L. S., & Downs, R. M. (1989c). Understanding maps as symbols: The development of map concepts in children. In H. W. Reese (Ed.), *Advances in child development and behavior* (Vol. 22, pp. 145-201). New York: Academic.

McFee, J., & Degge, J. R. (1977). *Art, culture and environment: A catalyst for teaching*. Belmont, CA: Wadsworth Publishing Co., Inc.

Natoli, S. J., Boehm, R., Kracht, J. B., Lanegran, D., Monk, J. J., & Morill, R. W. (1984). *Guidelines for geographic education: Elementary and secondary schools*. Washington, DC: Association of American Geographers.

Neperud, R. W. (1978). The what and why of environmental design education. *Art Education*, 31, 4-7.

Neperud, R. W. (1991, March). *A propositional view of environmental experiencing*. Paper presented at meeting of the National Art Education Association, Atlanta, GA.

Newcombe, N. (1989). The development of spatial perspective taking. In H. W. Reese (Ed.), *Advances in child development and behavior* (Vol. 22, pp. 203-247). New York: Academic.

Piaget, J., & Inhelder, B. (1956). *The child's conception of space* (F. J. Langdon & J. L. Lunzer, Trans.). New York: Norton. (Original published 1948).

Chapter 19
A Cross-Cultural Study of Partial Occlusion in Children's Drawings

Chun-Min Su
University of Illinois at Urbana-Champaign

Strategies for Creating Spatial Relationship

When a picture is drawn on a piece of paper, the flat picture plane serves well to represent the two-dimensional view, as long as it is consistent with the projective view. The vertical dimension of the picture plane can be used to correspond to the up-down aspects of an object or scene and the horizontal dimension to the right-left aspects. Thus, young children's favorite subject matter—the human figure—translates into an upright object drawn clearly and characteristically in vertical space (Arnheim, 1974).

However, a problem arises with the representation of more than one plane, for example, the near-far dimension in which one object overlaps another. Solutions vary among cultures and through historical time. The ancient Egyptian artists, to express ideas of constancy and immortality, chose the most characteristic aspect of an object or part of an object and combined these aspects in one picture plane without regard to the consistency of viewpoint. In the Chinese landscape tradition, artists also adopted a multiple-viewpoint perspective for expressing the immensity and the manifest greatness of nature. In these two artistic traditions, objects are given whatever size and angle accords with their purposes.

In traditional Western art, the system most commonly used to represent near-far dimensions is linear perspective. However, when a picture is drawn from one particular focal point, as with linear perspective, the rest of the view is sacrificed, and the nearer objects may partially occlude those that are behind. The representation produced by linear perspective most nearly approximates the images imprinted on our retinas. Possibly because of this identity with retinal images, nonartists, many adults, and children recognize linear perspective as the most "realistic" strategy for visual representation. "Modern" art in the Western art world, however, is more eclectic. To the untutored, or visually unsophisticated, it seems that there are many similarities between modern art and children's art. Seen from a developmental viewpoint, however, modern artists' subjective interpretations and representations of space are essentially different from children's fusion of space in drawings, because the motives behind them are different.

Literature Review

Most experimental findings show that children before the age of 8 years are not able to represent two objects, one situated behind the other, by the strategy of partial occlusion (Clark, 1897; Freeman, Eiser, & Sayers, 1977). These findings seem to support the proposition that the transition from intellectual realism to visual realism occurs at about the age of 8 (Luquet, 1927). Piaget and Inhelder (1969) valued Luquet's stages as constituting a remarkable introduction to the study of the mental image, which obeys laws closer to those of conceptualization than to those of perception. According to Piaget, drawings are reflections of the child's concepts; that is, children draw what they know instead of what they see (Piaget, 1956; Rosenblatt & Winner, 1988).

Production difficulty and instructional effect are the two most common interpretations used to explain the age difference (Cox, 1978, 1981, 1985; Freeman, 1980; Light & Simmons, 1983; Smith & Campbell, 1987; Su, 1991). But the proposition that young children's inability to represent partial occlusion is caused by the production difficulty of hidden line elimination is not confirmed by experimental findings (Light & MacIntosh, 1980). In terms of instructional effect, communication game designs do not elicit more partial occlusion drawings from 5- and 6-year-olds (Light & Simmons, 1983; Smith & Campbell, 1987), but a "robber and policeman" format does promote more partial occlusion drawings from 4-year-olds (Cox, 1981). In this chapter, an alternative explanation, that production difficulty may include other factors, is suggested.

Junction Line and Configuration

When one object is situated behind another, the configuration of these two overlapping objects is influenced by the junction line which separates these two objects. If the nearer object, shorter and narrower than the rear form, cannot occlude the farther object with a simple junction line, obviously the configuration of these two objects becomes more complex and difficult to draw. In the study described in this chapter, the drawing problem of partial occlusion between two overlapping objects is emphasized. Therefore, the production difficulty of the junction line which may affect the configuration (such as the shapes and sizes of the stimuli used to construct the scene) and, subsequently the drawing problem, is addressed.

Objectives

A wall, a simple rectangular shape which is easily drawn, is used in Cox's (1981) study. In terms of production difficulty, the partial occlusion presented by a figure behind a rectangular shape is a relatively easy task. To investigate the effect of stimuli, objects in irregular and smaller shapes than the wall are also used to create complex junction lines in the task.

Freeman and Janikoun (1972) suggest that using a familiar object in a drawing task would enable the child to use a long-term mental image ready to be expressed and minimize the dramatic effect that might induce novel styles. Because the present study emphasizes the spatial relationship between two objects, using fairly commonplace models may simplify the criteria of the task. Therefore, junction-line effect and the use of familiar objects in a drawing task were considered when four different objects were selected to serve as the farther object in this study to investigate the possible effect of the stimuli characteristics. The four objects in this task are a wall, a school bus, a little boy, and a "tower" constructed from small blocks.

Due to the dramatic improvements of young children's performance, Cox's "robber and policeman" study is reinvestigated. Hiding/nonhiding becomes another parameter in the experiments, because the hiding condition might not be the crucial factor in the results in question.

A well-established tradition in cognitive psychology assumes that the developmental stages are universal. To investigate a possible culture effect on this particular drawing task, the subject pool included Chinese as well as American children. Lowry and Wolf (1988) suggest that learning the arts (including music, visual arts, and calligraphy) in China relies on rote methods and focuses on skill building. However, visual art activities for young children are often self-initiated and not as rigid as learning in music or calligraphy. The present study attempts to investigate the culture effect from a developmental viewpoint. Young children of ages 4, 5, and 6, who have no privileged art training experiences and may represent the standard experiences of general population, are chosen as subjects for this study.

Method

The subject pool was 96 children. Half (the American culture group) were drawn from one local school and one day care center, and the other half (the Chinese culture group) from two kindergartens in Taipei. They were divided into three age groups: 32 children with a mean age of 4 years 5 months (range 4:0-4:9 years); 32 children with a mean age of 5 years 5 months (range 5:0-5:10 years); and 32 children with a mean age of 6 years 8 months (range 6:2-6:11 years). Within each culture and age group, the children were randomly assigned to two different conditions: 48 children were assigned to the experimental (hiding) condition, and 48 children to the control (nonhiding) condition.

Each child was randomly assigned to either the hiding or the nonhiding condition and was tested individually in the drawing task. To avoid a possible order effect, four different order conditions of presenting the nearer objects to the subjects were used. The subjects were randomly assigned to each order. In the hiding condition, the task was introduced as a game of "robber and policeman." A toy policeman was introduced to the subject. A robber, trying to hide from the policeman, was placed behind the nearer object (a wall, a school bus, a little boy, or a tower). Because the robber was taller than the nearer object, his head was still visible above the top edge. The subject was asked to pretend to be the policeman and was asked to draw "what you can see." In the nonhiding condition, the policeman was never shown during the task, and the robber was introduced as a man. After the nearer object was placed in front of the man, the subject was asked to draw "what you can see."

Drawings were classified according to the depicted spatial relationship between the nearer and farther objects in one of two categories: "partial occlusion" and "non-occlusion" drawings. The non-occlusion category included subcategories of horizontal separation, vertical separation, transparency, and other.

Results and Discussion

The Effects of Age and Stimuli

The results demonstrate that there is a significant difference between age 4 and the other two age groups, ages 5 and 6, and that the transition from intellectual realism to visual realism at age 4 to 5 is more significant than age 5 to 6. In this study, 69% of 4-year-olds and 94% of 6-year-olds produced partial occlusion drawings in the robber/man-behind-wall condition. This suggests that there is more partial occlusion in young children's drawings than found in previous studies. Even though an age shift in the production of partial occlusion drawings is demonstrated, the hiding game is ineffective. An examination of the effects of stimuli indicates that the differences between the nearer and farther objects in terms of shape and size have significant effects. Particularly when the nearer object is smaller than the farther one, the drawing task becomes more difficult for the children.

It is observed that children at these ages rarely use partial occlusion in their free drawings. However, the experiment results indicate that when the task demand is specified and salient, most children are able to solve the visual problem successfully. Vygotsky (1978) proposes that the developmental process lags behind the learning process, and this sequence results in "zones of proximal development." Under teacher guidance, children at these ages are ready to take the learning process of using partial occlusion for space representation. Once this process is internalized, as Vygotsky suggests, the skill becomes part of the child's independent developmental achievement.

The Effect of Culture

The experimental findings also show that there is a significant difference in the drawing task between the two culture groups. Of the American children, 78% produced partial occlusion drawings, while 57% of Chinese children did so. According to our observation during the experimental procedure, 4-year-olds in the Chinese culture show more hesitation in drawing activities. They tend to say, "I am not sure how to draw" before they start drawing, and they tend to show more caution in trying to make drawings look right. This phenomenon is reflected in the frequency of using erasers. The findings show significant differences: 40% of the Chinese children used erasers compared to only 15% of American children.

A possible explanation lies in how the Chinese children learn to write Chinese characters (the system of pictographs), a process which seems similar to draw-ing practice and starts early in kindergarten. Although the reading and writing practices start from simple letters and the child's own name (which unfortunately may not be simple), the sophisticated family relationship among Chinese characters makes it a tough task for all learners. Until the child has memorized several hundred characters, the written language is not ready for the child to use. Carlisle (1989) suggests that the nature of the written Chinese language may be one reason why Chinese teaching over the centuries has been based on imitating models. According to Carlisle's observation, the memorization system becomes the foundation of learning and affects all other schooling and adults' dealing with new technologies.

Eng (1954) suggests that the development of drawing at this stage may be regarded as an example of a natural process of learning. However, as Gardner (1990, 1991) suggests, the values and priorities of a culture can play an important and influential role in learning. Not only is it possible that the writing practice might enhance Chinese children's sense of right or wrong when using pencils to draw, but their strong sense of correctness may be also influenced by cultural values. Generally speaking, Chinese society emphasizes collectivism: The individual must behave correctly according to social norms. In addition, in Confucian tradition, Chinese teachers represent authority to their students and the students are expected to behave respectfully toward their teachers. Consider a situation in which a Chinese 4-year-old is asked to draw by the experimenter who is introduced by the teacher. Under these cultural influences, the child not only hesitates, but also feels obligated to draw correctly. The child's murmur of "I don't know how to draw," as well as his or her frequent erasures, indicate both an eagerness to perform correctly and habits derived from writing practice.

On the other hand, young American children pick up crayons or markers for free drawings more frequently than Chinese youngsters. During the drawing task, they draw with more confidence and use more bold and spontaneous lines. Besides the influence from American cultural values which emphasize individualism and free expression, the differing perspectives on using pencils to draw also explains the American children's drawing style in this task. Freeman (1980) regards drawing processes and spatial skills as problem-solving exercises for children. The more frequent free drawing activities by American children give them more opportunities to explore the strategies of representing depth and encourage them to feel free and confident to solve visual problems in the task.

Other possible factors may include Chinese children's familiarity with the multiple-viewpoint landscapes through traditional Chinese paintings or illustration books in their environment. For centuries, multiple-viewpoint perspective has been the most common strategy used by Chinese artists for expressing the immensity of nature. The illustrations in Chinese children's books frequently use multiple-viewpoint perspective to express the background scene of traditional Chinese stories. Possibly, the cultural artistic heritage also influences young children's perspective toward space representation. According to Winner (1989), in China, Chinese painting is taught in kindergarten and in elementary school by teaching children to imitate traditional schema used by the ancient masters. However, this kind of art lesson is not common in Taiwan, and the subjects in this study had not been given systematic instruction in Chinese painting. In the present study, the artistic heritage can not be concluded as the most significant factor contributing to the performance differences in the drawing task; however, it may be a secondary one.

The findings also show that the differences of producing partial occlusion drawings between the two culture groups decrease along with the increase of age. The 22% discrepancy between 4-year-olds of the two culture groups reduces to 12% between 6-year-olds. It suggests that American children develop the use of partial occlusion earlier than their Chinese counterparts, but the Chinese children catch up to the developmental stage of realism in a few years.

To summarize:

- The practice of writing Chinese characters in early childhood may reflect on the frequency of using erasers by Chinese children.

- The multiple-viewpoint perspective shown in the environment may have a certain influence, if not a dominant one, on Chinese children's space representation.

- The frequency of free-drawing activity by American children may account for their using more partial occlusion than their Chinese counterparts.

To further clarify the cultural effect on the drawing task, experiments along with a systematic survey and measurement of the frequency and types of children's drawing activities may be necessary for investigation.

Notes

Kindergarten education in Taiwan is not included in the public school system. A private kindergarten is a combination of kindergarten curriculum and day-care service. Children in a private kindergarten are grouped by age in different classes.

One subject consistently insisted on drawing the nearer object on one page and the farther object on another page to express the spatial relationship of front and behind. The four drawings made by this subject were classified under the category of "other."

References

Arnheim, R. (1974). *Art and visual perception*. Berkeley: University of California Press.

Carlisle, B. (1989). The fourth good: Observations on art education in China. *Journal of Aesthetic Education, 23*(1), 17-39.

Clark, A. B. (1897). The child's attitude towards perspective problems. In E. Barnes (Ed.), *Studies in education* (Vol. I, pp. 283-294). Stanford, CA: Stanford University Press.

Cox, M. V. (1978). Spatial depth relationships in young children's drawings. *Journal of Experimental Child Psychology, 26,* 551-554.

Cox, M. V. (1981). One thing behind another: Problems of representation in children's drawings. *Educational Psychology, 1*(4), 275-287.

Cox, M. V. (1985). One object behind another: Young children's use of array-specific or view-specific representations. In N. H. Freeman & M. V. Cox (Eds.), *Visual order: the nature and development of pictorial representation,* (pp. 188-200). London: Cambridge University Press.

Eng, H. (1954). *The psychology of children's drawings*. London: Routledge & Kegan Paul.

Freeman, N. H. (1980). *Strategies of representation in young children*. London: Academic Press.

Freeman, N. H., Eiser, C., & Sayers, J. (1977). Children's strategies in producing 3-D relationships on a 2-D surface. *Journal of Experimental Child Psychology, 23,* 305-314.

Freeman, N. H., & Janikoun, R. (1972). Intellectual realism in children's drawings of a familiar object with distinctive features. *Child Development, 43,* 1116-1121.

Gardner, H. (1990). *Art education and human development*. Los Angeles: The Getty Center for Education in the Arts.

Gardner, H. (1991). *To open minds*. New York: Basic Books.

Light, P. H., & MacIntosh, E. (1980). Depth relationships in young children's drawings. *Journal of Experimental Child Psychology, 30,* 79-87.

Light, P. H., & Simmons, B. (1983). The effects of a communication task upon the representation of depth relationship in young children's drawings. *Journal of Experimental Child Psychology, 35,* 81-92.

Lowry, K., & Wolf, C. (1988). Art education in the People's Republic of China: Results of interviews with Chinese musicians and visual artists. In H. Gardner & D. Perkins (Eds.), *Art, mind & education,* (pp. 89-98) Urbana & Chicago: University of Illinois Press.

Luquet, G. H. (1927). *Le dessin enfantin*. Paris: Delachaux & Niestle.

Piaget, J. (1956). *The origins of intelligence in children*. New York: International University Press,Inc.

Piaget, J., & Inhelder, B. (1969). *The psychology of the child*. New York: Basic Books.

Rosenblatt, E., & Winner, E. (1988). The art of children's drawing. In H. Gardner & D. Perkins (Eds.), *Art, mind & education,* (pp. 3-16). Urbana & Chicago: University of Illinois Press.

Smith, L., & Campbell, J. (1987). One thing behind another: A school based study of children's drawing abilities. *Educational Psychology, 7*(4), 283-293.

Su, C. M. (1991). One object behind another: Problems of partial occlusion in children's drawings. *Visual Arts Research, 17*(1), 52-64.

Vygotsky, L. S. (1978). *Mind in society: The development of higher psychological processes*. Cambridge, MA: Harvard University Press.

Winner, E. (1989). How can Chinese children draw so well? *Journal of Aesthetic Education, 23*(1), 41-63.

Chapter 20
Educating the Artistically Gifted Student in Early Childhood

Andra L. Nyman
University of Georgia at Athens

Although extensive research has been conducted on the nature of creativity and intellectual giftedness (Guilford, 1956, 1967; Parnes, 1963; Renzulli, 1977, 1978; Torrance, 1976), the developmental patterns and characteristics of the young artistically gifted individual have not been fully investigated. Unfortunately the lack of research has contributed to the low status and funding for programs of early education in the visual arts.

Over the past 50 years, scholars in the field of art education have provided recommendations for programs for school-aged students. Research by Lowenfeld (1957), Lansing (1967), Lark-Horowitz, Lewis and Luca (1973), Kellogg (1969), Gardner (1980), and Golomb (1981), as well as others, endeavored to identify patterns of development and describe characteristics of the artwork created by young children. Only in recent years has the focus turned towards the development of the preschool-aged child. Herberholz and Hanson (1985), Smith (1983), Colbert and Taunton (1990) and others have brought the importance of such goals into clearer focus.

The question of whether one should identify and program differentially for the student who shows indications of early artistic ability has not been resolved. Some educators and researchers believe that the developmental process should not be interfered with and that identification need not occur until later during the elementary school years. Clark and Zimmerman (1984) question whether evidence of artistic talent will be apparent until the student has fully matured into adulthood or whether "the early display of artistic talent" will "persist into adulthood" (p. 46).

Although this viewpoint is still open to debate, the rapidly growing number of programs for early childhood education along with increased numbers of students in preschool and kindergarten programs should provide rich ground for further study. These questions call for both short-term and longitudinal studies of artistically gifted individuals.

An alternative view suggests that early ability in any area of artistic (or intellectual) functioning should be recognized and fostered in order to provide the most supportive and responsive learning environment possible for children to grow to their fullest capacity (Karnes, 1987; Torrance, 1976). Voicing support for the early identification of intellectually advanced children, Robinson, Roedell, and Jackson (1979) stated:

> Early identification creates the opportunity for early intervention. The parent who is aware of a child's special abilities can plan intelligently for appropriate, challenging educational experiences. The educator who has direct information about a child's advanced abilities can develop programs geared to the child's actual level of competence rather than to a level calibrated on the basis of chronological skills alone (p. 141).

This latter viewpoint, which supports the value of early identification of artistic talent, will serve as the foundation for the following discussion and will guide the investigation of issues related to this process.

Issues Related to Education of the Artistically Gifted

Three main questions will provide structure for the argument that early artistic ability should be identified and fostered. The first question, "What is known about the young artistically gifted child?", will be examined through discussion of the research on identification of early talent in art. The second question, "What is known about the characteristic traits of young artistically talented children?", will be examined through discussion of current educational practices and programs for the artistically gifted. Finally, the question "How can these students best be served?, will be answered through summarization of the literature on current educational practices for the artistically gifted. These issues will, it is hoped, provide guidance for teachers who may be interested in possible models and methods for working with young artistically gifted students. After a review of the literature on characteristics and identification procedures and programs, recommendations for further research related to issues associated with education for the artistically gifted will be offered.

Because the terms used in the literature on education for the gifted and talented vary greatly, a brief comment may be needed to clarify the choice of terms used in the following discussion. According to Passow (1980), "the more than fifty-one different terms used to designate children with potential for outstanding achievement in the areas of intellectual, artistic or mechanical areas, reflects the lack of a uniformly accepted definition by either school practitioners or researchers" (p. 1).

This variation parallels the many labels that have been used to describe students with special needs. Unfortunately, the need for terms that refer to educational strengths or needs is a reality in the current educational bureaucracy, in which the formula for funding programs for the special needs of students is directly related to identification, labeling, and head counts. As Passow states, "identification is for the purpose of educational planning, not simply for the purpose of discovery and record keeping" (1980, p. 3). Zimmerman warns that further study of the effects of labeling should be conducted in order to avoid negative outcomes. She recommends that "approaches to labeling of students can [then] be formulated that nurture student's art talents and encourage them to develop their abilities in programs designed for their specific needs and eventually help them to contribute to society" (1985, p. 40).

For the sake of this discussion, the term "artistically gifted" will be used to refer to students who have special or advanced abilities or skills related to the visual arts, unless the use of a different term is required by a direct quotation or specific context.

Characteristics of the Artistically Gifted Child

According to one definition accepted widely by educators, gifted and talented children are those identified by professionally qualified persons who by virtue of outstanding abilities are capable of high performance. These are children who require differentiated educational programs and services beyond those normally provided by the regular school program in order to realize their contribution to self and society. Children capable of high performance include those with demonstrated achievement and/or potential ability in any of the

following areas: 1) general intellectual ability, 2) specific academic aptitude, 3) creative or productive thinking, 4) leadership ability, 5) visual and performing arts and 6) psychomotor ability (Marland, 1972, p. 10).

Early evidence of giftedness in art may be noticed in either behavioral traits and/or in characteristics of artwork created by the child (Hurwitz, 1983). An early interest in art and in art-related activities is often exhibited by the artistically gifted child. Students may also exhibit evidence of a rapid transition through the usual stages related to artistic development and graphic representation. According to Hurwitz, students who are visually gifted may have extended periods of concentration, may be highly self-motivated, and "may prefer art activity to television, sports and other forms of entertainment" (1983, p. 20).

The artwork created by children as young as preschool age may show an intuitive sophistication in terms of composition or may be highly complex and elaborate. Hurwitz states that "complexity and elaboration are directly related to sensitivity to detail and the use of memory" (1983, p. 24).

Other possible indicators may be the child's love for drawing, painting, sculpting, or the like; the child's deep absorption and great joy in those activities; the child's development of an "understanding" of the subject matter gained through the process of drawing it; skillful communication through visual arts media; and/or the ability to "capture the essence of whatever he draws or otherwise interprets through visual arts" (Torrance, 1980, p. 54). Other traits which may be characteristic of the artistically gifted child or the child's artwork are:

- Advanced fine motor skills.
- Unusually keen observation skills.
- Advanced graphic representational ability shown in elaborate, highly detailed, and accurate drawings.
- The capacity of creating artwork displaying an advanced level of narrative quality.

The identification of a child as "gifted" or "talented" is most often initiated by the teacher, or possibly by the teacher and the child's parents. Unfortunately, most teachers do not receive adequate training to enable them to understand the special characteristics and needs of the gifted and talented. There is documented evidence that little training of this sort is provided during the educational coursework for teachers preparing for elementary school teaching, with even less emphasis in this aspect of training for teachers for the preschool levels. Although the identification of "children who show their giftedness through the visual arts" is often difficult at the preschool and primary levels, according to Clark, "such identification is important if the proper encouragement is to occur" (1983, p. 286). Presently, research is inconclusive with regard to the procedures for, and the value of, identification of students at the early childhood levels. Further study of the identification process may be necessary if appropriate preparation for such responsibilities is to be included in the training for teachers.

The following discussion focuses on the findings of research on beliefs and knowledge held by teachers concerning the nature of giftedness and talent. In a study conducted by Wolfle and Southern (1989), teachers who taught in preschool and primary grade programs in Ohio and Virginia were asked to respond to a questionnaire that listed traits indicative of giftedness. The items related to the following categories: cognitive, talent, personality, physical and social. The survey conducted by Wolfle and Southern included items related to behaviors frequently associated with giftedness, as well as behaviors thought to have low correlation to giftedness. The teachers in this study rated cognitive traits as more indicative of giftedness. Traits associated with talents in creativity or the arts were not as highly rated nor as frequently cited, even though specific directions were given to consider characteristics which might indicate artistic or musical abilities.

The items cited most frequently as "most likely indicators of giftedness," in both open-ended and research-generated tasks, were:

1. Understands abstract concepts.
2. Is curious.
3. Reads and was self-taught.
4. Has an ability to generate unusual comparisons and categorizations.
5. Learns exceptionally rapidly.
6. Possesses insight into cause and effect relationships.
7. Possesses a large storehouse of information.
8. Chooses advanced or challenging activities or hobbies.
9. Has diverse, frequently self-directed activities.
10. Is highly imaginative (Wolfle & Southern, 1989).

While most of these traits or behaviors reflect the intellectually gifted individual, some have also been mentioned in the literature on the creative or artistically talented (Renzulli, 1977; Torrance, 1976, 1979). Many artistically talented students possess traits such as the ability to generate unusual comparisons and to perform in self-directed and highly imaginative ways in art activities.

The Identification Process

One common rationale for identification and programming has focused on the arguments made by Gallagher (1975), Passow (1980) and others, which support the premise that gifted children who have not been provided with challenging educational opportunities by the middle elementary grades often become underachievers. This situation is often impossible to reverse and students are not as likely to meet their full potential (Karnes, 1987, p. 12).

The work of Karnes and associates supports the need for early identification of both intellectual and artistic abilities. Extensive research on early childhood education conducted since 1970 in the area of special education, education of the culturally disadvantaged, and more recently, gifted education, has served to guide the development of programs for early childhood education throughout the nation (Karnes, 1987; Shwedel & Stoneburner, 1978). Programs for preschool and primary-level gifted children have been developed on the basis of conceptual models which reflect approaches ranging from Guilford's Structure of the Intellect (Guilford, 1956) to the open classroom (Karnes, 1987).

In the models developed by Karnes, teachers play an important role in the identification of students in the areas of talent as well as intellectual, social, or psychomotor abilities. Although originally designed for use in the program called Retrieval and Acceleration of Promising Young Handicapped and Talented children (RAPYHT), the talent screening instrument may provide guidance for the teacher who is looking for a composite list of some of the behaviors which might be used in identification of young children with talents.

The following screening instrument is used as an assessment tool for identifying strengths and needs in the area of artistic talent (Karnes, 1987, p. 45). Items which appear on the screening instrument are:

1) Works seriously on art projects and gets much satisfaction from them, 2) experiments with different art materials and uses them in original ways, or produces art which is very original, 3) has advanced skills in using art materials and does art work which is exceptional in composition (balance, unity, use of space), design, color, and 4) shows a very strong interest in and remembers in great detail what she or he has seen. (Karnes, 1987, p. 48)

This instrument is designed to identify children who exhibit signs of early ability and also includes traits in the areas of creative, intellectual, and leadership areas (p. 45-48). The traits which are used to serve as indicators for creative abilities are:

1) Often has many ideas or solutions to problems for a given situation, 2) elaborates or adds detail to artwork or conversation, 3) is highly imaginative in artwork, use of materials, or ideas, and often gives unusual responses, 4) is flexible (i.e., able to approach a problem or use materials in more than one way) (Karnes, 1987, p. 45).

Investigation of methods used in the identification process in a variety of programs indicates a range of assessments including;

- Portfolios or sets of art works.
- Identification checklists based on theoretical constructs developed by Renzulli, Torrance and others.
- Interviews.
- Visual arts tests (based on painting and drawing experiences).
- Creativity tests.
- Auditions.
- Nominations by the teacher, self, or professional artists and community people. (Moody, 1983)

Observation of performance and evaluation of products may provide for better assessment of art ability than tests (Torrance, 1980).

Programs for the Young Artistically Gifted Child

During the early 1970s, interest in the development of programs for children with both special needs or talents increased, as laws were enacted which supported the student's rights to an appropriate education in the least restrictive environment. Under the direction of Sidney Marland, then U.S. Commissioner of Education, a subgroup of gifted and talented students was specifically identified who showed capabilities of high performance in the visual and performing arts. From the document generated as the Marland Report (Marland, 1972), Public Law 93-380, the Special Projects Act of 1975, was enacted. This law established the term, gifted and talented, as applicable for youth identified at the preschool through secondary levels as learners with potential for high performance in the areas of the visual arts. Furthermore, it established their rights to educational services geared specifically towards their special abilities and needs.

Recommendations by leaders in the field of education for the gifted and talented called for the development and identification of a range of services which could provide the opportunities needed for these students. Currently, models for programs exist in school programs, museums, magnet schools, and afterschool and Saturday school programs (both community- and university-supported), and through individual or small group instruction conducted by artists and art teachers. As Torrance states,

Schools cannot provide all of the needed resources for creative children and adults. Frequently, the needed resources may not even be available in the community. Thus policies and practices are needed at all levels—community, city, county, regional, national, and international—that facilitate access to the resources needed by creative children and adults (1979, p. 370).

It is important to recognize that the goals, structure, curriculum and identification processes may vary from one setting to the next (see Hurwitz, 1983, and Moody, 1983, for examples). Recommendations for program design, goals, and objectives of leaders from the fields of gifted education and art education can provide valuable directions for program development.

According to Clark and Zimmerman (1984), curriculum for the high-ability art student should be more demanding, be offered at an accelerated pace, and require a higher level of achievement and a greater amount of material to be learned, than the program offered to average or below-average students. This program should be implemented in a manner that allows students to work independently, at their own pace, in order to optimize learning. Valuable experiences can be provided for "sophisticated inquiry based on role models of the artist, art critic, art historian, or aesthetician", as well as through "a related series of learning experiences in one media or about one major skill or concept" (Clark & Zimmerman, 1984, p. 34). Although the recommendations made by Clark and Zimmerman are aimed towards programs for older students, many of the recommendations may also serve as principles for programs for the young artistically gifted child.

Teaching strategies may also be adopted from a variety of sources. One strategy which lends itself effectively to classroom use is the center-based approach. Chetelat (1981) suggested one such application for individual investigation of visual arts concepts and art works through an independent learning environment. The study of drawings and paintings created by great artists can be stimulated through the independent examination of books and reproductions in combination with guided activities for exploration and direct application of observed techniques. One such lesson, suggested by Chetelat (1981), focused on landscape drawings created by Cezanne and Van Gogh. It directed the students to create drawings of scenes in their own community using line to create contours of objects, as well as textured and patterned surfaces, in much the same ways that the artist had done. This model might be adapted for use in a regular classroom and might be monitored by an art specialist to provide opportunities for the artistically gifted student. This activity might also be simplified and integrated into a program for younger children by using art works and narratives which have special meaning for the young child.

The most important goal in the education of the gifted and talented is that students receive educational opportunities designed for their specific strengths and needs. This differentiation of instruction can be accomplished through the means of an organized program or the use of an Individualized Education Plan (IEP). The IEP allows the teacher to identify the present level of functioning and set both annual goals and short-term objectives which are focused on the special needs of the student (Whitmore, 1985). The IEP can be specific in terms of recommendations for activities and services and can be used to ensure differentiation from the regular program of instruction.

Recommendations for Further Research

Although much of the research in the education of artistically gifted students has focused on primary- and secondary-level students, there is recognition that the early years are important to the development of graphic capabilities and artistic strengths. Presently, increased numbers of young children are attending preschool and kindergarten programs, and the education of teachers has changed, placing a strong emphasis on the importance of early intervention and learning. Although successful programs are currently being implemented, further study into issues surrounding identification and assessment of early abilities will assist in defining the nature and scope of future programs for the education for the artistically gifted.

Research is needed into the nature of early giftedness and appropriate methods of identification. There is also a need for the art field to further examine the nature of creativity in the visual arts. LaChapelle (1983) and others have expressed concern over the lack of focus on creativity in the visual arts, as most existing research has been conducted on the nature of creativity as it relates to intellectual abilities or academic subject areas. There has been little research on artistically talented students as a whole, and further inquiry into the unique abilities and needs of this population is warranted.

Research into the nature of the performance of the gifted on spatial tasks such as drawing, as well as the development of the process of organizing knowledge for

depiction, would further our understanding of the process of the development of graphic representation. This area of research, which has been the focus of work by Smith (1981), Wilson and Wilson (1977, 1982), Colbert and Taunton (1988), Golomb (1981), Gardner (1980), and others would serve to further our ability to effectively address program needs for the artistically gifted during early childhood. It would be helpful to understand what effects language and socialization play in the development of artistic abilities. Further research of the sort which has been conducted by Thompson and Bales (1991) may help to define the interaction of the intellectual abilities associated with language development with the development of artistic skill. Research is also needed to address questions of whether students are best served in programs based on acceleration or enrichment. Current and future programs for artistically gifted young children would benefit greatly from further research in these many areas.

Finally, the importance of providing specialized training for teachers in the areas of gifted education can not be stressed strongly enough. The role of a teacher for the gifted and talented ranges widely and includes:

- Serving as major organizer of enrichment activities.

- Gathering and disseminating information about resources, opportunities and innovative practices.

- Promoting integration between special programs and regular curricula.

- Identifying and directly instructing individuals in need of special services.

- Advising students, parents, and other teachers on the best ways to provide opportunities for optimal learning and achievement. (Jenkins-Friedman, Reis & Anderson, 1984)

Serving the needs of young artistically gifted students may, indeed, become a larger issue with the increased interest in early childhood education and the growing numbers of students in programs at that level.

References

Chetelat, F. (1981). Visual arts education for the gifted elementary level art student. *Gifted Child Quarterly, 25* (4), 154-158.

Clark, B. (1983). *Growing up gifted.* Columbus, OH: Charles E. Merrill Publishing Company.

Clark, G. & Zimmerman, E. (1984). *Educating artistically talented students.* Syracuse, NY: Syracuse University Press.

Colbert, C. & Taunton, M. (1988). Problems of representation: Preschool and third grade children's observational drawing of a three-dimensional model. *Studies in Art Education, 29* (2), 115-125.

Colbert, C. & Taunton, M. (1990). *Discover art: Kindergarten.* Palo Alto, CA: Davis Publications.

Gallagher, J. J. (1975). *Teaching the gifted child* (2nd ed.). Boston: Allyn and Bacon.

Gardner, H. (1980). *Artful scribbles*. New York: Basic Books.

Golomb, C. (1981). Representation and reality: The origins and determinants of young children's drawings. *Review of Research in Visual Arts Education, 14*, 36-48.

Guilford, J. P. (1956). The structure of the intellect. *Psychological Bulletin, 53*, 267-293.

Guilford, J. P. (1967). *The nature of human development*. New York: McGraw Hill.

Herberholz, B & Hanson, L (1985). *Early childhood art*. (3rd Ed.). Dubuque, IA: W. C. Brown.

Hurwitz, A. (1983). *The gifted and talented in art: A guide to program planning*. Worchester, MA: Davis Publications, Inc.

Jenkins-Friedman, R. Reis, S. M., & Anderson, M.A. (1984). Professional training for teachers of the gifted and talented. Reston, VA: Eric Clearinghouse on Handicapped and Gifted Children.

Karnes, M. (1987). Issues in educating young gifted children: Promising practices. (Leadership accessing monograph: Education of gifted and talented youth. Indianapolis: Indiana Department of Education. Eric Document Reproduction Service (ED 315 946).

Kellogg, R. (1969). *Analyzing children's art*. Palo Alto, CA: National Press Books.

LaChapelle, J. R. (1983). Creativity research: Its sociological and educational limitations. *Studies in Art Education, 24* (2), 131-139.

Lansing, K. M. (1967). *Art, artists and art education*. New York: McGraw-Hill Book Company.

Lark-Horowitz, B., Lewis, H. & Luca, M. (1973). *Understanding children's art for better teaching*. (2nd ed.). Columbus, OH: Charles E. Merrill Publishing Co.

Lowenfeld, V. (1957). *Creative and mental growth*. (3rd ed.). New York: Macmillan.

Marland, S. (1972). Education of the gifted and talented. Report to the Congress of the United States by the U. S. Commissioner of Education. Washington, D.C.: U.S. Government Printing Office.

Moody, B. J. (1983). *Visual arts in gifted programs: Thirty-one current programs described*. Greeley, CO: Creative Arts Center.

Parnes, S. (1963). Education and creativity. Teachers College Record, 64, 331-229.

Passow, A. H. (1980). *Education for gifted children and youth: An old issue—A new challenge*. Ventura, CA: Ventura County Superintendent of Schools Office.

Renzulli, J. S. (1977). *The enrichment triad model: A guide for developing defensible programs for the gifted*. Mansfield Center, CT: Creative Learning Press.

Renzulli, J. S. (1978). What makes giftedness? Reexamining a definition. *Phi Delta Kappan, 60* (3), 180-184, 261.

Robinson, H. B., Roedell, W. C. & Jackson, N. E. (1979). Early identification and intervention. In A. H. Passow, (Ed.), *The gifted and talented: Their education and development*. (pp. 138-154) Chicago: National Society for the Study of Education.

Shwedel, A. M. & Stoneburner, R. (1978). Identification. In M. B. Karnes (Ed.), *The underserved: Our young gifted children*. (pp. 19-39) Reston, VA: The Council for Exceptional Children.

Smith, N. R. (1981). Developmental origins of graphic symbolization in the paintings of three to five year olds. *Review of Research in Visual Arts Education, 13*, 9-17.

Smith, N. R. (1983). *Experience and art: Teaching children to paint*. New York: Teachers College Press.

Thompson, C. & Bales, S. (1991). Michael doesn't like my dinosaurs: Conversations in a preschool art class. *Studies in Art Education, 33* (1), 43-55.

Torrance, E. P. (1976). *Guiding creative talent*. Melbourne, FL: Robert E. Krieger Publishing Co., Inc.

Torrance, E. P. (1979). Unique needs of the creative child and adult. In A. H. Passow, (Ed.), *The gifted and talented: Their education and development* (pp 352-371). Chicago: National Society for the Study of Education.

Torrance, E. P. (1980). Extending the identification of giftedness: Other talents, minority and handicapped groups. In *Educating the preschool/primary gifted and talented* (pp. 43-58). Ventura, CA: Office of the Ventura County Superintendent of Schools.

Whitmore, J. R. (1985). Developing individual education programs (IEPS) for the gifted and talented. Reston, VA: Eric Clearinghouse for the Gifted and Talented.

Wilson, B. & Wilson, M. (1977). An iconoclastic view of the imagery sources in the drawings of young people. *Art Education, 30* (1), 5-12.

Wilson, B. & Wilson, M. (1982). *Teaching children to draw*. Englewood Cliffs: NJ: Prentice-Hall.

Wolfle, J. and Southern, W. T. (1989). Teachers' assessment of preschool and primary giftedness. The United States Department of Education, Office of Educational Research and Development: (Eric Document Reproduction Service ED 315 945).

Zimmerman, E. (1985). Towards a theory of labeling artistically talented students. *Studies in Art Education, 27* (1), 31-42.

Chapter 21
Multiculturalism and the Tender Years: Big and Little Questions

Elizabeth Manley Delacruz
University of Illinois at Urbana—Champaign

Art educators are currently reexamining the content and methodology of their programs of study, and reasserting basic questions about the nature and function of the visual arts curriculum with respect to an emerging focus on multiculturalism. As a larger social movement, multiculturalism is a framework for thinking about American society in which ethnic, religious, and cultural diversity are recognized as social realities to be embraced (Banks, 1984). Within the context of public and private schooling, multicultural education is dedicated to the realization that we live in a pluralistic society, one that is based, at least in principle, on the ideals on which our nation was founded: freedom, equality, and opportunity (Chapman, 1978).

Multiculturalists advocate a reconceptualized program of art education that deals specifically with the concepts of pluralism, globalism, and multicultural education as ways to focus on questions about knowledge, values, aesthetics, and opportunity. These concepts, although related, need to be distinguished (Daniel, 1991).

Pluralism refers to the idea that there are many truths, many lifestyles, and many products of human productivity and aesthetic sensibility that merit study (Blandy & Congdon, 1991). Pluralists look at art from a variety of perspectives and consider varying points of view. Globalism focuses on the world at large and the many unique peoples who inhabit it. Enhancing positive interhuman relations is an educational goal of globalism. Multicultural education generally refers to teaching children about the diverse ethnic groups that make up this country (Daniel, 1991). Cultural and ethnic diversity are celebrated and nurtured as unique and positive features of American society. A framework based on democracy, equality, and social responsibility underlies the multiculturalist's agenda as does fostering such a conceptual framework in the minds of students.

Art and Human Thought: The Humanities

Democracy, regard for individual differences, celebration of human potential, and a desire to explore questions and possibilities—these are the themes of a multiculturalist art program. These themes become clearer and more coherent when children interact in meaningful and connected ways with the intellectual, social, spiritual, and artistic endeavors of the diverse cultures that make up humankind. These endeavors are embodied in the humanities: the arts, philosophy, religion, and history. The organization of the humanities into coherent bodies of knowledge is the accomplishment of culture. Art educators may derive meaningful content and instructional strategies from these bodies of knowledge in developmentally appropriate and intellectually honest ways for children of all ages (Bruner, 1960; Katz & Chard, 1989).

Like their counterparts in the other humanities, art educators apply the best and most challenging ideas from various fields of professional inquiry. These include not only selected art disciplines (Clark, Day & Greer, 1987), but also related areas which inform and are informed by these art disciplines: archaeology, anthropology, psychology, mythology, structural and poststructural linguistics, and political science (Beyer, 1987). These disciplines, like the arts, are undergoing major revision (Margolis, 1987): Concepts and propositions once held to be immutable are now open to question, notably by those not in power. Approaching knowledge itself as provisional and contextual, multicultural educators may promote the advancement and proliferation of worthy ideas and make a lasting contribution to the storehouse of human thought.

Art works—as exemplars of cultural knowledge and desire, selected with diversity in mind—provide teachers with a rich source of human thought about the big and little questions of life, a source that should be shared with young learners before their attitudes become solidified in early adolescence (Chapman, 1978). Multicultural thinking may become the foundation on which young children build regard for the inherent potential of others and develop the motivation to act upon these beliefs. First and foremost, teachers must model the dispositions they wish to foster in their students (Katz & Chard, 1989).

The Moral Mandate: Diversity, Intercultural Understanding, and Social Action

Art education in a multicultural curriculum is morally committed to intercultural understanding (Lanier, 1980). Understanding art through culture and understanding culture through art are the educational objectives that reinforce multiculturalist goals. The multicultural art educator explores the ways in which values and meanings in art operate in the lives of people from both familiar and unfamiliar ethnic cultures, both within and outside the United States, understanding that these cultures are arenas of both stability and change (Clifford, 1987; McFee & Degge, 1977). Glaeser (1973) calls this a "celebration of cultures," a means of cherishing the uniqueness and integrity of cultures while also recognizing the shared dimension underlying all human experience.

Chapman (1985) and other advocates of multicultural education believe that the art curriculum should acknowledge the achievements of non-Western cultures, minority groups, and women and reflect the significance of folk art, the crafts, mass-produced objects, and mass-circulated images. These latter art forms until recent years were considered neither "fine" nor "exemplary" enough to merit serious study (Lanier, 1987). Chapman maintains that the underrepresentation of such groups' artistic accomplishments in the traditional art disciplines and in the art curriculum should be remedied because American society itself is unusually diverse and the underlying principle of equity must be served.

The moral mandate underlying multiculturalism will remind art educators of the picture-study curriculum at the turn of the 19th century, with its emphasis on human virtues and moral character (Chapman, 1978). But significant differences also exist. Artists are not romanticized as suffering geniuses, students are not trained solely on the imagery of aristocracies, and appreciation is no longer seen as a frill. Rather, interhuman understanding and an appreciation and support for the "artistry in varied lifestyles" is fostered. Intelligent, informed appreciation of the aesthetic and cultural similarities and differences that exist among us is the multiculturalist's educa-

tional goal. This is a different kind of appreciation, however, because this goal fosters not only purposeful thought but also purposeful behavior (Jagodzinski, 1982). In this view, multicultural education is not only about cultural facts but also about social issues, and the moral obligation of every citizen to work toward the American ideal of equity for all.

Curriculum development, like any institutionalized practice, is inherently a political venture. The programs of study employed legitimize and perpetuate selected beliefs and attitudes for future generations (Cherryholmes, 1987). Interest in this political dimension will continue to grow as more educators realize that when people of different traditions come in contact, differing values must be accommodated. For art educators, interest in multiple definitions of artistic value and significance will likewise grow as understanding increases that:

- The aesthetic framework in lived experience is inseparable from the moral and social frameworks (Lanier (1980).

- Each culture invents and preserves artistic traditions that re-present that culture's important concerns about the meaning and value of life.

Art, Culture, and Knowledge: Questions Becoming Curriculum

Multicultural art education enables children to make important connections between themselves and others by tapping into the rich artistic traditions of different cultures. For teachers, multiple perspectives offer the opportunity to guide young minds on the path of seeking answers to the big and little questions of human experience, questions that artists in every culture have asked (either directly or implicitly): Who am I? Where did I come from? How can I gain better control of my world? What will happen to me, to my family? What are my dreams, my wishes, my fears? Am I loved? Am I safe? These questions, simple and naive, form the basis of human thought and feeling about the nature and meaning of life. They creep—silently or not so silently—into the concerns of young minds and enter centuries-old philosophical, theological, and ethical traditions, perhaps steeped in mysticism, or even organized into dogmas, or made arcane in academic rhetoric, but certainly posed once again in the mute relics that populate the world's ethnological and art museums.

These questions underlie many (if not all) of the greatest intellectual, artistic, and cultural achievements of humanity. They transcend time and place, obliterate the distinctions between East and West, and narrow the gap between young and old. World art embodies these questions and provokes them in the viewer. Many educators believe that it is the opportunity to explore life's big and little questions that makes the school curriculum a meaningful venture for children (Giroux, Penna, & Pinar, 1981).

If we accept art as the aesthetic embodiment of human concern and desire, then the artistic and aesthetic traditions of all people become content worthy of study, notable not only for their underlying attention to big questions and universal problems, but for the unique and rich solutions presented in a tapestry of tools, bowls, blankets, healing implements, helmets, pendants, statues, paintings, carvings, songs, dances, dramatic enactments, poems, myths, and histories, both oral and written (Vogel, 1986). Art becomes not only the thing, the end product of refined craftsmanship or extraordinary vision, but also the vehicle or medium, the process by which closure is brought, if only temporarily, to human concerns.

Questions the teacher could ask of students might move from "What is this artist's work about?" and "Where do you think these artists got their ideas?" to "How many ways can we think about art?" and "How does art itself expand our thinking?" Countless examples of children's remarkable capacities for complex intellectual and philosophical reasoning suggest that these kinds of questions can become part of the curriculum (Anderson, 1986; Ecker, 1973; Matthews, 1984). Examining the objects and objectives of many cultures, young children may explore questions of concern not only to philosophers (What is the essence of life? What is truth? What is good? How do I know what I know?) or aestheticians (How is it art?), but questions directly relevant to themselves and to all of us: Am I safe? Am I loved? Is my family secure?

Other fundamental questions underlie the curriculum:

- How do we define art?
- What constitutes an understanding of art and its role in society?
- What learning experiences best foster or promote this understanding?

As we approach these questions, McFee (1987) asks us to consider both universal and culturally specific qualities of art. More importantly, she asks us to consider artistic traditions that support democratic values, including the institutions that sponsor, support, and maintain art: governmental agencies, museums, local civic centers, the mass media, public/private schools, and universities. Katz and Chard (1989) tell us that in the preschool and early elementary years, fostering dispositions, attitudes, and inclinations are primary educational objectives. For early childhood teachers, elementary teachers, and art teachers this means getting students involved in thinking about works of art in terms of the roles art plays in all aspects of life, particularly in the lives of its creators.

Art embodies important human concerns. In the contemplation of these concerns, as they are posed in aesthetic form, the lines between object and subject, between the objective and the subjective, are delightfully blurred. It is here that questions from many perspectives about art, and the questions of art, become the center of the curriculum. It is from this stance that a viable educational program may progress toward more academic questions such as:

- What does this art mean?
- How does this art form convey meaning?

To children, such questions may be posed in many forms:

- What is my art about?
- What events, experiences, objects, and desires are re-presented?
- What about this other work of art?
- What could it be about?
- How is it like my art?
- How is it different?
- What makes this work of art powerful, gentle, meaningful, enjoyable, disturbing?

These questions then inform and become the content of the curriculum by leading to open-ended and/or more structured studio explorations, the examination of design concepts, the development of skills in materials and processes, the motivations for critical analysis and reflection, and the connections to contextual, historical, and intercultural understanding.

Centering the Multicultural Art Curriculum

In a multicultural art curriculum the art, artifacts, crafts, ritual and domestic objects fashioned by generations of artisans become the subjects of interest that inform and expand children's frames of reference. The subject of interest is not limited, however, to formal and technical accomplishments, but includes meaning, symbolism, intention, function, and both relative and universal values. The subject is the artist, the culture, the purposeful processes and products of human concern. The subject is, finally, the student, centered in her or his own personal space of curiosity and intentionality, and in his or her interactions with others.

104   The multicultural curriculum does not center on design processes, criticism, history, and social studies per se; rather these disciplines become vehicles, like art-making itself, for enhancing and extending each child's ability to make sense of life, to attach value to certain aspects of life, to seek solutions to the problems of living, and to act upon them. The center is the self as it acts upon and within its intercultural realities. This is the instrumental value of art, and the ultimate goal of multicultural art education programs.

Art becomes the second center of the curriculum as it touches the lives of children and as it both carries and informs philosophy, religion, science, and history. For the very young, art making is a means of acting upon the world within the safety of personal space. Eisner (1978) observes that art making provides children with a sense of their own power to create desired effects and to explore concerns. Art making is inherently pleasurable in that it allows for unrestricted exploratory possibilities and experiences. Smith and Smith (1970) recognize this as the beneficial role of play. These authors see art making as a special mode of thinking and acting upon the world.

Art making is by its nature a construction of meaning and, as such, provides the evidence of meaningful inquiry. This is true for children, for adult artists, for artists and artisans in all cultures. The art of young children reflects "the flow of life around them, including social changes and technological advances" (Lark-Horovitz, Lewis, & Luca, 1973, p. 21). Their early symbol-making activities arise out of their relationships to their world, beginning with family and extending to home and community life and finally to the natural and constructed environments surrounding their homes (Gaitskell & Hurwitz, 1975). They favor themes that center around family, love and security, animals, natural scenery, and fantasy. In their own art, children depict the customs of everyday living, the surrounding world of plants and animals, and the imaginative world of dreams, spirits, and other-worldly entities.

Wilson and Wilson (1982) describe the art making activities of children as a self-defining process devoted to exploring the essential self, its consciousness, memories, desires, experiences, impressions, and feelings. "The questions Who am I? What am I? How am I? and What will I become? however implicitly asked, require a lifetime to answer" (Wilson & Wilson, 1982, p. 28). These questions connect children to artistic traditions and innovations in all times and places.

But art making should be only one part of the curriculum, even in the early years. Heightened and deepened artistic and aesthetic reflection and response are equally efficacious educational goals, and multiculturalists see them as crucial elements in the educational pro-

gram for young children. Looking back upon the experience of constructing their own meaningful art works, children develop personal perspective, attach values, and perhaps are motivated toward further, more refined, inquiry. Contemplating the art of others, children look beyond themselves and enhance their capacities for understanding. Finally, as they glimpse connections between art making and reflection and other organized bodies of knowledge, a bigger picture emerges in children's minds: the realization that things fit together, that people have similar questions all over the world, and that the process of asking questions is perhaps the most human characteristic of all.

Implementation Problems: From Theory to Practice

Although curriculum development has far to go, some notable work has already been done by veteran art educators (Chapman, 1978, 1985; Feldman, 1985, 1987; McFee & Degge, 1977) and others who have dedicated themselves to the idea that, for art education, educational reform means a complete reconceptualization of the art curriculum (Blandy & Congdon, 1987; Daniel, 1991; Stuhr, Petrovich-Mwaniki, & Wasson, 1992). These individuals call for art curricula which are more inclusive and, in multicultural terms, more authentic.

Interest in the meaning and significance of the art of other cultures presents several conceptual and practical problems for teachers. Which cultures and which art forms should be studied, and how should these art forms be studied? Attention to the formal and expressive qualities of these art forms is not enough; exploration of the symbolic meanings intended by their creators is equally crucial to an adequate appreciation of these works.

With the recent deluge of publications centering on one culture after another, the sheer magnitude of choice is enough to paralyze a teacher's attempts to be sensitive to ethnicity and to be authentic to the meaning, function, and artistic value of ethnic art. This problem is compounded by the fact that adequate and comprehensive educational resources dealing with minority, ethnic, women's and other "outsider" art have become available only recently. Teachers interested in implementing multicultural education must filter through seemingly incomprehensible volumes of incorrect, misinformed, or shallow representations of people and their art. These teachers must conduct research themselves in order to evaluate and use these resources, before they begin to design a meaningful and coherent program. Anyone who has taught in the public schools knows what a formidable task this really is, given the demands of the profession.

This is further complicated by a climate seemingly hostile to any hint of "values education" (Park, 1980; Parkay, 1985) or teaching about the spiritual or belief systems of other cultures. Multiculturalists need to respond cautiously. Indeed, some of the art forms appearing in museum collections and in the vastly expanding literature on world art are profoundly ritualistic objects used in connection with religious practices which Westerners find difficult to appreciate. Should such objects be censored from the curriculum, treated solely as aesthetic objects without attention to their spiritual meanings, or given patriarchal treatment as "practices conducted by less advanced cultures"? Or should they be treated equally, as meaningful objects whose meanings, however controversial, merit full disclosure?

Equally problematic are works of art created by many ethnic-American artists, works that deal with sexism, racism, poverty, violence, destruction of the natural environment, and genocide. Most teachers will look for "nice art," finding it inappropriate to expose impressionable young children to disturbing sexual, religious, or violent content.

Add to these problems the developmental question: What concepts, skills, and dispositions are desirable educational goals for the very young with respect to intercultural understanding and art appreciation? It is commonly held that the very young are not naturally inclined to take the perspective of another, that young children are centered solely on self (Parsons, 1987). Art educators do not even agree that the early learner needs exposure to art in activities beyond their own art making experiences. And if such exposure is deemed important, how much and in what kinds of learning encounters? Motivational and instructional questions now come into play, presenting complex choices.

Some Provisional Recommendations

For those teachers who, like me, are perplexed by the magnitude of the task of developing and implementing a multicultural curriculum, I can only offer the simplest of advice. Center your instruction on the reasons children make art (Leeds, 1986). Focus on those timeless human concerns posed as questions in this chapter, and build learning activities around the exploration of these themes and questions.

Start with a few good books written by contemporary scholars in the art of other cultures and become familiar with some of those scholars who have focused on multicultural education for the past two or three decades. Contact area agencies and individuals with a background in ethnic studies. Purchase some reproductions, audiotapes, videotapes, and children's books that deal with ethnic art and culture. Publishers are discovering that there is a market for these instructional resources and more resources are rapidly becoming available. Borrow ideas from the published art curricula that address, if only peripherally, the art of other cultures but do not be limited to their content and structure. Reshape your curriculum to fulfill your own educational goals.

It is not enough to just do art with the very young. It is also important to talk about art with them. Educators should value questions as much as answers (Giroux, Penna, & Pinar, 1981) and encourage children to pose their own questions. "Teacher talk" (Good & Brophy, 1978) should not drown out what children have to say.

Multicultural curricula must be infused into the art and school curricula throughout the academic year, throughout the early elementary years, and throughout the K-12 program and not, as Feldman (1987) advises, added on as occasional tokens, separate projects that give "special attention" to the "exotic" art of "other people." Nothing could be more irrelevant, even racist, than asking a group of little white kids to make "African" masks or "Indian" sand paintings. Focus each child on the richness of her or his family heritage, the wonders of the neighborhood, and the many kinds of people who live there. Let children tame the wild and untamed animal world and pay tribute to the delicate and powerful ecology in which they thrive.

Bring children's art making back to their own lives, as these lives are motivated by, and made more meaningful in, their own cultural contexts. The contextual perspective makes the familiar more meaningful and the unfamiliar more concrete. It is a manner of approaching art works that allows children to see art in its own light. Finally, return again and again to the art of diverse cultures to explore commonalities and differences.

For multiculturalists, a major goal of art education is to teach students about the role of art in all aspects of life:

- To help them understand the relevance and significance of art in the larger context of human experience.

- To consider perspectives posed by people of different backgrounds.

- To develop a sense of both the commonality and the diversity of humankind.

- To reinforce each student's own sense of personal power and the social responsibility that comes with power.

The goals of multicultural art education reinforce those of the nation as a whole as it struggles and strives toward its original democratic ideals: freedom and equity based on an abiding respect for the integrity and dignity of every individual life (Chapman, 1978). Such regard for the inherent potential of the individual is made concrete in the art of the very young and underlies a multicultural art curriculum.

Note: The author wishes to acknowledge and thank Mary Stokrocki for her thoughtful commentary and generous assistance on an early draft of this paper.

References

Anderson, T. (1986). Talking about art with children: From theory to practice. *Art Education, 39* (1), 5-8.

Banks, J. A. (1984). *Teaching strategies for ethnic studies* (3rd ed.). Newton, MA: Allyn and Bacon.

Beyer, L. E. (1987). Art and society: Toward new directions in aesthetic education. *Journal of Curriculum Theorizing, 7*(2), 72-98.

Blandy, D., & Congdon, K. G. (1987). *Art in a democracy.* New York: Teachers College Press.

Blandy, D. & Congdon, K. G. (1991). *Pluralistic approaches to art criticism.* Bowling Green, OH: Bowling Green State University Popular Press.

Bruner, J. S. (1960). *The process of education.* Cambridge, MA: Harvard University Press.

Chapman, L. H. (1978). *Approaches to art in education.* New York: Harcourt Brace Jovanovich.

Chapman, L. H. (1985). Curriculum development as process and product. *Studies in Art Education, 26* (4), 206-211.

Cherryholmes, C. H. (1987). A social project for curriculum: Poststructural perspectives. *Journal of Curriculum Studies, 19*,(4), 295-316.

Clark, G. A., Day, M.D., & Greer, W. D. (1987). Discipline-based art education: Becoming students of art. *Journal of Aesthetic Education, 21*(2), 129-197.

Clifford, J. (1987). Of other peoples: Beyond the "Savage" paradigm. In H. Foster (Ed), *Discussions in contemporary culture* (Vol. 1, pp. 121-130). Seattle: Bay Press.

Daniel, V. A. (1991, September). *Beyond the traditional in art: Facing a pluralistic society.* Address given at the United States Society for Education Through Art Symposium, Columbus, OH.

Ecker, D. W. (1973). Analyzing children's talk about art. *Journal of Aesthetic Education, 7*(1), 58-73.

Eisner. E. W. (1978). What do children learn when they paint? *Art Education, 31*(3), 5-12.

Feldman, E. B. (1980). Anthropological and historical conceptions of art curricula. *Art Education, 33*(6), 6-9.

Feldman, E. B. (1985). *Thinking about art.* Englewood Cliffs, NJ: Prentice-Hall.

Feldman, E. B. (1987). *Varieties of visual experience,* (3rd Ed.).Englewood Cliffs, NJ: Prentice-Hall.

Gaitskell, C. D., & Hurwitz, A. (1975). *Children and their art.* New York: Harcourt Brace Jovanovich.

Giroux, H. A., Penna, A. N., & Pinar, W. F. (1981). *Curriculum & instruction: Alternatives in education.* Berkeley, CA: McCutchan.

Glaeser, W. (1973). Art, concepts of reality, and the consequences of "The Celebration of Peoples." *Studies in Art Education, 15*(1), 34-43.

Good, T. L., & Brophy, J. E. (1978). *Looking in classrooms.* New York: Harper & Row.

Jagodzinski, J. (1982). Art education as ethnology: Deceptive democracy or a new panacea? *Studies in Art Education, 9*(3), 5-7.

Katz, L. G., & Chard, S. C. (1989). *Engaging children's minds: The project approach.* Norwood, NJ: Ablex.

Lanier, V. (1980). Six items on the agenda for the eighties. *Art Education, 33*(5), 16-23.

Lanier, V. (1987). Misdirections and realignments. In Blandy, D., & Congdon, K. G. (Eds.), *Art in a democracy* (pp. 175-183). New York: Teachers College Press.

Lark-Horovitz, B., Lewis, H., & Luca, M. (1973). *Understanding children's art for better teaching* (2nd ed.). Columbus, OH: Charles E. Merrill.

Leeds, J. A. (1986). Teaching and the reasons for making art. *Art Education, 39*(1), 17-21.

Margolis, J. (1987). *Philosophy looks at the arts: Contemporary readings in aesthetics.* Philadelphia: Temple University Press.

Matthews, G. (1984). *Dialogues with children.* Cambridge, MA: Harvard University Press.

McFee, J. K. (1987). In D. Blandy & K. G. Congdon (Eds.), *Art in a democracy* (pp. ix-xii). New York: Teachers College Press.

McFee, J. K., & Degge, R. M. (1977). *Art, culture and environment.* Dubuque, IA: Kendall/Hunt.

Park, J. C. (1980). Preachers, politics, and public education: A review of right-wing pressures against public schooling in America. *Phi Delta Kappan, 61,* 608-612.

Parkay, F. W. (1985). The authoritarian assault upon the public school curriculum: An additional indicator of risk. *Phi Delta Kappan, 57,* 3-9.

Parsons, M. J. (1987). *How we understand art: A cognitive developmental account of the aesthetic experience.* Cambridge: Cambridge University Press.

Smith, R. A., & Smith, C. M. (1970). Justifying aesthetic education. *Journal of Aesthetic Education, 4*(2), 37-51.

Stuhr, P. L., Petrovich-Mwaniki, L., & Wasson, R. (1992). Curriculum guidelines for the multicultural art classroom. *Art Education, 45*(1), 16-24.

Vogel, S. M. (1986). *African aesthetics.* New York: Center for African Art.

Wilson, M., & Wilson, B. (1982). *Teaching children to draw: A guide for parents and teachers.* Englewood Cliffs, NJ: Prentice-Hall.

Additional Resources

Bancroft-Hunt, N., & Forman, W. (1979). *People of the totem: The Indians of the Pacific Northwest.* Norman, OK: University of Oklahoma Press.

Beardsley, J., & Livingston, J. (1987). *Hispanic art in the United States: Thirty contemporary painters and sculptors.* New York: Abbeyville Press.

Heller, N. G. (1987). *Women artists: An illustrated history.* New York: Abbeyville Press.

Lippard, L. R. (1990). *Mixed blessings: New art in a multicultural America.* New York: Pantheon Books.

Roselle, R. V., Wardlaw, A., & McKenna, M. A. ((1989). *Black art, ancestral legacy: The African impulse in African-American art.* New York: Abrams.

Sullivan, C. (1991). *Children of promise: African-American literature and art for young people.* New York: Abrams.

Wade, E. L., & Strickland, R. (1981). *Magic images: Contemporary Native American art.* Tulsa, OK: Philbrook Art Center.

Young, B. (Ed.). (1990). *Art, culture, and ethnicity.* Reston, VA: National Art Education Association.

Liora Bresler is an Associate Professor in the Department of Curriculum and Instruction at the University of Illinois at Urbana-Champaign. Dr. Bresler teaches courses in Aesthetics and Curriculum, The Arts in Early Childhood, and Qualitative Research Methodology.

Cynthia B. Colbert is Chair of Art Education and Professor of Art at the University of South Carolina, Columbia. Dr. Colbert has written extensively on early childhood art, and is co-author, with Martha Taunton, of "Developmentally Appropriate Practice in Early Art Education," a recent policy statement of the National Art Education Association (NAEA).

Elizabeth S. Cole is Professor and Chair of The University of Toledo Department of Art at the Toledo Museum of Art, Ohio. Codeveloper of the museum's nationally recognized early childhood program, Dr. Cole has focused her research and teaching on the design of developmentally appropriate methods for teaching art and art appreciation to young children.

Elizabeth Manley Delacruz is an Assistant Professor of Art Education in the School of Art and Design at the University of Illinois at Urbana-Champaign. Recipient of the Vice Chancellor's Teaching Scholars Award for her work in multicultural education, Dr. Delacruz is at work on a text on instructional theory and practice to be published by NAEA.

Mary Erickson is Professor of Art Education at Arizona State University, Tempe. A curriculum consultant to school districts across the United States and co-author of a series of art learning games, Dr. Erickson's writings and presentations focus primarily on teaching art history and aesthetics.

Kathryn Gaspar is Head of Children's Programs in the Creative Workshop, where she teaches and designs materials for young children and their teachers. The Creative Workshop is the studio school of the Rochester Memorial Art Gallery, Rochester, New York.

Joanne K. Guilfoil is an Assistant Professor in the Department of Curriculum and Instruction, College of Education, at Eastern Kentucky University, Richmond. Dr. Guilfoil's research focuses on the built environment as an educational concern.

Karen Kakas is Chair of the Division of Art Education/Art Therapy in the School of Art at Bowling Green State University, in Ohio. Dr. Kakas has conducted research on communication in classrooms, on the relation of contemporary and folk art to studio and art criticism curricula, and on art education and special populations.

Larry A. Kantner is a Professor in the Departments of Art and Curriculum and Instruction at the University of Missouri-Columbia where he serves as Coordinator of the Art Education Program and Director of Graduate Studies in Curriculum and Instruction. Dr. Kantner's research interests include art in early childhood and multicultural education.

Priscilla Lund is an Assistant Professor of Art Education in the Department of Education at Montana State University, Bozeman. Dr. Lund also serves as a Research Associate at the Museum of the Rockies.

Marianne Sykes Kerlavage is an Assistant Professor of Art Education at Millersville University in Pennsylvania. Dr. Kerlavage serves as curriculum coordinator for an arts-based education program recently implemented in a local elementary school.

Anna M. Kindler is an Assistant Professor of Art Education at the University of British Columbia, Vancouver and coordinator of the Arts Research Program at the University of British Columbia Child Study Centre. Dr. Kindler's research interests include artistic and aesthetic development in early childhood, curriculum, and the perception of art in a cross-cultural context.

Suzanne Kolodziej is an early childhood educator in the preschool program of the Rochester Museum and Science Center and an art educator at the Rochester Memorial Art Gallery in New York State.

Florence Swindell Mitchell taught art and art education at the university level for 25 years. Currently a freelance writer in Florida, Dr. Mitchell is working on a book on architecture for children.

Connie Newton is an Associate Professor and Director of Graduate Studies in the School of Visual Arts at the University of North Texas, Denton. Dr. Newton has published and presented papers on children's aesthetic responses to national and international audiences.

Andra L. Nyman currently serves as Associate Head of the Department of Art at the University of Georgia in Athens. Dr. Johnson edited the recently published NAEA anthology, *Art Education: Elementary*, and continues to serve as editor of the *NAEA Advisory* series.

Sandy Osborne is an Associate Professor in Child Development and Family Science in the Department of Health and Human Development at Montana State University in Bozeman.

Mary Stokrocki is an Associate Professor of Art Education at Arizona State University, Tempe. Recipient of the Mary Rouse Award for outstanding performance in research, teaching, and leadership in art education, Dr. Stokrocki conducts ethnographic studies of art teachers in diverse cultural settings.

Chun-Min Su is a researcher who focuses on children's drawings, cognition, and development. Dr. Su recently completed a doctoral degree in art education at the University of Illinois at Urbana-Champaign.

George Szekely is Professor of Art Education and Director of Graduate Studies at the University of Kentucky. Dr. Szekely is the author of several books, including *Encouraging Creativity in Art Lessons, Music and Art in the Elementary School*, and, most recently, *From Play to Art*.

Pat Tarr teaches early childhood and elementary art methods courses in the Department of Art at the University of Calgary, Alberta. Dr. Tarr recently completed a doctoral degree in art education at the University of British Columbia, with a specialization in early childhood art.

Christine Marmé Thompson is an Associate Professor of Art Education at the University of Illinois at Urbana-Champaign. Dr. Thompson teaches methods and practicum courses to students majoring in early childhood, elementary, and art education, and graduate courses in artistic development. Her research focuses on teacher education and on early childhood concerns.

Marilyn Zurmuehlen was Head of Art Education and Professor of Ceramics at The University of Iowa, Iowa City until her death in 1993. Dr. Zurmuehlen was author of *Studio Art: Praxis, Symbol, Presence*, co-author of *Understanding Art Testing*, and editor of *Working Papers in Art Education*, the journal for graduate students in art education and their mentors.